The New Instructional Leadership

Co-published with UCEA, this exciting new textbook is the first to tackle the ISLLC Standard 2—Instructional Leadership. In light of recent curriculum reforms, accountability policies, and changing demographics, today's leaders must not only have expertise in culture building and supervision skills, but also in adult learning, cultural funds of knowledge, curriculum, and the role of politics. *The New Instructional Leadership* helps aspiring school leaders examine their beliefs and practices about instructional leadership in relation to ISLLC Standard 2 and provides the theory, learning experiences, and analytical tools for effective leadership in today's world. Chapters cover issues of collaboration, curricular programming, motivation, supervision, accountability, capacity building, use of technology, monitoring, and evaluation.

Special Features:

- **Case Studies**—encourage readers to reflect and actively engage with instructional leadership beliefs and practices.
- **Fieldwork** and **Extended Reflections**—a range of inquiry activities provide students with opportunities to consider problems of practice related to the standard.
- **Strategies for Leaders**—offers students practical and accessible ideas in order to transform their practice to address the complex challenges facing contemporary schools.

Theoretically grounded and research-based, this unique volume will help aspiring and current leaders to understand instructional leadership and help them to sustain strong curricular and instructional programs in their increasingly diverse schools and communities.

Rose M. Ylimaki is Associate Professor of Educational Leadership at the University of Arizona, USA.

ISLLC LEADERSHIP PREPARATION SERIES

Series Editors: Michelle Young, Margaret Terry Orr

The New Instructional Leadership
ISLLC Standard Two
Edited by Rose M. Ylimaki

Political Contexts of Educational Leadership
ISLLC Standard Six
Edited by Jane Clark Lindle

The New Instructional Leadership

ISLLC Standard Two

Edited by Rose M. Ylimaki

Routledge
Taylor & Francis Group

NEW YORK AND LONDON

First published 2014
by Routledge
711 Third Avenue, New York, NY 10017

and by Routledge
2 Park Square, Milton Park, Abingdon, Oxon OX14 4RN

Routledge is an imprint of the Taylor & Francis Group, an informa business

Library of Congress Cataloging in Publication Data
A catalog record for this book has been applied for

ISBN: 978-0-415-53517-5 (hbk)
ISBN: 978-0-415-53518-2 (pbk)
ISBN: 978-0-203-11288-5 (ebk)

Typeset in Aldine 401 and Helvetica Neue
by Florence Production Ltd, Stoodleigh, Devon, UK

Index by Indexing Specialists (UK)

A co-publication of Routledge and the University Council for Education Administration—UCEA

Printed and bound in the United States of America by Sheridan Books, Inc. (a Sheridan Group Company).

For my students—instructional leaders—who are engaged in the gritty, theoretically grounded work to transform Arizona schools every day. This book represents your work as well as mine.

Contents

Figures

Tables

Series Foreword

As with the evolution of schooling in the US, the history of educational administration can be traced in a variety of ways. One of the most important of these avenues is the examination of major pieces of reflective scholarship and seminal professionally sponsored reports. Much of this work has left few fingerprints on the profession. But some has had robust influence on shaping choices made in school administration at critical junctions in its development. The best of this work has also provided action maps for once those choices were selected.

We know some things about this work. It is always context sensitive. There is a time to galvanize action and times when proposed stakes in the ground and new architectural designs will be ignored. The cardinal reports in the history of educational leadership arrived when people were ready for them. We also know that except for historians few people are aware of these foundational analyses. Once new pathways are chosen, it is difficult to remember that there were alternative possibilities. By achieving the goal of becoming deeply embedded in the fabric of the profession, new ideas lose their uniqueness and singular position as markers. Finally, we know that pathways that seem illuminatory sometimes turn out to provide less than salutary designs and building materials. Only time can provide the scale to assess this point.

Historical analysis shows us that there are a small handful of these critical markers in educational administration. One is the development of the ISLLC Standards for School Leaders, itself an outgrowth of an earlier historical marker, the National Commission on Excellence in Educational Administration (NCEEA). Founded in 1985 under the leadership of UCEA, the NCEEA laid out a broad framework of improvement for educational leadership writ large, with particular attention to the education of school administrators. One of its cornerstone recommendations was for the creation of the National Policy Board in Educational Administration (NPBEA), a new guiding body for the profession consisting of ten national associations with considerable interest in school leadership. Created in 1988, the NPBEA elected to make the development of national standards for the profession its signature work. Between 1994 and 1996, half of the states in the nation and the ten associations that comprised the NPBEA worked to forge an empirically and value-based vision for school administrators. That effort culminated in the publication of the ISLLC Standards in 1996. A dozen years later the NPBEA commissioned work that produced an update of those Standards, ISLLC 2008. It was my privilege to chair all this work.

It is safe to say that the ISLLC Standards have had a significant influence on the shape and texture of school administration in the US. As noted above, some of this had to do with context. The profession was unquestionably ready for a recentering of academic and practice work, away from an organizational foundation built up over the 20th century and toward one that would honor a steadfast focus on student success broadly defined—success achieved through an ethic of care, a commitment to community, and a strong sense of academic press.

The Standards by design operate at a high level of guidance. Based on best research and commitment to non-negotiable values they establish a distinct infrastructure for the profession. But most of the heavy lifting began after the Standards were crafted. They need to be yoked to essential leverage points for improvement, e.g., program accreditation, licensure, administrator evaluation, and so forth. Equally important they need to be fleshed out, deepened and to be brought to life, made accessible. Much commendable work has been occurring over the last 15 years on these two intertwined needs in every domain of the profession—policy, research, development, and practice.

This UCEA-sponsored project to provide heft, meaning, and concreteness to the ISLLC Standards is a cardinal example of this heavy lifting work. Designed to support preparation programs by helping their students understand and use the Standards, this series of textbooks, one for each of the six standards, provides a critically needed, unique, and powerful tool to rebuild educational leadership around what we know works and what we value as a profession.

Joseph Murphy
Leipers Fork, TN
May 2013

Preface

BACKGROUND AND RATIONALE

This book grew out of a recognition that rapidly changing times demand a new instructional leadership. The context for instructional leadership work has changed rapidly in the wake of recent policies, economic pressures, technological advances, and demographic shifts. Today's instructional leaders must implement new teacher (and principal) evaluation systems with effectiveness defined by student outcomes. At the same time, districts and schools face pressures to keep pace with technology and rigorous curriculum standards in spite of severe budget reductions. Many schools now serve increasingly diverse populations, including recent immigrants who must learn English as a second or third language, as well as a growing number of poor (even homeless) students. According to Interstate School Leaders Licensure Consortium (ISLLC) Standard 2, instructional leaders advocate, nurture, and sustain a school culture and instructional program conducive to student learning and staff professional growth. In this volume, we present a *new* instructional leadership prepared for the instructional leadership standard in the context of accountability, economic pressures, national curriculum standards, and demographic changes.

The principal's role as instructional leader emerged during the 1970s and 1980s effective schools literature conducted in the wake of the Coleman Report that suggested socioeconomic status (SES) as the largest contributor of student performance. And while schools have been under pressure to improve academic performance for decades, accountability pressures and related economic and demographic changes have only intensified in the wake of the No Child Left Behind Act. Principal Leah Rodriguez summarized the prevailing concern over the present condition of instructional leaders well when she said:

> I had a good preparation program. We learned a lot of leadership theories and practical strategies to implement the ISLLC standards, but as time goes on, I feel like I need more. We have children from many different countries coming to school. Our budget has been cut again, and we need to raise standards to prepare for new

tests . . . again. I feel like I need a new way of leading or new theories and strategies for all this complexity.

This book not only provides aspiring instructional leaders with leadership models and strategies but also background in broader theories regarding the sociocultural, political, and cultural dimensions of today's instructional leadership work. Beyond instructional leadership models and frameworks, chapter authors draw on theories from curriculum studies, social foundations, anthropology, and organization studies. These theories/lenses and related research studies provide a backdrop to powerful learning experiences designed to prepare new instructional leaders to implement the ISLLC standards in complex times. Indeed, some chapters refer to "curriculum" leadership as a broader term beyond leadership of classroom practice to encompass historical, political, cultural, and social dimensions of the work.

The instructional leadership descriptions and learning experiences presented in this volume consider demographics, school/community cultures, historical influences, and broader cultural political shifts as essential for the new instructional leadership. Moreover, through problem-posing cases and other learning experiences derived from broader theories (e.g. Funds of Knowledge, Curriculum Theories, Learning Theories), this volume helps school leaders examine their beliefs and the negotiated meanings of curriculum, learning, accountability, leadership, and politics in daily school practices; identify the values and goals that they want to encourage; and determine the purposes on which they ground their work, and the actions or reactions they prompt in teachers, parents, and students. In sum, this is the first instructional leadership volume, to my knowledge, that attempts this leadership preparation or pedagogical task in relation to the ISLLC standards.

In examining the literature, I recognized that many studies have been conducted on exemplary principals' instructional leadership practices but very little had been written about how principals *acquire* instructional leadership understandings and practices. Educational Administration Professor Rich Halverson and colleagues (2005) recently called for a new instructional leadership prepared in data-driven decision-making in an accountability era. Elsewhere I have called for a new curriculum/ instructional leadership prepared with deep understandings of curriculum and social theories. In his presentation at a recent Bergamo Curriculum conference, Professor James Henderson likewise argued that we need curriculum leaders with the self-understanding and open-mindedness to deal with the social and cultural aspects of today's educational prospect. Therefore, I decided to draw on multiple theories as backdrop for powerful learning experiences, including fieldwork, reflective inquiry, and case studies.

This book is written to provide a deeper (theoretically informed) understanding of the pressures related to the principal position and its changing instructional leadership role and expectations. Through background information and learning experiences, the reader gets a firsthand sense of what it feels like to serve in this critically important position, and of what must be done if this position is to support an improved American school system. Through case studies, the reader feels the challenges, frustrations, joys, and stresses of school leadership. Each chapter of this book focuses on a particular aspect of the ISLLC Standard 2, providing new lenses and learning experiences to help prepare today's principals for instructional leadership.

PEDAGOGICAL FEATURES

The contributors begin each chapter with a reflection or inquiry activity in order to provide students with opportunities to consider problems of practice related to the featured dimension of ISLLC Standard 2. The chapters then discuss background theories and research studies that help illuminate each aspect of Standard 2. Finally, each chapter contains learning activities that help readers/students reflect and actively engage with instructional leadership beliefs and practices. More specifically, each book chapter follows a similar format and includes a particular set of pedagogical features.

- **Theory and Research Background:** Each chapter provides aspiring principals with theory, research, and background information to illuminate each particular aspect of ISLLC Standard 2. Importantly, chapter authors or contributors provide background information to help readers consider multiple dimensions of the standard aspect, including social justice, organizational learning, and curriculum.
- **Extended Reflection:** Each chapter begins with an extended reflection where readers consider their prior experiences with that standard aspect. Readers are also asked to keep track of how their understandings develop and change as they engage with the chapter. Each chapter concludes with an extended reflection designed to help readers internalize the chapter content in relation to his/her experiences.
- **Fieldwork:** All of the chapters include fieldwork that provides readers with data-based experiences in classrooms and schools. Many of the activities ask readers to collect data, interviewing principals, teachers, students, and parents about how they implement that ISLLC standard aspect, both in terms of successes and challenges. Readers are asked to use the background information to consider the data gathered in the field. Further, readers are asked to compare what they learned from interviews and observations with their own experiences.
- **Strategies for Leaders:** Each chapter concludes with suggestions for how to implement all of the chapter information into practice. Specifically, this section provides aspiring leaders with summary suggestions for what they need to know and be able to do as new instructional leaders implementing that particular aspect of the ISLLC Standards.
- **Cases:** Each chapter contains examples or case studies designed to help aspiring leaders consider the challenges and struggles of the new instructional leadership.

OVERVIEW OF CHAPTERS

Chapter 1: Introduction: Overview of ISLLC Standard 2 and the New Instructional Leadership

Rose M. Ylimaki

This chapter provides the overarching theoretical framework and relevant research for understanding the new instructional leadership described in subsequent chapters. To begin, the chapter further posits a rationale for why we need a broader and deeper theoretical base for instructional leadership work, including policy trends, demographic shifts, cultural political shifts, and economic pressures. Following a brief analysis of instructional leadership work that emerged from effective schools literature, the chapter widens the lens on instructional leadership to consider curriculum, social and cultural perspectives, and the politics of leading curriculum and instruction in the current accountability era and beyond.

Chapter 2: Nurture and Sustain a Culture of Collaboration, Trust, Learning, and High Expectations

Brendan H. O'Connor, Vanessa Anthony-Stevens, and Norma González

This chapter illuminates the sociocultural context for the new instructional leadership. More specifically, it explores one facet of ISLLC Standard 2—a collaborative learning culture as a nested concept of schools, communities, and broader culture. Specifically, this chapter examines "funds of knowledge" (Moll et al., 2005) as a way to build trust, learning, and high expectations in culturally diverse schools and communities. Assuming that classroom cultural and linguistic patterns should be congruent with the cultural and linguistic patterns of the community, "funds of knowledge" seeks to bridge the discontinuity between classroom and community practices by utilizing strengths from students and their households (González et al., 2005). Funds of knowledge is also concerned with understanding the social networks between households in the community that facilitate the development and collaborative exchange of resources including knowledge, skills, and labor (Moll et al., 2005). When schools enter into collaboration (*confianza*) with the families through inclusion in the social network and practices, parents become cognitive resources for the classroom. By building funds of knowledge into the curriculum and utilizing social networks, schools can work with students, their families, and the community to provide students with an additive form of schooling rather than the subtractive schooling, which has led to inequities in outcomes for many minority populations historically.

Chapter 3: Create a Comprehensive, Rigorous, and Coherent Curricular Program

Rose M. Ylimaki

Considering the broader sociocultural context for curriculum described in Chapter 2, this chapter focuses on curriculum or the content of education. More specifically, this chapter examines how instructional leaders negotiate the politics behind curriculum decisions to foster a rigorous, coherent, and comprehensive curricular program across five dimensions:

1. intended
2. enacted
3. assessed
4. learned
5. hidden.

All of these curriculum dimensions are shaped by individual beliefs, values, external cultural politics, and policies. Curriculum content is also shaped by broader cultural politics and local expectations. According to the ISLLC standards, curriculum is also characterized by rigor, relevance, and coherence. Rigor should be addressed in terms of texts, instruction, and outcomes as well as cognitive demands. Yet instructional leaders must balance students' interests, cultural funds of knowledge, and rigorous (tested) curriculum expectations. Curriculum coherence helps principals and teachers attain this balance by organizing the curriculum in ways that connect rigorous expectations with other ideas, students' interests, and cultural backgrounds. Curriculum content is also shaped by broader cultural politics and hegemony. In other words, instructional leaders must help teachers and others think about how policy and cultural political rhetoric affect curriculum content, what we consider legitimate knowledge, and what is hidden in the curriculum.

Chapter 4: Create a Personalized and Motivating Learning Environment for Students

Rose M. Ylimaki

This chapter focuses specifically on how leaders provide personalized and motivating student learning environments, both physical and virtual. When psychologists write about motivation, they typically refer to the reasons that students are engaged in learning to a point that they are aroused to action. Students are driven to act for extrinsic reasons when they anticipate some kind of tangible payoff, such as good grades, recognition, and so forth. These rewards are said to be extrinsic because they are unrelated to the action. In effect, the activity becomes a means to an end. By contrast, students are said to be intrinsically motivated when they engage in activities for their own sake. This chapter applies these understandings of motivations to the dimensions of a motivating learning environment, including research about how motivation and learning environments affect student learning, and offers a framework for understanding the conditions and factors that enable 21st century learning environments. Leaders must also consider how motivation affects teachers' work environments. Thus, classic and more recent motivation theories are presented.

Chapter 5: Supervise Instruction

Peter Burke and Henry St. Maurice

This chapter is an examination of instructional leaders' practices as supervisors of instruction, in the context of debates over mass public schooling. Much of the literature on instructional supervision has been conducted primarily in teacher education rather than the educational administration field. Drawing on instructional supervision literature, this chapter defines and distinguishes types of instructional supervision, compares theoretical models, and analyzes supervision as persuasive discourse among professionals enmeshed in local, national, and global political relations. Specific criteria and rubrics are presented for further study of supervisors' knowledge and skills. In brief, this chapter helps leaders understand and improve supervisory practices to enhance performance in learning communities in which they lead.

Chapter 6: Develop Assessment and Accountability Systems to Monitor Student Progress

Rose M. Ylimaki

Today's instructional leaders must use formative and summative assessment measures as essential components of a comprehensive accountability system that connects assessments, instruction, and curriculum for increasingly diverse students. Drawing on Skrla et al.'s (2004) reconception of equity audits and the Funds of Knowledge research tradition (see Chapter 2), this chapter provides instructional leaders with strategies to examine data with regard to teacher quality, programmatic quality, and overall academic opportunity. As schools and communities become increasingly diverse, curriculum rigor and accountability has increased. The new instructional leader must integrate their assessment literacy skills with understandings of equity and intercultural education to develop and sustain a comprehensive assessment system aimed at improved teaching and learning for *all* students.

Chapter 7: Develop the Instructional and Leadership Capacity of Staff

Catherine Hackney and James Henderson

This chapter suggests that curriculum leaders can build their capacities to provide their students with learning experiences that offer hope for a better personal, vocational, cultural, and global future. They are fulfilling Dewey's 1897 vision of educational work:

> Education . . . marks the most perfect union of science and art conceivable in human experience. The art of thus giving shape to human powers and adapting them to social service is the supreme art; one calling into its service the best of artists; that no insight, sympathy, tact, executive power, is too great for such service.
>
> (Dewey, 1897/2009, p. 40)

Thus, today's curriculum leadership must be both *warm-hearted* in the spirit of Noddings' (2003) ethic of care and *open-minded* in the spirit of a Socratic love of wisdom. Noddings (2002) writes that, "As Dewey filled out his moral theory, he moved rapidly to problem solving—surely one aim of communication. As school leaders fill out an ethic of care, they concentrate on the needs and responses required to maintain caring relations" (p. 22). Such curriculum leadership is grounded in *caring transactions* with its four "components" of relational self-reflection, open-ended dialogue, interpersonal attention, and personal confirmation (Noddings, 2002, pp. 15–21).

Chapter 8: Maximize Time Spent on Quality Curriculum and Instruction

Rose M. Ylimaki and Lynnette Brunderman

This chapter is designed to help principal candidates/readers (re)think about the various dimensions of both time (during the day, week, and year) and the nature and influences on quality instruction. It begins by exploring the nature of time in schools and then reviews the definitions of quality curriculum and instruction presented in Chapter 3. Next, the chapter outlines areas of opportunity that leaders have to rethink time and the relationships among time, curriculum, and instruction. It provides a framework on areas of action for using time effectively during and around the school day, while uncovering key issues and dilemmas that must be navigated.

Chapter 9: Promote the Use of the Most Effective and Appropriate Technologies to Support Teaching and Learning

Seann M. Dikkers

This chapter provides aspiring leaders with background in technology and its uses to meet the goals of a 21st century education. Pressure to educate youth to engage and master these technologies comes alongside the need for 21st century skills in the workplace. This chapter highlights the most effective use of learning technologies, appropriate application of those technologies, and leverage points for student learning and teacher professional development. Aspiring school leaders learn about new technologies and how they are being used to build unique, engaging, and high-performing learning spaces for students and professionals.

Chapter 10: Monitor and Evaluate the Impact of the Instructional Program

Lynnette Brunderman and Thad Dugan

This chapter brings all the aspects of ISLLC Standard 2 together in a focus on systemic program evaluation. More specifically, this chapter provides an organizational learning perspective on program evaluation, highlighting personal, interpersonal and organizational capacity for instructional improvement. Such program evaluations shift from a focus on the merit of a single program to assessments of impact of programs within the whole organization. To understand the impact of a single instructional program (e.g. a new reading series) or how a program fits within the entire system, a more holistic, organic approach is needed. "Systems thinking" offers a broad view by exploring program interactions and relationships, including key aspects of the ISLLC standards (e.g. collaboration, curriculum, school culture, supervision approaches, assessments, technology, time, and capacity).

In a broad sense, these chapters help aspiring leaders cultivate their curriculum and instructional leadership capabilities. As Maxine Greene (1998) put it, "I know the challenges are always new. The questions still gather, and I relish my sense of incompleteness. I can only live, it seems to me, with a consciousness of possibility, of what might be, of what *ought* to be" (p. 256). The next chapter provides an overview of ISLLC Standard 2 and possibilities for a new instructional leadership.

REFERENCES

Dewey, J. (1897/2009). *How we think*. Digireads.com.

González, N., Moll, L., & Amanti, C. (2005). *Funds of knowledge: Theorizing practices in households, communities, and classrooms*. New York: Lawrence Erlbaum Associates.

Greene, M. (1998). *The dialectic of freedom*. New York: Teachers College Press.

Halverson, R., Grigg, J., Prichett, R., & Thomas, C. (2005, July). The new instructional leadership: Creating data-driven systems in schools. A paper presented at the annual meeting of the National Council of Professors of Educational Administration, Washington, D.C.

Moll, L., Amanti, C., Neff, D., & González, N. (2005). Funds of knowledge for teaching: Using a qualitative approach to connect homes and classrooms. In N. González, L. Moll, & C. Amanti (Eds.). *Funds of knowledge: Theorizing practices in households, communities, and classrooms* (pp. 71–88). Mahwah, NJ: Lawrence Erlbaum Associates.

Noddings, N. (2002). *Educating moral people: A caring alternative to character education*. New York: Teachers College Press.

Noddings, N. (2003) *Caring: A feminine approach to ethics and moral education, second edition*, Los Angeles, CA: University of California Press.

Skrla, L., Scheurich, J., Garcia, J., & Nolly, G. (2004). Equity audits: A practical leadership tool for developing equitable and excellent schools. *Educational Administration Quarterly*, *40*(1), pp. 133–161.

Acknowledgments

My conceptualization of instructional leadership has been influenced and supported by a number of people. To begin, many of my colleagues have contributed greatly to my understanding of curriculum/instructional leadership. Specifically, I am grateful to David Gurr, Jim Henderson, and Chris Day for supporting and challenging my thinking about curriculum and instructional leadership over the years. Routledge editor Heather Jarrow and my colleague Lynnette Brunderman read several chapter drafts, and their comments greatly improved the quality of this book. I am also deeply thankful for the support of Dean Ron Marx and my colleagues in the intellectual community of the Department of Educational Policy Studies at the University of Arizona. My colleague Jeff Bennett and students from the Spring Curriculum Leadership course also enhanced my understandings about curriculum and leadership in relation to broader cultural politics and institutions. Finally, I would like to acknowledge many sources of inspiration (large and small) that encouraged and supported me through this project, including the sights, sounds, and tastes of Rome and Spain, Arizona sunshine, and good friends.

CHAPTER 1

Introduction: Overview of ISLLC Standard 2 and the New Instructional Leadership

Rose M. Ylimaki

A 2007 report by Linda Darling-Hammond and colleagues at Stanford University found that exemplary pre- and in-service development programs for principals have a set of common components, including a comprehensive and coherent curriculum aligned to state and professional standards. Similarly, Ken Leithwood, Karen Seashore Louis, Stephen Anderson, and Kyla Wahlstrom (2004) noted three core system elements that determine the quality of school leadership—standards, training, and context/conditions. This volume is a resource for developing principals in Standard 2 Instructional Leadership with particular attention to the broader conditions that surround principals' work today and into the future. In so doing, this volume goes beyond traditional managerial paradigms used to prepare instructional leadership to consider the personal and sociocultural and political aspects of today's leadership work. Standard 2 and its specific functions are identified below. Each function is fully described in subsequent chapters.

Standard 2

An education leader promotes the success of every student by advocating, nurturing, and sustaining a school culture and instructional program conducive to student learning and staff professional growth.

Functions
A. Nurture and sustain a culture of collaboration, trust, learning, and high expectations
B. Create a comprehensive, rigorous, and coherent curricular program
C. Create a personalized and motivating learning environment for students
D. Supervise instruction
E. Develop assessment and accountability systems to monitor student progress
F. Develop the instructional and leadership capacity of staff
G. Maximize time spent on quality instruction
H. Promote the use of the most effective and appropriate technologies to support teaching and learning
I. Monitor and evaluate the impact of the instructional program

These instructional leadership functions are grounded in effective schools literature described below.

INSTRUCTIONAL LEADERSHIP LITERATURE

Many scholars (e.g. Bossert et al., 1982; Edmonds, 1979; Hallinger & Murphy, 1986) have provided extensive research support for the importance of instructional leadership and its core functions. Across this literature, instructional leaders were described as *strong, directive leaders* who had been successful at "turning their schools around" (Bossert et al., 1982; Edmonds, 1979; Hallinger & Murphy, 1986). Hallinger and Murphy (1986) identified three broad categories of instructional leadership practice:

1. defining the school mission
2. managing the instructional program
3   promoting school climate.

Associated with these broad categories are a total of 21 more specific functions such as supervising instruction, culture building, and fostering deep understandings of subject matter content. Similarly, Hallinger and Murphy (1986) conducted a survey of principals and identified instructional leadership tasks that distinguished low-performing and high-performing schools. According to Murphy's findings, effective instructional leaders:

1. develop mission and goals
2. promote quality instruction through supervision
3. promote a positive learning culture through rewards, high expectations and professional development
4. develop a safe and orderly environment with appropriate economic and community resources.

Other studies (Blasé & Blasé, 1998) likewise identified principal's instructional leadership behaviors that contributed to improvements in classroom practice. These instructional leadership behaviors dominated leadership certification training for decades. Yet the most fully tested instructional leadership models (e.g. Hallinger & Murphy, 1986) were developed in the mid-1980s prior to the recent intensified accountability systems, teacher/leader evaluation systems, economic downturn, technological advances, demographic shifts, and decentralization trends toward collaboration.

One of the major impediments to effective school leadership is trying to carry the burden alone. This point was captured by Lambert (2003) who contends that, "The days of the lone instructional leader are over. We no longer believe that one administrator can serve as the instructional leader for the entire school without the substantial participation of other educators" (p. 37). Thus, several different writers have attempted to integrate these constructs into a variant they refer to as "shared instructional leadership" (Jackson, 2000; Lambert, 2003; Marks & Printy, 2003). Recent studies have also demonstrated that "instructional" leadership is not the exclusive domain of the principal since teachers and other support professionals play a vital leadership role in the improvement of teaching and learning (e.g. Hallinger, 2004; Jackson, 2000; Marks & Printy, 2003). Such a shared or integrated model conceptualizes instructional leadership as a *capacity* for school improvement in which the principal models appropriate instructional leadership behaviors and invites teachers and others to join their efforts to change and improve their teaching practices.

A growing number of scholars have also expanded instructional leadership to focus on social justice (e.g. Oakes et al., 2012; Scheurich, 1998; Theoharis, 2009; Touchton & Acker-Hocevar, 2001). For instance, Touchton and Acker-Hocevar (2001) examined schools that were restructured to improve academic performance for students from traditionally marginalized groups. Likewise, Dantley and Tillman (2006) examined school restructuring and policy change efforts aimed at transforming procedures that perpetuate social inequalities and marginalization attributable to race, class, gender, and other markers of otherness. Focusing more specifically on the leader, Theoharis (2009) studied principals' social justice orientations and argued that leaders must create inclusive instructional programs that account for race, class, gender, disability, sexual orientation, and other historically and currently marginalizing conditions (p. 223). These and other social justice leadership studies move the needs of traditionally marginalized groups to the center of instructional leaders' efforts and push instructional leadership to incorporate dispositions and practices from curriculum studies, critical education studies, and anthropology.

Marshall (2004) argues that leaders must have "more skills beyond scientific management or quick fixes" (p. 43) to address complex educational dilemmas steeped in an array of social, cultural, and political contexts. More specifically, McKenzie and colleagues (2008) posit three goals for educational leaders who seek educational equity and excellence: (a) They must believe that high test scores matter and raise the academic achievement for *all* students in the school, (b) they must prepare their students to live as critical citizens in society, and (c) they must recognize that both of these goals can be achieved only when leaders assign students to inclusive, heterogeneous classrooms that provide all students with access to a rich and engaging curriculum. In light of this research, instructional leadership preparation has expanded to include a clear focus on social justice and equity as well as pedagogical excellence and learning.

At the same time, even most recent social justice oriented instructional leadership models do not explicitly consider the complex context of policy, cultural politics, or students'/communities' funds of knowledge (O'Connor, Anthony-Stevens, & González, this volume) as these affect curriculum, instruction, and learning in schools. A few curriculum scholars have examined questions of leadership, with teachers and students most often serving as primary participants (e.g. Breault & Breault, 2005; Dentith, 2004). Drawing from empirical findings of youth leadership and identity among Las Vegas adolescents, Dentith (2004) studied youth leadership and identity among Las Vegas adolescents and argued for a curriculum that problematizes issues of identity, and culture. Similarly, Brady and Dentith (2001) conducted a qualitative study of curriculum leaders (teachers and students) with curriculum leadership defined as a shared phenomenon that has unique expressions at each teaching site. Brady and Dentith's findings indicate the importance of readiness for leadership, content knowledge, and context. With curriculum leadership defined as a shared phenomenon, Brady and Dentith's definition assumes that various people who have a stake in curriculum will have a voice in it. However, Brady and Dentith do not give explicit attention to the role of school leadership and the broader cultural context of such curriculum work. As demographics shift across the U.S., Luis Moll and Norma González' work on funds of knowledge is increasingly relevant for schools (and leaders thereof). In Funds of Knowledge research, teachers entered students' homes as ethnographers—in effect, as anthropologists studying the students' cultural "lifeworlds" (the everyday spaces, suffused with social relationships, in which they live, learn, and grow)—in order to investigate the "historically accumulated and culturally developed bodies of knowledge and skills" present in households (Moll et al., 2005, p. 72). Changing contexts for instructional leadership are further described in the next section.

CHANGING CONTEXTS FOR INSTRUCTIONAL LEADERSHIP STANDARDS

Accountability Policy Trends and Cultural Political Shifts

Since the time many instructional leadership studies were conducted in the 1980s and early 1990s, curriculum and instructional decisions have been heavily influenced by accountability policies and cultural political shifts. For example, recent U.S. federal policies (i.e., the No Child Left Behind Act and Race to the Top) require the testing of curriculum standards at each grade level, with serious consequences for schools that fail to make "adequate yearly progress" on state tests over a series of years, including conversion to a charter school or dismissal of the administration. Most states have also adopted more rigorous Common Core Standards aimed at developing students who are ready for college or career and able to compete globally. Moreover, many states and districts have mandated principal and teacher evaluation systems linked, at least in part, with student outcomes. Thus, U.S. schools now operate in a context of high-stakes testing accountability and public visibility as a result of the federal No Child Left Behind Act, its more recent iteration, Race to the Top (2009), related state testing mandates, and the most recent move toward national curriculum standards—Common Core and Partnership for Assessment of Readiness for College and Careers (PARCC) assessments.

Such policy trends are linked to cultural political shifts toward a particular set of ideologies, beliefs, and values about what we teach in schools (Apple, 2013). Curriculum historian Herbert Kliebard asserts that tensions between what knowledge a society *values* and what gets *taught* are universal. He continues, "The route between the knowledge a society values and its incorporation into the curriculum becomes infinitely more tortuous, however, where we take into account the fact that different segments in any society will emphasize different forms of knowledge as most valuable for that society" (Kliebard, 1986).

According to Apple (2004), dominant groups have recently been successful in shifting the way many people think about schools, curriculum, instruction, and assessments by circulating a particular set of discourses. These discourses have affected our common sense about what is most valuable in the curriculum. The four groups include: (a) dominant economic and political elites intent on "modernizing" the economy; (b) largely white working-class and middle-class groups who mistrust the state and are concerned with security, the family, and traditional knowledge and values (e.g. the Tea Party); (c) economic and cultural conservatives (such as Bill Bennett) who want to return to "high standards", discipline, and competition in schools; and (d) a faction of the new middle class who may not totally agree with these other groups, but who have the technical expertise to support their agendas. It is important to note that Apple is not talking about Republican vs. Democratic political arguments here as agendas for standardization and testing cut across both political parties in many ways.

And while there are elements of good sense in their arguments about the need for accountability and high standards, the next generation of instructional leaders must have the dispositions and analytical tools to advocate for a comprehensive curriculum beyond dominant groups' values about knowledge. Recent demographic shifts and economic pressures have heightened the need for such dispositions and analytical tools.

Demographic Shifts and Economic Pressures

Across the United States, Latino(a)/Hispanic populations are increasing dramatically; it is projected that between 1990 and 2050, the percentage of the U.S. population of Hispanic origin will almost triple, growing from 9 percent to 25 percent (making them the largest minority group by far) and the percent of Asian will more than double, growing from 3 percent to 8 percent. During the same period, the percent Black will remain relatively stable, increasing only slightly from 12 percent to 14 percent while the percent White will decline sharply from 76 percent to 53 percent (U.S. Census Bureau, 2009).

At the same time, a growing number of children are living in poverty; nearly 16 million children or 22 percent of all children live in families with incomes below the U.S. poverty line at $23,021 for a family of four (National Center for Children in Poverty, 2013). Approximately one million students were identified as homeless in the United States during the 2009–2010 school year (Miller, 2011). Although this number represented only a fraction of the students who actually experienced homelessness that year (many more were unidentified), it was startling because it was 41 percent greater than just two years earlier (National Center for Homeless Education, 2010). Further, 70 percent of school districts throughout the United States reported local increases in student homelessness during the period (National Association for the Education of Homeless Children and Youth/First Focus, 2010). Many schools need to provide holistic kinds of services beyond the curriculum, including health care and social services. Moreover, the new instructional leadership cannot mean that principals or teacher leaders have the sole power and responsibility to determine what "counts" as academically valuable for increasingly diverse populations and then decide how to transmit that knowledge to students (O'Connor, Anthony-Stevens & González, this volume).

TOWARD A "NEW" CURRICULUM/INSTRUCTIONAL LEADERSHIP

The complex and rapid political, economic, and demographic shifts described above demand wider and deeper lenses on curriculum and instructional practice, and some of these lenses are situated within disciplines and fields outside of educational administration. Anthropology, curriculum studies, and critical education studies offer explicit attention to the role of policy, cultural political shifts, and students' funds of knowledge, all of which help new instructional leaders address academic and social inequities. Each discipline or field offers its own frame of reference, its own structure of knowledge that contributes to our understanding of leadership. Through the study of educational administration, we can understand the capacities for leadership influence on inclusive, socially just classroom practice (e.g. Murphy & Hallinger, 1984; Hallinger 2004; Marks & Printy, 2003). The curriculum studies field is committed to deep understandings of curriculum subjects, history, the process of self-formation, and social transformation (e.g. Pinar et al., 1995; Breault & Breault, 2005; Henderson & Hawthorne, 2000). Moreover, drawing on critical education studies of cultural politics—with its underlying social theories (e.g. Foucault, 1980; Habermas, 1991)—we can engage in critical reflection of the historical, sociocultural, and political realities that shape our leadership narratives, lives, and ultimately, the content of education (curriculum). Critical education studies (e.g. Apple, 2004; Giroux, 2001; Pedroni, 2007) offer the potential for researchers and practitioners to examine and understand cultural political shifts that affect our common sense about curriculum and, more importantly, how to support substantive change in our schools. As curriculum theorist William Pinar (2004) argued, the point of the public school curriculum is understanding—understanding the relations among academic knowledge, the state of society, the processes of self-formation, and the character of the historical moment in which we live, in which others have lived, and in which our descendants will someday live. Thus, this volume provides aspiring leaders with a range of literature (e.g. history, curriculum studies, anthropology, learning theory) and practical application strategies to meet and transform the complex challenges facing contemporary schools.

BIBLIOGRAPHY

Anyon, J. (2005). *Radical possibilities: Public policy, urban education, and a new social movement.* New York: Routledge.

Apple, M. (1993). *Official knowledge: Democratic education in a conservative age.* New York: Routledge.

Apple, M. (1996). *Cultural politics and education.* New York: Teachers College Press.

Apple, M. (2004). *Ideology and curriculum.* New York: Routledge.

Apple, M. (2013). *Can education change society?* New York: Routledge.

Banks, J. & Banks, C. (2007). *Multicultural education: Issues and perspectives, 4th Edition.* Needham Heights, MA: Allyn & Bacon.

Blasé, J. (1991). *The politics of life in schools: Power, conflict, and cooperation.* Thousand Oaks, CA: Corwin Press.

Blasé, R. & Blasé, J. (1998). *Handbook of instructional leadership: How really good principals promote teaching and learning.* Thousand Oaks, CA: Corwin Press.

Bossert, S. T., Dwyer, D. C., Rowan, B., & Lee, G. V. (1982). The instructional management role of the principal. *Educational Administration Quarterly, 18*(3), 34–64.

Brady, J. & Dentith, A. (2001). Critical voyages: Postmodern feminist pedagogies as liberatory practice. *Teaching Education, 12*(2), 165–176.

Breault, D. A. & Breault, R. (Eds.). (2005). *Experiencing Dewey: Insights for today's classroom.* Indianapolis, IN: Kappa Delta Pi Publications.

Dantley, M. & Tillman, L. (2006). Social justice and moral transformative leadership. In C. Marshall & M. Oliva (Eds.). *Leadership for social justice: Making revolutions in education* (pp. 16–30). Boston, MA: Allyn and Bacon.

Darling-Hammond, L., LaPointe, M., Meyerson, D., Orr, M. T., & Cohen, C. (2007). *Preparing school leaders for a changing world: Lessons from exemplary leadership development programs.* Stanford, CA: Stanford Educational Leadership Institute.

Deal, T. & Peterson, K. (1999). *Shaping school culture: The heart of leadership*. Somerset, NJ: Jossey-Bass.

Dentith, A. (2004). Female adolescent subjectivities in Las Vegas: Poststructural thoughts on the intersections of gender, sexuality, consumer logic, and curriculum. *Gender and Education, 16*(4), 455–472.

Dewey, J. (2008/1916). *Democracy and education*. New York: Seven Treasures Publications.

Edmonds, R. (1979). Effective schools for the urban poor. *Educational Leadership, 37,* 15–24.

Foucault, M. (1980). *Power/knowledge: Selected interviews and other writings, 1972–1977*. New York: Vintage.

Freire, P. (1993). *Pedagogy of the oppressed*. New York: Continuum.

Giroux, H. (2001). *Theory and resistance in education*. New York: Praeger.

Glatthorn, A., Boshee, F., & Whitehead, B. (2006). *Curriculum leadership development and implementation*. Thousand Oaks, CA: Sage.

González, N., Moll, L., & Amanti, C. (2005). *Funds of knowledge: Theorizing practices in households, communities, and classrooms*. New York: Lawrence Erlbaum Associates.

Habermas, J. (1991). *The structural transformation of the public sphere: An inquiry into a category of bourgeois society*. Cambridge, MA: MIT Press.

Hallinger, P. (2004). Reflections on the practice of instructional and transformational leadership. Paper presented at the Annual International Congress for School Effectiveness and School Improvement, Nottingham, UK, January, 2004.

Hallinger, P. & Heck, R. (1996). Reassessing the principal's role in school effectiveness: A review of empirical research, 1980–1995. *Educational Administration Quarterly, 32*(1), 5–44.

Hallinger, P. & Murphy, J. (1986). The social context of effective schools. *American Journal of Education, 94*(3), 328–355.

Heck, R. H. & Hallinger, P. (2005). The study of educational leadership and management. *Educational Management Administration & Leadership, 33*(2), 229.

Henderson, J. & Gornik, R. (2006). *Transformative curriculum leadership* (3rd ed.). Upper Saddle River, NJ: Prentice-Hall.

Henderson, J. & Hawthorne, R. (2000). *Transformative curriculum leadership* (2nd ed.). Upper Saddle River, NJ: Prentice-Hall.

hooks, b. (1991). *Essentialism and experience*. Oxford, UK: Oxford University Press.

Jackson, D. (2000). The school improvement journal: Perspectives on leadership. *School Leadership and Management, 20*(1), 61–78.

Johnson, B. & Johnson, B. (2007). *High-stake: poverty, testing, and failure in American schools*. New York: Rowan & Littlefield.

Johnson, L. (2007). Rethinking successful school leadership in challenging U.S. schools: Culturally responsive practices in school-community relationships. *International Studies in Educational Administration, 35*(3), 49–58.

Kliebard, H. (1986). *The struggle for the American curriculum: 1893–1958*. New York: Routledge.

Kliebard, H. (1992). *Forging the American curriculum*. New York: Routledge.

Lambert, L. (2003). *Leadership capacity for lasting school improvement*. Alexandria, VA: Association for Supervision and Curriculum Development.

Leithwood, K., Seashore Louis, K., Anderson, S., & Wahlstrom, K. (2004). *How leadership influences student learning*. New York: The Wallace Foundation.

Leithwood, K., Jacobson, S., & Ylimaki, R. (2011). Converging policy trends. In R. Ylimaki & S. Jacobson (Eds.). *US and cross-national policies, practices, and preparation: Implications for successful instructional leadership, organizational learning, and culturally responsive practices*. Dordrecht, Netherlands: Springer-Kluwer.

Marks, H. & Printy, S. (2003). Principal leadership and school performance: An integration of transformation and instructional leadership. *Educational Administration Quarterly, 4*, 293–331.

Marshall, C. (2004). Social justice challenges to educational administration: Introduction to a special issue. *Educational Administration Quarterly, 40*(1), 3–13.

Marshall, C. & Oliva, M. (2006). *Leadership for social justice: Making revolutions in education.* New York: Pearson.

McCarthy, C. & Teasley, C (2008). *Transnational perspectives on culture, policy, and education: Redirecting cultural studies in neoliberal times.* New York: Peter Lang.

McKenzie, K. B., Christman, D., Hernandez, F., Fierro, F., Capper, C., Dantley, D., Gonzalez, M. L., Cambron-McCabe, N., & Scheurich, J. (2008). From the field: A proposal for educating leaders for social justice. *Educational Administration Quarterly, 44*(1), 111–138.

Miller, P. (2011). A critical analysis of the research on student homelessness. *Review of Educational Research, 81*(3), pp. 308–337.

Moll, L., Amanti, C., Neff, D., & González, N. (2005). Funds of knowledge for teaching: Using a qualitative approach to connect homes and classrooms. In N. González, L. Moll, & C. Amanti (Eds.) *Funds of knowledge: Theorizing practices in households, communities, and classrooms* (pp. 71–88). Mahwah, NJ: Lawrence Erlbaum Associates.

Murphy, J. & Hallinger, P. (1984). School leadership studies: Where do we go from here? *American Secondary Education, 13*(4), 18–21.

National Association for the Education of Homeless Children and Youth/First Focus. (2010). *A critical moment: Child & youth homelessness in our nation's schools.* Washington, DC: National Association for the Education of Homeless Children and Youth.

National Center for Children in Poverty. (2013). *Putting research to work for children and families.* Retrieved April 10, 2013 from www.nccp.org

National Center for Homeless Education. (2010). *Education for Homeless Children and Youth program data collection summary.* Washington, DC: U.S. Department of Education.

Noddings, N. (1992). *The challenge to care in schools: An alternative approach to education.* New York: TC Press.

Oakes, J., Lipton, M., Anderson, L., & Stillman, J. (2012). *Teaching to change the world.* Boulder, CO: Paradigm Publishers.

Oja, S. N. (1980). *Developmental theories and the professional development of teachers.* (ERIC Document Reproduction Service No. ED 248–277).

Pedroni, T. (2007). *Market movements: African American involvement in school voucher reform.* New York: Routledge.

Pinar, W. (2004). *What is curriculum theory?* New York: Routledge.

Pinar, W., Reynolds, W., Slattery, P., & Taubman, P. (1995). *Understanding curriculum: An introduction to historical and contemporary curriculum discourses.* New York: Peter Lang.

Purkey, S. & Smith, M. (1983). Effective schools: a review. *The Elementary School Journal, 83*(4), 427–452.

Robinson, V. M. J., Lloyd, C. A., & Rowe, K. J. (2008). The impact of leadership on student outcomes: An analysis of the differential effects of leadership types. *Educational administration quarterly, 44*(5), 635–674.

Scheurich, J. (1998). Highly successful and loving, public elementary schools populated mainly by low-SES children of color: Core beliefs and cultural characteristics. *Urban Education, 33*(4), 451–491.

Theoharis, G. (2009). *The school leaders our children deserve: Seven keys to equity, social justice, and school reform.* New York: TC Press.

Touchton, D. & Acker-Hocevar, M. (2001). Using a lens of social justice to reform principals' practices from high-poverty, low-performing schools. A paper presented at the annual meeting of the University Council for Educational Administration, Cincinnati, Ohio, November, 2001.

U.S. Census Bureau. (2009). State and county quickfacts: Arizona. Retrieved August 8, 2013 from http://quickfacts.census.gov/qfd/states/04000.html

U.S. Congress. (2001). No Child Left Behind Act. Retrieved September 28, 2003 from www.ed.gov/nclb/landing.jhtml

Wahlstrom, K. L. & Louis, K. S. (2008). How teachers experience principal leadership: the roles of professional community, trust, efficacy, and shared responsibility. *Educational Administration Quarterly, 44*(4), 458–495.

Waters, J. T., Marzano, R. J., & McNulty, R. A. (2003). *Balanced leadership: What 30 years of research tells us about the effect of leadership on student achievement.* Aurora, CO: McREL.

Ylimaki, R. M. (2007). Instructional leadership in challenging US schools. *International Studies in Educational Administration, 35*(3), pp. 11–19.

Ylimaki, R. (2011). *Critical curriculum leadership: A framework for progressive education.* New York: Routledge.

Ylimaki, R. & Jacobson, S. (Eds.). (2011). *US and cross-national policies, practices and preparation: Implications for successful instructional leadership, organizational learning, and culturally responsive practices.* Dordrecht, Netherlands: Springer-Kluwer.

Nurture and Sustain a Culture of Collaboration, Trust, Learning, and High Expectations

Brendan H. O'Connor, Vanessa Anthony-Stevens, and Norma González

---

KEY TOPICS
───────────

- Connecting to Family and Community Funds of Knowledge
- Challenging Deficit Thinking
- Understanding Culture as Practice
- Instructional Leadership for Intercultural Education

CONNECTING TO FAMILY AND COMMUNITY FUNDS OF KNOWLEDGE

In this chapter, we propose that instructional leadership need not, and should not, mean that administrators or teacher-leaders have the sole power and responsibility to determine what knowledge "counts" as academically valuable and to decide how to transmit this knowledge to students. According to ISLLC Standard 2, effective instructional leaders nurture and sustain a culture of collaboration, trust, learning, and high expectations. These leadership processes identified in the ISLLC Standard 2 are best conceived as a multidirectional, dialectical process. We use "dialectical" to underscore the open-ended, back-and-forth, conversational character of this process: instead of assuming they have all the answers (when it comes to issues of academic knowledge and family/community involvement), instructional leaders take the knowledge, values, and viewpoints of family and community members seriously. This kind of communication is sometimes called "transformative dialogue" because, as families and communities come to reconsider the relationship between their world and the too-often-distant world of the school, we teachers and administrators may find ourselves questioning our *own* assumptions about our students and the resources that exist in their homes and neighborhoods. Below, we outline some ways that schools, families, and communities can collaborate to define what kind of school culture—and, therefore, what kind of leadership—is likely to serve the needs of unique students in specific communities.

To illustrate this, we appeal to an educational research tradition known as the Funds of Knowledge (FofK) paradigm. In the original FofK research, teachers entered students' homes as ethnographers—in effect, as anthropologists studying the students' cultural "lifeworlds" (the everyday spaces, suffused with social relationships, in which they live, learn, and grow)—in order to investigate the "historically accumulated and culturally developed bodies of knowledge and skills" present in households (Moll et al., 2005, p. 72). The teachers then had the opportunity to meet in study groups to share what they had discovered, and to explore possibilities for drawing on existing knowledge and strengths in households and communities as a resource for academic learning. This project amounted to an attempt at "theorizing practices": in other words, taking families' everyday activities and know-how and "making them academic"—recognizing their potential, for example, to connect to the forms of knowledge valued in school curricula and state standards. Before you continue reading this chapter, take a few minutes to reflect on your current experiences with theorizing practices.

EXTENDED REFLECTION 2.1

- What do you think of when you hear the word "culture"?
- How have you, if at all, taken families' everyday activities and know-how to make them "academic"?
- How, if at all, do you and your colleagues draw upon students' existing cultural knowledge in the curriculum?
- How, if at all, does your school use culturally relevant pedagogy?

TRANSFORMING RELATIONSHIPS, TRANSFORMING INSTRUCTION

Teachers who participated in this research reported that it transformed their view of their students and their households and communities in two principal ways. First, it overturned the assumption, shared by many teachers and administrators, that what happens at home, or what students learn from their families, is *detrimental* to their school success. We refer to these types of attitudes or beliefs as *deficit discourses*. When given the opportunity to examine students' lifeworlds in detail, rather than concluding that what lower-income, minority students learned at home was a deficit to be overcome, teachers found a wealth of knowledge and skills with potential to inform instruction and in-school interaction (González et al., 1995, pp. 452–453). Second, while many of the teachers involved had no doubt heard of the desirability of "culturally relevant" or "culturally responsive" pedagogy, FofK research allowed them to consider "culture" in a different light. For example, for teachers who worked with a large number of Mexican-American students,

> viewing households within a *processual* view of culture, rooted in the lived contexts and practices of their students and families, engendered a realization that culture is a dynamic concept, and not a static grab bag of tamales, quinceañeras and cinco de mayo celebrations ... [Instead, teachers] found that students acquired a multidimensional depth and breadth from their participation in household life.
>
> (p. 456)

Emphasizing culture as *practice*, and not just as a "grab bag" of traditions or a list of stereotypical traits that people in a certain culture must share, empowered teachers to ground their efforts to "bring students' culture into the classroom" in an authentic understanding of which cultural practices actually had meaning in their students' lives.

However, FofK research was not conceived just as a convenient way for school personnel to "access" household or community knowledge and "translate" it into an acceptable form for the school's purposes. It also sought to transform the relationships among teachers, students, families, and communities, which are too often characterized by confusion, anxiety, and mistrust. An additional outcome of the teachers' home visits was the realization that students' family and community learning takes place in the context of very different kinds of relationships than the traditional student-teacher relationship. Children's relationships with their out-of-school "teachers" are usually "thick" and "multi-stranded":

> the person from whom the child learns carpentry, for example, may also be the uncle with whom the child's family regularly celebrates birthdays or organizes barbecues, as well as the person with whom the child's father goes fishing on weekends.
>
> (Moll et al., 2005, p. 74)

Such "teachers" are more likely than most in-school teachers to "know the child as a 'whole' person, not merely as a 'student,'" since they encounter the child in a variety of different settings and engaged in a variety of activities. Of course, teachers are not family members, and do not, except in rare cases, have such close, long-term relationships with their students, but the question remains: What can teachers and administrators learn from students' out-of-school learning experiences, and what steps can they take to get closer to knowing their students—intellectually, emotionally, and socially—as "whole people"? More to the point, what impact might this have on instruction?

Instructional leaders will be effective in creating a culture of collaboration and trust if they keep relationships at the center of their efforts to redress educational inequity and achievement gaps (González, Wyman, & O'Connor, 2011, p. 488). Doing so means having the will and making the time to engage directly with families, through observation and dialogue, so that the accumulated knowledge and experience contained in households and students' social networks can be brought into conversation with the school's values and priorities. We know that principals, along with teachers, are under a great

FIELDWORK 2.1

Choose a student whom you have gotten to know fairly well, but only in an academic context. Ask permission to visit the student's home, at a convenient time for the family, and, once there, spend some time talking to the student's parents or other family members. You might begin by sharing some stories about what the student is working on at school, how s/he is doing, and if there are upcoming opportunities for family members to be involved with school activities, before (respectfully) inquiring about the family's history. (Commenting on family photos or other objects on display in the family's house and yard can be a good way to start this conversation.)

Hearing about the family's labor and educational history can be especially useful for revealing elements of the family's—and student's—funds of knowledge, but you might also ask about other activities that family members participate in on a regular basis—anything from playing in a band (or singing in a choir), to coaching a baseball team, to cooking, to telling stories, to attending Sunday school or catechism classes, to selling goods at yard sales or flea markets, to fixing cars, to going to the movies. Think about how family expertise in any of these areas might be connected to the kinds of curricular goals expressed in state learning standards for content areas like Math, Science, and Social Studies. Think also about how, as an instructional leader, you could use one or more of these activities as a starting point for family-school-community collaboration.

If possible, on another occasion, observe the student participating in one of these activities or in any out-of-school activity where learning is taking place. How does the student's out-of-school learning look similar to, or different from, the learning s/he does in school? What specific activities or forms of participation does it involve? What social roles exist in the informal educational setting, and what role(s) does the student take on? What changes do you note in her/his behavior (compared with her/his behavior at school)? Be prepared to share: (1) your observations about the differences between learning in family/community contexts and in-school learning, and (2) your thoughts on how understanding family histories and out-of-school learning—in effect, where students come from and what they know how to do—might push us to rethink our approach to curriculum.

deal of pressure to implement state standards and to ensure that certain amounts of material are "covered" in certain amounts of time, but we argue that this need not result in a "narrowed curriculum" that is of little relevance to students' lives (see Chapter 3).

Giving teachers opportunities to explore the funds of knowledge that exist in students' households, and develop a more nuanced understanding of culture, is a starting point for countering the tide of standardization and "de-skilling" of teachers that currently afflicts schools (González et al., 2011). But, as the scenario in the following section demonstrates, nurturing a culture of collaboration and trust, in order to promote learning and maintain high academic expectations, is not *just* about improving instruction. Making a real effort to understand where students and families are coming from does not begin and end with decisions about what and how to teach. It requires the slow, careful building of what participants in the original FofK research called *confianza,* deep trust that implies "serious obligations" to families—for example, the obligation to promote children's well-being in ways that may include, but also transcend academic success. In this way of thinking, instructional leadership means becoming aware of the complex social situations in students' households and communities, and thinking critically about what implications they might have for instruction and students' and families' ability or willingness to benefit from instruction at school.

Instructional leaders and teacher-leaders are positioned to encourage and sustain an educational climate of trust, learning and high expectations. The educational literature documents many examples of how the implementation of policies varies directly with the administrative ethos that is constructed within schools. As illustrated in the following case study, principals and leaders may transform and actively enact policies for the benefit of students, families and communities.

CASE 2.1 DIMENSIONS OF COMMUNITY COLLABORATION IN INSTRUCTIONAL LEADERSHIP

Ms. Gutiérrez, an elementary school principal in a majority Mexican-American community in the Southwest, has actively fostered, nurtured and sustained a sense of community that transcends school walls. Dissatisfied with superficial approaches to multicultural education that rely on traditions, holidays, and so on, she gives interested teacher-leaders at the school structured opportunities to do ethnographic observations of their students' households, and to work on finding ways to integrate family/community funds of knowledge with the standards-based curriculum at the school.

Her approach has already begun to pay dividends: for example, one teacher discovered that her student bought and sold candy that he brought from his grandparents' ranch in Mexico. The teacher took this small nugget of information and developed an elaborated unit on candy, which addressed all of the core curriculum standards in several areas. She was able to bring in mathematics by having students conduct surveys about favorite candies and graph the results; science, by having students determine the ingredients in candy and how they differed between the United States and Mexico; and language arts and social studies in the form of investigating the development of different forms of candy across time and across countries and writing up reports. In this way, one student's small international business venture, and the family know-how that made it possible, became the basis for an academic unit that expanded upon what students already knew and found interesting, rather than ignoring their funds of knowledge or merely seeking to reproduce them. With Ms. Gutiérrez's support, the teacher also emerged as an instructional leader by pursuing family/community collaboration in ways that transformed curriculum and re-framed out-of-school knowledge as academic (Moll et al., 2005).

Additionally, this principal took her leadership role as a protector of students and a creator of safe space for students very seriously. She was highly attentive to the image of the school as a place where students could feel secure in their learning environment. One of the teachers at her school recounts that once, when a Border Patrol officer pulled into the parking lot after school, simply because he had a flat tire, Ms. Gutiérrez went out to the parking lot saying, "Get out, get out, move it, get out!" According to the teacher, she did this because she didn't want any of the students to tell their families, "Hey, I saw *la migra* [immigration authorities] at school!" (Rabin, Combs, & González, 2008). Although the Border Patrol agent was on school property as a coincidence, Ms. Gutiérrez was keenly aware of what his presence would represent symbolically.

Is this an example of instructional leadership? In this case, building a culture of collaboration means deeply understanding the concerns of family and community members and what consequences particular acts and situations could have for them. In other words, it entails a certain degree of intersubjectivity, or mutual understanding, between educators and community members that puts instructional leaders in the shoes of others, and allows them to comprehend how political and social realities outside school can affect students' opportunities to learn.

The example of Ms. Gutiérrez illustrates different dimensions of what it means to nurture a culture of collaboration and respect as an instructional leader. There is no one way to connect meaningfully to communities and to be responsive to concerns beyond the school, but in responding to the contingencies of life beyond school walls, and encouraging her teachers to do so, Ms. Gutiérrez sent the message that school-family-community relationships do matter in instructional leadership. Attaining a more authentic understanding of what *culture* means in the lives of students goes hand in hand with building these relationships, but many teachers and administrators enter schools with little preparation to do so. In the following section, we discuss approaches to culture and collaboration that are not as well-informed or successful as Ms. Gutiérrez's, and offer suggestions as to how instructional leaders can engage more productively with culturally "different" families and communities.

EXTENDED REFLECTION 2.2

- As you are talking with a colleague about investigating students' household and community funds of knowledge, she says, "What's the point? Why would we teach students what they already know?" How would you respond?
- Think of activities at your school (or another school where you have worked) that are considered "cultural." Next, make a list of group activities in which students participate on a regular basis (daily, weekly, or less frequently) *outside* of school. You can include family, community, or peer group activities. How does the sense of "culture" captured by your list compare to the sense of "culture" embodied in the school-based "cultural" activities?
- What does Ms. Gutiérrez's interaction with the Border Patrol agent have to do with instructional leadership? It doesn't seem to relate directly to instructional decision-making—but does it? Or *could* it?

CHALLENGING DEFICIT DISCOURSES AND UNDERSTANDING CULTURE AS PRACTICE

Too often, school failure is theorized as stemming from cultural "difference" or the absence of what dominant society considers to be legitimate cultural values, a perspective that erases the knowledge possessed (and continually reinvented) by economically and socially marginalized families as means of survival and meaning-making in their daily lives. Such a convenient explanation for why many minoritized students do not achieve success in school both allows educators to theorize what they often know little about, and to fall into the common pitfalls of misunderstanding and mistrust bred, in part, by the "poverty" of cultural analysis (Ladson-Billings, 2006) in the field of education. On the other hand, questioning shallow assumptions about culture (Pollock, 2008) promotes the opening up of critical space for educators to pose questions and seek out deeper understandings of the many actions, relationships, and types of practice that contribute to the ways we enact similarity and difference in our schools and communities.

When we refer to "challenging deficit discourses" through these critical conversations, we use *discourses* to mean ways of speaking that people—in this case, educators—routinely use when interacting with one another (Gee, 2005). Because the forms of language we use reflect our values and beliefs about the world and those around us, "deficit discourses" can be understood as common ways of characterizing minoritized families and students, in relation to school, based on what they are perceived to lack or in which ways they are "deficient". For example: "Those parents don't even speak English to their kids! I guess they don't ever want their kids to get ahead!", or "It's the kids from the reservation who bring our test scores down," are oft-repeated statements that portray English language learners or students from an Indian reservation (to give two examples) as problems and obstacles to their own success in education.

Teachers are seldom given space to engage in critical interrogations that can help them move beyond an understanding of culture as deficit. It is more common, probably, for pre-service teachers to be given multicultural methods textbooks (e.g. Farris, 2007) where subtitles such as "Understanding Mexican Culture" are followed by two pages of essentializing statements—simplistic but innocuous at best, offensive and instructionally harmful at worst—about Mexican-American students, such as that men have a higher status than women in Mexican culture (and that the teacher should take this into account when assigning classroom jobs to boys and girls) or that *quinceañera* celebrations are important to every girl of Mexican heritage. If instructional leaders are able to move the school conversation about culture away from stereotypes and generalizations about this or that culture, and encourage teachers to "adjust their lenses" to consider culture as practice, support can be provided for teachers to reconceptualize everyday educational interactions—the what, when, how and from whom students learn—as moments of learning opportunity, rather than moments of alienation from learning (Pollock, 2008).

As a starting point, instructional leaders might think about how to challenge deficit discourses with more practice-based, ethnographically informed conceptions of culture. Drawing on textbooks and curriculum materials already in use at your school and/or drawing on teachers' knowledge of specific discourses about students' or families' supposed cultural "traits" are good ways of beginning the conversation. Here are a few questions that instructional leaders could use to give other educators the opportunity to begin to interrogate commonly-circulating deficit discourses:

FIELDWORK 2.2

1. Have teachers reflect on comments they commonly hear made about minority students in their school and/or other schools. Ask teachers to choose one or two of the comments they have on their lists and then discuss with their colleagues how those comments relate to student achievement in school. Are the comments generally positive or negative? What types of comments portray deficits and what types of comments portray strengths? (Since discussing culture can veer uncomfortably close to discussing "race", be prepared with a few common statements to share with the group in the event that educators exhibit reluctance or tentative distrust toward dialoguing about perceptions of cultural deficit in an open forum.)

2. Select two or three common textbooks, posters, or children's stories that portray a particular cultural group (e.g., Native American). In groups, ask educators to analyze the words, images or story and summarize what types of messages are being conveyed through the document. Are these messages favorable or unfavorable to the cultural group being portrayed? What experiences have educators had personally that challenge or contradict the messages being conveyed through the texts?

The following are three examples of the static treatment of culture in real school settings. These examples highlight educators' failing to *see* students and communities in their complexity, and consequently missing meaningful opportunities for relationship-building and collaboration in the construction of academic knowledge. While these examples may be written off as insignificant in themselves, the totality of their daily repetition in schools across the U.S. is cause for alarm, as it contributes to maintaining static, stereotypical definitions of who a group of people are and what values define them.

Examples

As Pollock (2008) exhorts (in words she claims to have "pilfered" from Ray McDermott), "Think about all the acts that get a child to the graduation stage"—or, by contrast, the accumulated acts that may contribute to keeping a child off that stage, some of which might look like this:

• Students attending an urban charter middle school designed to serve Native American youth are lining up to receive their hot lunch. One of the teachers, an experienced teacher, non-Native, but born and raised near the students' community is attempting to settle students down and organize them in the line. A few of the students do not heed the teacher's instructions, continuing to talk loudly and move freely. Becoming frustrated the teacher tells the disobedient students, "Well, aren't you Native American?! Your culture teaches you to be respectful to your elders—I'm your elder. You should have learned to respect me."

- Many textbooks offer supplemental content-area materials. In Vanessa's case (as a middle school science teacher at the charter school in the first example) she purchased a grade-appropriate Science text to help teach her curriculum. The text came with boxes of additional teaching resources (e.g., inquiry units, targeted reading lessons) designed to complement the primary lesson objectives. Among these supplemental resources was a sliver of materials entitled "Culturally Relevant Lessons". Upon opening this workbook she found examples of non-White groups and individuals, past and present, making contributions to science. She looked at the table of contents to see how the lessons were arranged and found a section titled "Native American medical healers". As her students were nearly all members of a southwestern Indian tribe, she tried to imagine how this worksheet about a doctor of a Midwestern tribal affiliation was relevant to their own experiences. She imagined how the publisher had intended that this lesson be used. On more than one occasion, she observed worksheets like it photocopied and circulated to students as teachers made comments to the effect of, "Well, they're Native American, too, so now they have no excuse to not be engaged in completing THIS work."
- A different school, also with a majority of Native American students, celebrates an annual Culture Week where teachers and students engage in sharing practices central to the local Indian tribe. Every year, American Indian and non-American Indian teachers alike plan a cultural activity or artifact for their students to create in the classroom. The week culminates with an exposition where classes share their work with the entire school, inviting parents and community members. Outside of the school building, in this rural Southwestern community, evidence of local cultural practice is apparent in linguistic repertoires, family relationships, labor, traditions, and physical structures, to say the least. Yet every year, without fail, many of the teachers in the school place orders in the Oriental Trading Company catalog to get the supplies they desire for their "cultural" activity. One year, a teacher ordered dreamcatcher kits for her students to make, despite the fact that making dream-catchers is not a traditional activity for this tribe. Nevertheless, the students glued together the feathers and beads sent from a factory in China, and posted them on the wall for their families to see.

All three of these examples involve teachers and curriculum developers making problematic assumptions about what is culturally relevant or meaningful to students, since the working definition of culture in each case was not based on firsthand knowledge gained from observation (as with the teacher at Ms. Gutiérrez's school) but on a simplistic conception of culture as an unchanging set of behaviors, characteristics, or activities, without any internal diversity (for instance, even among different American Indian tribes). In the first example, a teacher employs the word "respect" while simultaneously failing to question what respect may mean for those individual students, their families, and their community (i.e., What actions are deserving of respect? What words or actions would a young person use to demonstrate respect?) The teacher assumes that he knows something without actually getting to know his students or the ways that elders and youth interact to form the framework of "respectful" interaction.

The second and third examples likewise demonstrate a failure to recognize what makes anything "culturally relevant" to students. Relevance is in relationships. In our daily lives, our relationships to one another are at the core of what make us relevant to one another. That truth is no different at school. "Alternative" or "enrichment" activities mass-produced for wide-scale distribution to appeal to broad audiences cannot capture the immediacy of the social relationships that give cultural activities, traditional or otherwise, meaning in students' lives. Social relationships of reciprocity, and pathways for developing mutual trust, are the muscles and ligaments that attach to objects and activities and give them life—movement, and the ability to act and interact with other forms of knowledge. Starting with relationships, then, rather than starting with preconceived ideas about someone's culture, should be at the center of creating critical opportunity spaces that "can transform students, teacher, and parents, and their relationships, and can provide intellectually challenging alternatives to the 'skill and drill' pedagogies that have always been meted out to minority children in poverty" (González et al., 2011, p. 488).

This is not to say that the science materials highlighted in the second example are necessarily without value. Encountering varied perspectives is part of what it means to live in a multicultural and democratic society, and we certainly do not mean to suggest that students from a certain cultural group should *only* learn about people and practices from that group. Far from it: for the students at Vanessa's school, reading the story of one American Indian medical doctor who approaches medicine from both Western paradigm and the paradigm of his community could be valid and potentially enriching. The problem comes when we assume that this medical doctor can speak for all American Indians, or that his perspective automatically coincides with or reflects the practices and lived experience of diverse people who identify themselves as American Indian, urban and rural, young and old.

Furthermore, the pre-packaged quality of lessons like those in the second and third examples ignores active forms of cultural practice that could potentially facilitate the development of *confianza* (the deep level of trust associated with one's obligations to family members) (González et al., 1995). If educators are encouraged only to rely on a book, we perpetuate the colonial notion that schools generate the only valid form of knowledge, rather than looking to schools as a place to engage in collaborative knowledge construction, even in these times of standardization and high-stakes testing pressures. Moreover, the appropriation of Native American "cultural" perspectives in these examples suggests that the school is continuing to produce and authorize particular forms of legitimized knowledge, and marginalize other forms (Giroux, 1992). For the actual students in Vanessa's science class, their real experiences with medicine and healing, both in traditional tribal practice and institutionalized Western medicine, cannot be voiced when she photocopies the story of a Native American, from an unidentified tribe in a different region of the country, who uses his grandmother's teachings in his modern medical practice. The lived experiences the students may have with medicine men and women, or of attending family members in the local hospital, are not validated. Instead, there is an easy assumption that "This lesson will be relevant to Native American students because it talks about people from their culture," or, equally problematic, "This lesson will educate non-Native students because it describes (representative) Native American approaches to medicine."

The example of the dreamcatcher project similarly relies on and perpetuates stereotypes about culture. It assumes that one Native American tribe's practice is equivalent to any other, disregarding geographic and historical heterogeneity. This activity, cloaked as a feature of "local" culture within the school's curriculum, ignores and devalues the everyday experiences of the students and their families (see Amanti,

2005; Hensley, 2005 for FofK-based alternatives). The dreamcatcher project was not presented in a way that invited critical perspectives on the use and meaning of such an object (for example, on its rise to visibility during the civil rights-oriented Pan-Indian movement of the 1970s; see Jenkins, 2004). Certainly, the dreamcatcher as a symbol of Native solidarity or as a protector against harmful dreams could have meaning for individual students. However, to assume that the dreamcatcher in some way constitutes these students' "culture" imposes a prescriptive view of culture, marginalizing the participation of the students and community, and reinforcing the belief that pervades many marginalized communities: that schools are institutions that do not work for the community, but are imposed upon the community.

Many instructional leaders and teacher educators may find it challenging to push teachers and the educational establishment to go beyond the Oriental Trading catalogs, culturally relevant supplemental materials, and ossified ideas about cultural values to engage practices in households. Household engagement strategies require being willing to listen and learn, and *making* the time to listen and learn. And not listening just one time, but creating and taking advantage of many opportunities to listen. Important, nuanced aspects of how or why a family constructs a basket (for example), its use and meaning in their lives, would potentially all need to be unpacked. The complexities of historical struggle, life experience, nagging questions about cultural authenticity, and the sometimes contradictory ways students perform their identities do not easily transfer to addressing existing standards-based curricular demands. However, as our

---

FIELDWORK 2.3

Select an out-of-school community event to attend. This could be a public institutional event or a large private event—for example, a local veterans' parade, beauty pageant, community open house, a sports activity at the recreation center, etc. Attend the event as an observer and fellow community stakeholder. Taking on the role of learner, seek out casual interactions with others at the event. If parents and students recognize you as their teacher, engage them in casual ways and invite conversation and informal interaction with them.

Building upon your discussion of "challenging deficit discourses" (pp. 16–17) reflect on the following questions: What social roles exist in the setting of the event, and what role(s) do the students/parents/family members take on? How are these roles similar to or different from roles *you* play in your everyday life (i.e., outside of your "teacher" role)? What kinds of things do people speak with you about? How do those conversations expand or change your understandings of student/parent out-of-school practices? Be prepared to share: (1) your observations about the differences between participation in family/community contexts and in-school participation, and (2) your thoughts on how understanding family activities and out-of-school participation—in effect, what students do and how they spend out-of-school time—might push us to rethink our approach to identifying families' practices and ultimately making relevant curricular choices.

educational choices have an impact on our students and their communities, it becomes imperative that instructional leaders help teachers pursue the types of collaborative, unscripted and complicated exchanges that make schools and families relevant to one another, and, in doing so, provide inroads to developing reflexive and dynamic forms of human capital—the potential for students to achieve their goals, building upon the abilities and strengths they bring with them to schools.

Impoverished conceptualizations of culture and the cultural deficiencies of families and households erase the resources, resiliency and knowledge that families possess—knowledge that could serve school learning and be served by school learning. Our hope here is that by *problematizing* the examples presented here, and similar examples, the beginning of an important dialogue about relationships and collaboration can take shape. Coming to see the primacy of relationships—for learning, listening, and collaborating—pushes educators away from relying on multicultural methods textbooks and uninformed (and often baseless) assumptions about the unknown, and toward seeing school interactions and school curriculum with "place-based excitement," endowing the everyday practice, labor and activity of students, families and communities with the academic legitimacy that it is due (González et al., 2011).

INSTRUCTIONAL LEADERSHIP FOR INTERCULTURAL EDUCATION

In effect, the new instructional leader must move from multicultural education, as it has often been understood, to *intercultural* education. This may seem like a matter of semantics, but we feel it is much more than that. While multiculturalism in education has its roots in challenging the dominance of curricular approaches that ignore diversity, and making way for minority-sensitive curriculum, an intercultural approach highlights "contacts and relations, on both the individual and the collective levels . . . articulated in contexts of cultural diversity and heterogeneity" (Dietz & Mateos Cortés, 2011, p. 505). An intercultural approach to school-family-community engagement would imply that educators first recognize that cultural practices are dynamic—uneven, complex, and changing—and then begin to dig more deeply into the practices that form individual and collective repertoires of knowledge.

Our use of *interculturality* is intended to capture the fact that "'practice' supplies us with a panorama of activities that may or may not coincide with normative cultural behavior" (González, 2005, p. 43). For example, a Somali-American high school student who came to the U.S. as a teenaged refugee will almost certainly have "normative" elements of Somali cultural practice in her repertoire: she probably knows how to cook some traditional Somali dishes, is well-versed in Somali Muslim religious practices, knows what life is like in a refugee camp, and speaks a number of languages, like Maay Maay and Somali, "normatively" associated with her cultural identity. But her repertoire also probably contains cultural and linguistic practices, and knowledge, that would not necessarily be associated stereotypically with Somali-American teenagers: she may be a fan of hip hop, or of Bollywood movies; she may know some Spanish from interacting with Spanish speakers at her school or workplace; she is probably skilled at using online social networking tools; she may have gained knowledge of particular jobs or trades from her parents' "labor history" (Moll et al., 2005) since the family arrived in the U.S.

Thus, to understand such a student's cultural world is to understand that households are intercultural, and that their inhabitants "[draw] on multiple cultural systems and [use] these systems as strategic resources" to accomplish their goals (González, 2005, p. 43). A FofK approach to instructional leadership and curriculum development does not seek to *reproduce* in the classroom what students and families already know; rather, it asserts that schools can be intercultural spaces, just as households are, in which students' existing cultural knowledge and strengths, normative or otherwise, are brought into conversation with new forms of learning and social practice, and not erased or treated as a deficit to be overcome.

Even when given the opportunity, however, it is not easy for many teachers to step out of their comfort zone and enter into possibly uncomfortable engagements with students and families, where they may be confronted with issues of power and privilege and unfamiliar cultural practices. Teachers struggle with profound questions about what difference their actions can make, given the long history of marginalization of racially and culturally diverse students in U.S. schools; they may also wonder whether they are personally up to the task of learning to "see" their students, and their students' "cultures", differently, in ways that will at least inform, and possibly transform, the daily work of teaching (Pollock et al., 2010). Not only that, but they may encounter confusion and suspicion from family and community members at first, perhaps because of "ongoing dynamics of distrust . . . [stemming] from local histories of schooling as well as contemporary inequalities" (Wyman & Kashatok, 2008, p. 302), or because of a more general apprehension of outsiders, owing to the family's immigration status or any number of other concerns.

Learning about family and community funds of knowledge, then, must go along with opportunities for self-reflexivity, as teachers learn to see themselves as racially and culturally positioned beings, and to explore the beliefs, biases, and experiences that lead them to respond in certain ways to what they discover in their students' households and communities—and to understand how family and community members see *them*. Enacting critical student engagement (see Chapter 3) may well result in a more "multi-stranded" teacher-student relationship, but getting to know a community truly becomes a critical stance when teachers' understanding of themselves, and their practice, is transformed.

Each of the authors has worked closely with students and families who have crossed geographical borders between countries (or between the U.S. and sovereign Indian nations), often in search of different kinds of educational opportunities. But we have also come to realize that so-called "non-mainstream" students cross many other linguistic and cultural borders—for example, the "border" between family knowledge about the natural world and the academic discourse used to talk about it in Science class—on a daily basis (Lee, 2003). Our task, then, as instructional leaders, is to meet our students at least halfway. As in the case of Mrs. Gutiérrez and the Border Patrol agent, it is possible for teachers to cross "the border between knowledge and power" (González, 2005, p. 42), to get a sense of how the world looks through their students' eyes, to appreciate the different "borders" their students cross in coming to school, and to consider how their teaching practice might "[transcend] the boundaries of the classroom" in order to "rupture the flow of circulating discourses of deficiency and difference" (González, 2005, p. 43, citing McIntyre, Rosebery, & González, 2001).

STRATEGIES FOR LEADERS

How do instructional leaders put all of this background on nurturing a culture of collaboration, trust, learning, and high expectations into practice? This section provides guidance for what today's instructional leaders need to know and be able to do, as well as example strategies for practice. Instructional leaders need to:

Know:

- their families
- their communities
- Funds of Knowledge research tradition
- culture as practice
- intercultural education.

Be able to:

- engage with families and communities through Funds of Knowledge traditions
- establish deep trust or *confianza*
- challenge deficit thinking and discourses
- transform community relationships
- develop intercultural education.

For principals and other instructional leaders juggling an ever-increasing set of demands, it is nonetheless crucial to provide teachers with time and space to explore the interculturality of their students' worlds, think and talk critically about what they find, and work out the implications of their new understanding of culture-as-practice for classroom instruction. Here, we present a number of additional ideas for how to start this process.

Strategies

- Have teachers read case studies from other Funds of Knowledge projects (see González et al., 1995; Moll et al., 2005; the papers collected in González, Moll, & Amanti, 2005), talk about the understanding of culture in FofK research, and then design their own, small-scale FofK project, focusing on the household of just one of their students. (The "Fieldwork" activity in this chapter is just an example of how such a project might be designed). Use professional development time to allow teachers to carry out a home visit and offer professional development credit for community events attended by teachers. In subsequent meetings, structure time for teachers to share what they have learned from observing the out-of-school practices of families and students, and to plan lessons or units connecting out-of-school knowledge with standards-based curriculum.
- Start a weekly parent-teacher journal exchange (with a manageable number of parents—just one or two) to give teachers and parents opportunities to ask questions in a respectful way, and to get to know each other "on a continuous basis . . . and

to make more informed assessments of one another" (García, 2008, p. 297). The purpose of the journal is not to provide traditional weekly updates on the child(ren)'s academic progress. Instead, the idea is to expand the parameters of understanding student growth by allowing teachers and parents to get to know each other beyond the traditional parent-teacher relationship. The teacher could structure the journal like this: Teacher writes a question, such as: What does your family enjoy doing together? The journal goes home with the student for one week, giving her/his parent a week to answer the question. The parent answers and then poses a question to the teacher—again, something related to their social worlds in and beyond the school house. The weekly exchanges can take on a life of their own based on the dialogue that emerges from the questions and answers. However, teachers must be careful to *invite* parents to formulate their own questions as they become more comfortable with the exchanges.

- Encourage teachers to spend time with students in the community, outside of school, in ways that connect to, but transcend in-school academic content. Orellana and Hernández (1999) describe taking "literacy walks" around the urban school neighborhood with elementary-age students, whose facility at "reading the world" around them opened their teachers' eyes not only to their emergent literacy abilities, but also to the reality of living in that neighborhood—for example, the students' need to be able to interpret gang-related graffiti tags from a young age as a matter of personal safety. Have teachers share ideas about possible activities like this, and, afterwards, insights from their interactions with the students.

- Support teachers' efforts to involve themselves in routine activities with community members (Wyman & Kashatok, 2008), such as joining a sports team, attending church, eating dinner with students' families, going to weddings, *quinceañeras*, or other celebrations, and patronizing family businesses. Such efforts may seem insignificant, but they "demonstrate a deep willingness to get to know individuals and local ways of doing things" (Wyman & Kashatok, 2008, p. 301) and can, over time, contribute to building the *confianza* that makes intercultural education possible. The fieldwork is one example of how to structure reflections as teachers participate in routine community activities.

- Work with teachers to identify community "experts" on different topics (e.g. making candy, hunting, laying tile, naming plants in the local language, fixing cars or computers, telling traditional stories or life histories) that might be connected to academic learning, and, with the community members' permission, share this information with the rest of the faculty as an instructional resource. Informed by the experience of the fieldwork assignments, for example, teachers might collaboratively design lesson plans on a particular topic of local interest with a community "expert". In addition to sharing the lesson with the school faculty, the community member and cooperating teacher offer this lesson to the students. Taking time to document student engagement and feedback on the lesson offers a dynamic way to guide future lessons based on student interest and local relevancy.

An intercultural approach to schooling provides opportunities for all of us—educational leaders, teachers, families, and students—to see our intersections of identity, and to examine the factors that inform how and why we meet, and in what ways we are similar and different, endowing respect through the very attention that we pay to one another in the process of coming to understand each other. This chapter makes the case that nurturing a culture of collaboration and trust is not at odds with sustaining a commitment to learning and high expectations. Paying attention to the "messy details" of students' lifeworlds does not mean sacrificing academic rigor or high standards in school curriculum, but enhances the engagement and academic achievement of students who can only benefit from the school's respect for, and recognition of, their diverse funds of knowledge (García, 2008).

SUMMARY

In sum, by making time and space for educators to pursue a deeper understanding of students and families beyond the school, instructional leaders can help teachers build upon the knowledge and strengths that students bring with them to school, while also engaging students in linking their knowledge with standards-based concepts. The examples that we have provided throughout this chapter are offered as possible starting points for conceptualizing a culture of collaboration. Future steps for specific schools will take shape around the local practices, interactions and forms of collaboration that emerge as relevant in particular school sites and communities.

REFERENCES

Amanti, C. (2005). Beyond a beads and feathers approach. In N. González, L. Moll, & C. Amanti (Eds.). *Funds of knowledge: Theorizing practices in households, communities, and classrooms* (pp. 131–142). Mahwah, NJ: Lawrence Erlbaum Associates.

Dietz, G. & Mateos Cortés, L. (2011). Multiculturalism and intercultural education facing the anthropology of education. In B. Levinson & M. Pollock (Eds.). *A Companion to the Anthropology of Education* (pp. 495–516). Malden, MA: Wiley-Blackwell.

Farris, P. (2007). *Elementary and middle school social studies: An interdisciplinary, multicultural approach.* Long Grove, IL: Waveland Press.

García, E. (2008). Valuing students' home worlds. In M. Pollock (Ed.). *Everyday antiracism* (pp. 294–298). New York: New Press.

Gee, J. P. (2005). Meaning making, communities of practice, and analytical toolkits. *Journal of Sociolinguistics, 9*(4), 590.

Giroux, H. (1992). *Border crossing: Cultural workers and the politics of education.* New York: Routledge.

González, N. (2005). Beyond culture: the hybridity of funds of knowledge. In N. González, L. Moll, & C. Amanti (Eds.). *Funds of knowledge: Theorizing practices in households, communities, and classrooms* (pp. 29–46). Mahwah, NJ: Lawrence Erlbaum Associates.

González, N., Moll, L., & Amanti, C. (2005). *Funds of knowledge: Theorizing practices in households, communities, and classrooms.* Mahwah, NJ: Lawrence Erlbaum Associates.

González, N., Moll, L., Tenery, M., Rivera, A., Rendon, P., Gonzáles, R., & Amanti, C. (1995). Funds of knowledge for teaching in Latino households. *Urban Education, 29*(4), 443–470.

González, N., Wyman, L., & O'Connor, B. (2011). The past, present, and future of "Funds of Knowledge". In B. Levinson & M. Pollock (Eds.). *A Companion to the Anthropology of Education* (pp. 481–494). Malden, MA: Wiley-Blackwell.

Hensley, M. (2005). Empowering parents of multicultural backgrounds. In N. González, L. Moll, & C. Amanti (Eds.). *Funds of knowledge: Theorizing practices in households, communities, and classrooms* (pp. 143–152). Mahwah, NJ: Lawrence Erlbaum Associates.

Jenkins, P. (2004). *Dream catchers: How mainstream America discovered Native spirituality.* New York: Oxford University Press.

Ladson-Billings, G. (2006). It's not the culture of poverty, it's the poverty of culture: The problem with teacher education. *Anthropology and Education Quarterly, 37*(2), 104–109.

Lee, O. (2003). Equity for linguistically and culturally diverse students in science education: A research agenda. *Teachers College Record 105*(3), 465–489.

Moll, L., Amanti, C., Neff, D., & González, N. (2005). Funds of knowledge for teaching: Using a qualitative approach to connect homes and classrooms. In N. González, L. Moll, & C. Amanti (Eds.). *Funds of knowledge: Theorizing practices in households, communities, and classrooms* (pp. 71–88). Mahwah, NJ: Lawrence Erlbaum Associates.

Orellana, M. & Hernández, A. (1999). Taking the walk: Children reading urban environmental print. *The Reading Teacher, 52*(6), 612–619.

Pollock, M. (2008). From shallow to deep: Toward a thorough cultural analysis of school achievement patterns. *Anthropology & Education Quarterly, 39*(4), 369–380.

Pollock, M., Deckman, S., Mira, M., & Shalaby, C. (2010). "But what can I do?": Three necessary tensions in teaching teachers about race. *Journal of Teacher Education, 61*(3), 211–224.

Rabin, N., Combs, M., & González, N. (2008). Understanding *Plyler*'s legacy: Voices from border schools. *Journal of Law and Education, 37*(1), 15–82.

Wyman, L. & Kashatok, G. (2008). Getting to know students' communities. In M. Pollock (Ed.). *Everyday antiracism* (pp. 299–304). New York: New Press.

CHAPTER 3

Create a Comprehensive, Rigorous, and Coherent Curricular Program

Rose M. Ylimaki

KEY TOPICS
———

- A Multi-Dimensional Curriculum
- Rigor and Cognitive Demands
- Relevance
- Coherence
- The External Environment

Never before have instructional leaders faced such urgent challenges in their curriculum work. Curriculum standards (Common Core) and assessments (PARCC) are now linked to college and career readiness goals. Further, in many states, principals and teacher effectiveness are judged by student performance on state tests. At the same time, many schools face declining enrollments and budget deficits while they serve increasingly diverse students. Amidst these policy and demographic trends, today's instructional leaders must quickly raise test scores, make curricula more rigorous, and market their schools to compete with surrounding charter and public schools. In other words, curriculum is highly influenced by external politics, policies, curriculum reform trends, and demographic shifts. This chapter is about effective leadership for curriculum or the content of education in the midst of a challenging economic and policy climate.

According to the ISLLC standards, instructional leaders develop rigorous, relevant, comprehensive, and coherent curricula that draw on children's experiences/funds of knowledge and national/state content standards. The new instructional leader must have deep and broad understandings of curriculum (*what* we teach), instruction (*how* we teach), and the cultural and political trends that influence decisions about both. Learning how to be an effective curriculum/instructional leader is an ongoing, reflexive practice that continually evolves with experience, research, teacher relationships, and student/community relationships. Thus, this chapter begins with an extended reflection.

EXTENDED REFLECTION 3.1

Before reading this chapter, write down your definition of "curriculum" and the role of the leader in the development, implementation, and use of curriculum. Keep the definition and ideas about curriculum leadership available and revise it as you read the chapter and participate in the various reflections, fieldwork activities and other learning experiences.

For many practicing teachers and administrators, curriculum is "what the district or state tells them to teach from lists of standards or scope-and-sequence charts". Curriculum is not a static document; rather, curriculum is an ongoing, dynamic interaction of content, teachers' instructional decisions, assessment requirements, and students' backgrounds, all of which occur in a cultural political, historical, and local context. In one sense, curriculum is a formalized document that articulates what students must know and be able to do in each grade level or subjects. Yet "whatever the school subject, the curriculum is historical, political, racial, gendered, phenomenological, autobiographical, theological, and international. Curriculum becomes the site on which the generations struggle to define themselves and the world" (Pinar, Reynolds, Slattery, & Taubman, 1995, pp. 847–848). For instance, some suggest that children must have extensive knowledge about the past while others argue that curriculum must encompass the needs of future (i.e., 21st century learning). Further, a quick glance in three different classrooms would suggest that the same curriculum documents (content) could be translated in varying ways through instruction and received in different ways by students. In other words, curriculum is dynamic, multidimensional process (Porter, 2006). Pinar (2004) agrees, noting that classroom instruction mediates between broader cultural traditions and schooled knowledge. As Pinar and colleagues put it:

> In classrooms, curriculum ceases to be a thing, and it is more than a process. It becomes a verb, an action, a social practice, a private meeting, and a public hope. Curriculum is not just the site of our labor; it becomes the product of our labor, changing as we are changed by it. It is an ongoing, if complicated, conversation.
>
> (Pinar et al., 1995, p. 848)

When instructional leaders engage in curriculum work, they should consider multiple dimensions, broader historical/cultural/political influences, complicated conversations about these dimensions, and how these dimensions affect learning for all children. The relevant curriculum dimensions are:

- Intended Curriculum (Expectations)
- Enacted Curriculum (Instruction)
- Assessed Curriculum (Formative and Summative)
- Learned Curriculum (Outcomes)
- Hidden Curriculum.

Regardless of district or school level, effective instructional leaders recognize that written policy requirements and curriculum standards are subject to interpretation by classroom teachers when they teach the curriculum to their students. More broadly, good instructional leaders understand how written curriculum expectations and instructional practices are shaped by diverse values, cultural politics, and dominant social norms. At the same time, instructional leaders must recognize that there is an intended curriculum written in guidelines and a hidden (often unspoken) curriculum that reflects the beliefs of the dominant society. Today's instructional leaders must have a critical awareness of how underlying belief systems, policy, and the political environment affect curriculum work in schools. Each of these curriculum dimensions is further explained below.

INTENDED CURRICULUM (EXPECTATIONS)

At a basic level, the intended curriculum refers to the *content* we expect students to learn, using standards (e.g. common core), frameworks, and other guidelines. Some practitioners may refer to pacing guides as "the district curriculum". The intended curriculum is overt, explicit, and written in some documentation of *what* is taught supposed to be taught in classrooms (Cuban, 1992; Porter, 2006). As noted curriculum historian Herbert Kliebard (1992) put it, curriculum is the content of education—what is taught and to whom. In other words, the intended curriculum is important to provide clear content targets for instruction and learning to particular students (Reeves, 2009).

Curriculum standards. In the past several decades, professional organizations of various disciplines (math, English/language arts, reading, science, and social justices, etc.) have established curriculum standards and guidelines for student learning. By the late 1990s, all states except Iowa had established content standards, and these content standards formed the basis for state assessments. Professional and state content standards have been hotly debated among scholars and educators, particularly after the standards were linked to state assessments and accountability systems. Most recently, all but five states have adopted the Common Core Standards developed from a foundation of standards from individual states. Common Core Standards communicate what students need to know and be able to do at each grade level and feature an emphasis on integration, disciplinary knowledge, and content learning strategies.

In order to comply with standards and accountability requirements, many districts and schools have also adopted strict curriculum implementation guidelines or pacing calendars. Pacing calendars ensure "coverage" of state or national standards during the academic school year. However, curriculum is multi-dimensional; instructional leaders must help teachers do more than "cover" academic standards. "Academic standards are not a curriculum; they are a framework for designing curriculum" (Erickson, 2007, p. 48). In other words, Common Core Standards provide important guidance with regards to content students must know and be able to do. At the same time, instructional leaders must help teachers and students recognize standards as one of many resources for academic knowledge and skills.

Curriculum expectations and standards evolve in relation to research and changing demands. As this chapter is written, teachers are responsible for Common Core Standards in most states. Common Core Standards are still relatively new, and in certain regards, they represent a drastic change in subject area content knowledge and rigor.

FIELDWORK 3.1

When curriculum expectations change (e.g. Common Core, new state or district standards), leaders must work with and through teachers to recognize the similarities and differences in the current and new intended content. Conduct a forensic analysis of your written (intended) curriculum, using standards and curriculum maps if available. Compare Common Core to your previous state standard/district curriculum. Be prepared to report your findings to the class.

Instructional leaders of all kinds must be able to help teachers and students adjust to curriculum changes, particularly when those changes are subject to high stakes testing. The above fieldwork provides a forensic analysis process (Reynolds, 2012) to help teachers recognize and plan for curriculum changes.

ENACTED CURRICULUM (INSTRUCTION)

The *enacted* curriculum refers to instruction of content or what is actually taught in all classrooms (Porter, 2006). According to Porter (2006), the enacted curriculum is the content delivered and presented by each teacher. The enacted curriculum (instruction) is important because what students are actually taught is a powerful predictor of student learning and achievement. Teachers must negotiate between curriculum standards/ expectations and how much content students can learn within the constraints of time, the teacher's pedagogical skill, and students' backgrounds/developmental levels (Porter, 2006).

Curriculum mapping. Curriculum mapping is a real-time, calendar based (monthly) ongoing process for collecting, reviewing, modifying, and maintaining a database of the enacted (actual), planned, and learned curriculum in an organization (Hayes-Jacobs & Johnson, 2009). More specifically, curriculum mapping addresses what teachers are teaching (the intended curriculum), what students truly experience (the enacted curriculum), and what students have learned (the learned curriculum). Over time, such mapping processes illuminate many curriculum dimensions in action and provide a basis for making decisions about teaching and learning. In order for maps to be used, principals and district leaders need to provide teachers with time to work on the maps on a regular basis, a common format, and a communication system that makes the maps (and ongoing changes) accessible and usable. Do you currently use curriculum maps? How clear and accessible are these maps? Do they really help your teaching or are they, as some teachers have found (Ylimaki, 2011), primarily another source of accountability or paperwork to complete?

ASSESSED CURRICULUM (FORMATIVE AND SUMMATIVE)

The *assessed* curriculum includes a system of tools that is used to determine the extent to which students are acquiring or have acquired the knowledge and skills listed in the curriculum and enacted in the classroom via instruction. More specifically, instructional leaders should consider four types of assessment decisions:

- Summative—Identifies student learning at a particular point in time, usually used to make cumulative decisions about student performance over a period of time
- Formative—Identifies if students are making progress and helps teachers make decisions about instructional adjustments
- Screening—Identifies potential academic or behavior concerns in need of additional assessment
- Diagnostic—Helps to determine why the academic or behavioral needs are occurring; identifies what the student needs to learn

Assessment is more fully considered in Chapter 6.

LEARNED CURRICULUM (OUTCOMES)

The learned curriculum refers to student outcomes on various assessments, including formative and summative (Porter, 2006). The learned curriculum is much more inclusive than the overt, intended curriculum and the assessed curriculum (Eisner, 1970). In other words, the learned curriculum is the effects (unintended and intended) of the educational program experiences. The goal of teaching is to minimize the gap between the enacted (taught) curriculum and the learned curriculum. Along with standardized test items, all student outcomes (including those from formative assessments and benchmarks) should be compared to the intended curriculum expectations to find out which parts of the curriculum have been learned by large numbers of students and which aspects require increased attention (Ainsworth & Viegut, 2006). Information from curriculum alignment processes helps teachers become aware of students' strengths, background experiences or funds of knowledge, and weaknesses so that instruction can be responsive to their needs. I recommend that teachers collaboratively examine student work as well as large-scale assessment results in order to plan effective instruction that meets all students' needs (see Chapter 6).

HIDDEN CURRICULUM

Beyond the written (intended) curriculum, students learn a hidden curriculum that is implied in curricular choices, exclusions, and the very ways in which schools are structured in daily educational routines. In several books, Michael Apple (e.g. 1996; 2000; 2004) argues that there is high-status and low-status curriculum knowledge. In *Ideology and Curriculum*, Apple (2004) argues that the poor and minorities are excluded from high-status knowledge, as they are encouraged into vocational courses that reinforce economic stratification. Apple expands his argument in *Teachers and Texts* where he demonstrates how textbooks and programs promote some knowledge and marginalize other knowledge. Consider, for example, how some knowledge is privileged in the main text and other knowledge is devoted to a sidebar or completely removed. Textbook authors, and eventually educators, must decide whether to teach one thing instead of another, and these choices are not value neutral.

FIELDWORK 3.2

Examine a Social Studies content textbook, noting the knowledge contained in the main part of the text and the knowledge contained in the sidebars. What do you notice? What knowledge is emphasized? What knowledge is mentioned? What do students learn about the type of knowledge that is privileged and the type of knowledge that is "mentioned"? Be prepared to share your observations with the class.

THE EXTERNAL ENVIRONMENT AND RECENT (BROADER) CULTURAL POLITICAL SHIFTS

The hidden curriculum can also be explained by recent (broader cultural political) shifts. As Michael Apple (2004) put it, "Curriculum decisions are political acts" (p. xi). Over the past two decades, educators and others have been increasingly consumed with accountability and a host of curriculum reforms. Data-driven decisions, scripted curriculum programs, pacing guides and fidelity to various instructional reforms, increasingly dominate school language and practices. Take a look at the newspaper headlines below. Do they look familiar? Do you and your colleagues frequently talk about these issues? Have you restructured the ways in which you make decisions to focus on the issues in these headlines?

- "Tea Party Candidate Calls for Character Education in Schools"
- "Common Core Raises the Bar on Nonfiction Reading Standards"
- "Los Angeles School District Test Scores Plummet in Math: District Adopts New Reading Program to Respond"
- "Aspirations District Ranks #1 in the State for Third Year: Parents Seek More Choice Options for District Schools"

Michael Apple (2004) explains these headlines and school responses to these trends (e.g. accountability, continually raising standards, standardization of back-to-basics ideas) in terms of *hegemony*. Hegemony occurs when a particular set of ideologies (e.g. standardization, privatization) promoted by dominant groups affect our common sense about what we should teach in schools. For instance, *back-to-basics* (neoconservative) groups have recently dominated educational conversations, calling for higher standards, accountability in the form of standardized tests. Such neoconservative groups typically posit that the best knowledge was developed in the past. In other words, students (and educators) should return to "the basics". Similarly, *authoritarian populist* groups (e.g. Tea Party) call for schools to teach basic family values or character education. *School choice* (neoliberal) advocates have advocated increased competition among schools whereby parents and students are customers in an educational marketplace. *Neo-nationalist* groups are also increasingly vocal about the need to assimilate immigrant students, help them quickly acquire English, and cultivate their appreciation for Eurocentric perspectives on history. Thus, many districts have experienced pressures to emphasize Eurocentric studies over intercultural education or ethnic studies. Finally, some groups may not support these agendas but they have the technical or professional skills to help these groups realize their agendas. Apple (2004) refers to these groups as the "New Middle Class".

These groups can compromise in the fact that standardized tests give parents an objective way (performance labels) to decide whether one school performs better than another one. In other words, parents have objective information (test scores) from which to decide whether one school is better than another; parents can be more informed educational consumers. Further, standardized tests require strong English proficiency and tend to measure basic kinds of skills easily tested in multiple-choice formats. At the same time, instructional leaders have agency to make a difference in their own schools and communities. Instructional leaders must have the knowledge, skills, and confidence to lead complicated conversations about the politics of curriculum.

Struggles and debates over disparate educational values play out in schools across the U.S. and many other countries. Curriculum continues to be a place where educators, community members, and scholars struggle over values. Social expectations regarding social opportunity, economic opportunity, and influence play out in what we teach and to whom. In sum, today's instructional leaders need to consider academic standards (intended curriculum expectations) in relation to effective instructional processes (the enacted curriculum), assessed curriculum expectations, and student outcomes (the learned curriculum) as well as broader cultural politics and the hidden curriculum. Today's instructional leaders need to recognize the relationships among policy requirements and the politics of curriculum decisions over whose knowledge counts as legitimate (Anderson, 2001). Beyond these curriculum dimensions, curriculum content varies in terms of the inherent rigor and cognitive demands.

RIGOR AND COGNITIVE DEMANDS

Rigor is a centerpiece of the common core, and indeed most curricula for over a century. But what is rigor? When asked to define rigor, teachers and administrators often respond in one of three ways: (1) texts, (2) instruction, and (3) outcomes (learning). Text difficulty has long been measured in terms of readability; however, text difficulty also resides in the structure, the reader's prior knowledge (or lack thereof), vocabulary, and related concepts. Instructional rigor involves teacher and student expectations for academic performance in any teaching activity. Beyond difficulty, rigor involves depth and complexity of a text or task. Finally rigor lies in the benchmark identified for student performance and how close students come to meeting that benchmark.

Rigor also involves cognitive demand or the levels of abstraction required in the text, instruction, and student outcome. Bloom (1956) developed one of the earliest taxonomies to categorize the levels of abstraction in questions that commonly occur in educational settings. Within this cognitive domain, he identified six levels, increasing in complexity and abstract mental levels, to the highest order, classified as evaluation. Bloom's taxonomy levels were:

1. Knowledge—recall data or information
2. Comprehension—understand the meaning or interpretation of text, instructions, or a problem

3. Application—use a concept in a new situation
4. Analysis—separate material or concepts into component parts to understand an organizational structure
5. Synthesis—put parts together to form a new whole and create a new meaning
6. Evaluation—make judgments about the value of ideas or materials.

Since Bloom's early work, many others have used various schemas to describe cognitive demand in different learning and assessment contexts, including the two that follow: Andrew Porter's (2006) work on the enacted curriculum and Norman Webb's (1997) Depth of Knowledge levels. See Table 3.1 below and the box that follows.

Table 3.1 Porter's Enacted Curriculum and Cognitive Levels (2002)

English Language Arts	Mathematics
Recall Provide facts, terms, definitions, conventions; describe; etc.	Memorize Recall basic mathematics facts; etc.
Demonstrate/Explain Follow instructions; give examples; etc.	Perform procedures Do computational procedures or algorithms; etc.
Analyze/investigate Categorize, schematize; distinguish fact from opinion; make inferences, draw conclusions; etc.	Demonstrate understanding Communicate mathematical ideas; use representations to model mathematical ideas; etc.
Evaluate Determine relevance, coherence, logical, internal consistency; test conclusions; etc.	Conjecture, generalize, prove Determine the truth of a mathematical pattern or proposition; write formal or informal proof; etc.
Generate/create Integrate, dramatize; predict probable consequences; etc.	Solve non-routine problems, make connections Apply and adapt a variety of appropriate strategies to solve problems; etc.

NORMAN WEBB'S DEPTH OF KNOWLEDGE LEVELS (1997)

1. **Recall**—Recall or recognition of a fact, information, concept, or procedure.
2. **Basic Application of Skill/Concept**—Use of information, conceptual knowledge, follow or select appropriate procedures, two or more steps with decision points along the way, routine problems, organize/display data.
3. **Strategic Thinking**—Requires reasoning, developing a plan or sequence of steps to approach problem; requires some decision making and justification; abstract and complex; often more than one possible answer.
4. **Extended Thinking**—An investigation or application to real world; requires time to research, think, and process multiple conditions of the problem or task; non-routine manipulations, across disciplines/content areas/multiple sources.

Webb's Depth of Knowledge (DOK) levels and Porter's schema are increasingly popular in district as instructional leaders work to develop instructional processes and formative assessments to demonstrate learning. It is important to note that the Webb levels do not necessarily indicate degree of "difficulty" in that Level 1 can ask students to recall or restate a simple or a much more complex concept, the latter being much more difficult. Conversely, depth of understanding a concept is required to be able to explain how/why a concept works (Level 2), apply it to real-world phenomena with justification/supporting evidence (Level 3), or to integrate one concept with other concepts or other perspectives (Level 4). Further, DOK levels name four different ways students interact with content. Each level is dependent upon how *deeply* students understand the content in order to respond, not simply the "verb" used in a particular instructional and/or assessment task. In other words, depth of knowledge is about depth and complexity, not difficulty. The intended learning outcome determines the depth. Ask yourself: What mental processing must occur? While Bloom's taxonomy suggests the importance of the verb (e.g. describe, evaluate), what comes after the verb is the best indicator of rigor in depth of knowledge.

- *Describe* the process of legislation.
- *Describe* how the two political parties are alike and different.
- *Describe* the most significant effect of the Civil War on states in the South.

Notice the above statements all begin with the same verb (*describe*). Yet when you look at what comes after the verb in terms of the expectation, the cognitive demand changes. The first description requires understanding a process. The second description requires a comparison of two entities, and the third description requires a deep understanding of the complex issues and effects in the Civil War in order to describe the most significant effect. Effective instructional leaders/administrators and teacher leaders use various teacher meetings (e.g. faculty meetings, grade-level meetings, cross-grade level meetings) to examine rigor in terms of instruction and materials as well as assessments.

RELEVANCE

Many school and district leaders rightly emphasize relevance along with rigor. Here relevance means how well curriculum content relates to students' lives, cultures, and communities. As Linda Darling-Hammond (2006) puts it, schools should be places where "the work students are asked to do is work worth doing" (p. 21). Similarly, William Daggett (2005) recommends that schools emphasize rigorous curriculum content, instructional processes that teach children to think and wonder, as well as application to real-world problems. His Rigor and Relevance Application Model is based upon two continua: (1) Bloom's taxonomy describing increasingly complex levels of thinking (described earlier) and (2) an application model that describes increasingly complex levels of putting knowledge into action in complex, real world problems. "Students will learn more and work harder if the content is related to something they already know something about and are interested in" (Daggett, 2005, p. 14). McNulty and Quaglia (2007) make a similar argument and put a greater emphasis on disciplinary concepts and skills. Rigorous and relevant curricula are characterized by content that is linked to a core disciplinary concept and requires students to do authentic work using methods that are specific to the discipline and appropriate to solve complex problems (McNulty & Quaglia, 2007, p. 14).

The notion of a relevant curriculum is not new. John Dewey (1956) called for a curriculum that involves a critical but balanced knowledge of the culture and the knowledge of the child in order to extend children's learning. Here Dewey alludes to cultural knowledge as well as experience and application. More recently, González, Moll, and Amanti (2005) wrote about the importance of building upon children's funds of knowledge in the school curriculum. Funds of knowledge refer to linking students' lives, local histories, and community contexts to curriculum and instruction. Drawing upon extensive qualitative studies in southern Arizona for over twenty years, González, Moll, and Amanti (2005) have identified communities that possess funds of knowledge (e.g. agriculture, mining, economics, household management, communications, collaboration) that educators can harness as resources in school and classroom settings. Their research suggested that all students entered school with experience, skill, and information learned at home and in the community. However, these funds of knowledge may or may not be supported in schools with heavy emphases on standardization and assessments. (For additional information on culture and funds of knowledge, see Chapter 2.) Many educators embrace culturally responsive pedagogy as a way to incorporate students' cultural backgrounds/funds of knowledge in the curriculum.

Gay (2000) defines culturally responsive pedagogy as using the cultural knowledge, prior experiences, and performance styles of diverse students to make learning more appropriate and effective for them; it teaches to and through the strengths of these students. Gay (2000, p. 29) also describes culturally responsive teaching as having these characteristics:

- It acknowledges the legitimacy of the cultural heritages of different ethnic groups, both as legacies that affect students' dispositions, attitudes, and approaches to learning and as worthy content to be taught in the formal curriculum.
- It builds bridges of meaningfulness between home and school experiences as well as between academic subjects and lived sociocultural realities.
- It uses a wide variety of instructional strategies that are connected to different learning styles.
- It teaches students to know and praise their own and each other's cultural heritages.
- It incorporates multicultural information, resources, and materials in all subjects and skills routinely taught in schools.

Literature in the culturally responsive classroom includes multiple ethnic perspectives and literary genres. Ladson-Billings (1992) explains that culturally responsive teachers develop intellectual, social, emotional, and political learning by "using cultural referents to impart knowledge, skills, and attitudes" (p. 382). That is, culturally responsive teachers realize not only the importance of academic achievement, but also the maintaining of cultural identity and heritage (Gay, 2000). As Shor (1992) explains,

> It is a student-centered program for multicultural democracy in school and society . . . The goals of this pedagogy are to relate personal growth to public life, to develop strong skills, academic knowledge, habits of inquiry, and critical curiosity about society, power, inequality, and change.

(pp. 15–16)

FIELDWORK 3.3

Knowledge and Ethnic Studies

View *Precious Knowledge* video on Mexican American Studies (MAS) curriculum debate (www.preciousknowledgefilm.com). Look for evidence of instructional leadership applied to the curriculum dimensions discussed in this chapter. What would you do if you were the principal/instructional leader of the school featured in this video and why? What would you do if you were the district curriculum/ instructional leader and why?

Further, in culturally responsive pedagogy, education is transformative, meaning that students develop the knowledge and skills to become social critics who can make reflective decisions and implement those decisions to affect personal, social, and political actions. Students learn to respond to inequities and to "read the world" (Freire, 1993). Yet, as many teachers and students in the Tucson Unified School District (TUSD) can attest, culturally responsive pedagogy and related approaches that teach children to work toward social change, requires leaders/advocates who can educate communities about the value of culturally responsive pedagogy.

When Mexican American Studies (MAS) was initially developed, university professors and teachers with backgrounds in critical perspectives (e.g. Freire, McLaren, Giroux) worked together to develop a strong culturally responsive curriculum aimed at empowerment and social justice. In some TUSD schools, however, principals did not have strong backgrounds in the critical perspectives and pedagogy necessary to fully advocate for this program in their schools and communities. And while the MAS program had strong results (increased attendance, graduate rate, and student outcomes), data did not save the program with the state or the district. This case is very complex, but it clearly illustrates curriculum as a site of struggle over knowledge, values, and the legitimacy of both. Further, it illustrates the need for principals/curriculum leaders of culturally diverse schools to have backgrounds in critical perspectives on culturally responsive pedagogy as one way to meet the Common Core and other rigorous academic standards. Further, in order for the curriculum to be coherent and effective, culturally responsive pedagogy must be integrated with other approaches.

COHERENCE

A coherent curriculum effectively organizes and integrates important ideas so students can see how the ideas build on or connect with prior experiences, background knowledge/funds of knowledge and enables students to develop new understandings and skills. In other words, curriculum coherence is in place when "policies, strategies, and content across subject areas and grade levels are consistent and aligned, reflect standards, and result in students, teachers, and parents positively perceiving the rationale, scope, and sequence of educational experience" (Liebling, 1997, p. 16). A coherent curriculum is one that holds together, that makes sense as a whole; and its parts are unified and connected by that sense of the whole. Coherence makes connections explicit, including developmental connections across grades and among content areas, such as literature and historical periods. Without a coherent curriculum, teachers often duplicate their instructional efforts and spend valuable class time on unnecessary review of the material students already know.

FIELDWORK 3.4

Ask a principal . . .

Interview a principal who facilitates curriculum development on a regular basis and share what you learned with the class. Ask the principal:

- How do you help teachers set priorities for instruction?
- How do you and the teachers ensure that curriculum priorities are taught to an appropriate depth?
- How do you and the teachers ensure vertical alignment of curriculum from one grade level to the next?
- How do you foster connections across various subject areas including the arts?
- How do you integrate students' cultures/ethnic backgrounds into the curriculum?
- Describe a typical meeting in which you work with teachers on curriculum.
- How do you assess coherence? How do you identify and address gaps and overlaps?

Did the principal talk about all of the curriculum dimensions discussed so far? What was emphasized and what was missing? Did the principal discuss the school culture or external politics?

STRATEGIES FOR LEADERS

How do instructional leaders put all of this background on curriculum rigor, relevance, coherence and cultural politics into the curriculum dimensions discussed in this chapter? This section provides guidance for what today's instructional leaders need to know and be able to do as well as example strategies for practice. Instructional leaders need to:

Know:

- professional, national, and state content standards
- content (and rigor) of assessments
- rigor of teaching materials and teaching approaches
- a range of teaching approaches to enact curriculum standards/content
- potential points of integration for coherence across content standards
- culturally responsive pedagogy.

Be able to:

- align curriculum expectations with assessments and instructional approaches
- provide professional development in various instructional approaches
- help teachers integrate children's interests and funds of knowledge/experiences into a relevant, comprehensive curriculum
- analyze rigor in instruction, content/materials, assessments
- recognize underlying assumptions and values of policies and related curriculum practices
- educate and advocate for culturally responsive curricula in their schools and communities.

Use effective strategies to ensure:

Rigor

- Cross-Grade Level Teams—of teachers working together to examine rigor in instruction documented on curriculum maps, texts, or materials and assessments. For example, teachers in grades 2, 3, and 4 may meet to examine rigor in their textbooks and other materials. Many textbook companies have leveled readers, but there is collective power when teachers work together and read their grade level materials looking for rigor in terms of text structure and difficulty (vocabulary and other markers of readability). See companion website for more information.
- Differentiation—teachers develop particular lessons that differentiate content for students with differing backgrounds, experiences, and ability levels.
- Benchmark Assessment Teams—teachers should meet in grade level and cross-grade level teams to examine benchmark assessments and other measures of student performance. In particular, teachers should look for the cognitive demand required of the assessment tasks used at their grade level, and use this information to make decisions about where to focus instruction.
- Equity Audits—are a systematic way for instructional leaders to assess the degree of equity or inequity present in key dimensions of their curriculum—teacher/instructional quality, curriculum expectations, and achievement. See Chapter 6.

Relevance

- Curriculum Interest Audits—even the most standard curriculum expectations or maps imply whose history is of most worth, whose books are worthy of reading, which curriculum and text selections include author diversity (e.g. gender, race/ethnicity) and multiple ways of knowing, experiencing and understanding content. Teachers meet in grade level teams to examine texts for culturally relevant topics, perspectives, diversity in the selection of authors, and topics that may connect with their students.
- Policy Rhetoric Analysis Teams—principals/instructional leaders model how to examine policy documents, newspapers, media, and other state requirements for underlying assumptions. Someone in the group keeps track of assumptions and policy language on large charts. Group members make note of when they see or hear the policy rhetoric or underlying assumptions on the same charts.

Coherence

- Online Resources (e.g. Atlas)—a number of computer programs help teachers align curriculum maps across content areas and grade levels. These programs illustrate possible points of content integration to ensure curriculum coherence.
- Cross-Grade Level and Cross-Disciplinary Teams—teachers meet with teachers who teach children in grade levels below and above the one they teach to discuss curriculum expectations/standards and maps and how those expectations are developed or reinforced across grade levels and/or across disciplines. To enable this process, district and school leaders must provide teachers with ample time to meet with their colleagues. Further, teachers need to meet to examine transitions (from elementary to middle and from middle to high school grade levels).
- Walk-Throughs and Other Strategies—to monitor curriculum implementation and coherence.

Provide:

- resources for curriculum materials, collaborative teacher work time, and professional development (see also Ylimaki & Brunderman, Chapter 8, this volume)
- teacher leadership through engagement in regional or national networks for curriculum
- opportunities for inter-visitation to other schools to see what is taught and how.

CASE 3.1 CHANGING CURRICULUM . . . AGAIN!

Elementary principal Karen Minor watched her teachers' skeptical reactions when she told them they needed to adopt the new common core curriculum. Over the past five years, the school's curriculum had revolved around the Title I literacy intervention program with all activities aimed at assessed literacy standards (e.g. fluency, phonemic awareness, comprehension). At the same time, the school demographics had shifted from a primarily stable middle class population to a more transient, working class, ethnically diverse population. Mrs. Minor and the teachers had agreed to Success for All (SFA) supplemented by leveled reading material to accommodate various student abilities. Naturally, many teachers had become comfortable with the existing program and believed it helped meet the needs of their increasingly diverse students.

On the one hand, as a result of this standardized SFA program, the school performed well on standardized tests, attaining "proficient" or "excelling" labels for the past three years. On the other hand, test scores revealed clear achievement gaps among students of color and their white peers. Teachers were often reluctant to discuss achievement gaps in terms of race/ethnicity, preferring to "teach all children the same" and "develop intervention programs so that *all* children could attain high proficiency levels". Difficult conversations were typically avoided in favor of collegiality norms.

Although the academic intervention courses were designed to support increased critical thinking, classes often focused on drill and practice activities aimed at improved state test scores. Further, according to the school members, consistency and coherence within and across grade-levels has largely been achieved. Yet when Mrs. Minor walked through classrooms, she wondered if the curriculum was sufficiently engaging and rigorous to accommodate changes toward the common core. Generally speaking, the common core standards were more holistic and promoted more rigorous non-fictional texts and critical thinking skills.

Mrs. Minor knew change would take time, but she had little time to lose. Even a brief glance at the common core revealed major changes, and teachers were slow to get on board. Her most recent faculty meeting illuminated more teacher resistance when she asked for changes to curriculum maps. As one teacher put it, "We have changed these maps so many times. What good does that do to help our students be able to read more difficult material in the common core books?" Another teacher added (quietly to the teacher next to her), "I can dust off any new maps she wants, but that doesn't mean I'm going to forget about developmentally appropriate practices and teach my students at their levels." A new teacher (who rarely spoke) quickly spoke up and said, "I don't think we have a choice. The common core is coming along with new tests. Our students will have to make the change, but I think we need to recognize that we have a major problem with achievement gaps now. That is only likely to get worse." The first teacher rolled her eyes, but before the conversation could go further, it was 4:30, the contractual end to the day. Mrs. Minor returned to her office and reflected on the day.

Questions

1. What would you do if you were Mrs. Minor?
2. How can the teachers' beliefs or assumptions be negotiated in ways that support the common core implementation without compromising the needs of an increasingly diverse student population?
3. Do you consider this curriculum to be rigorous, comprehensive, and coherent? Why or why not?

EXTENDED REFLECTION 3.2

Revisit your definition of curriculum that you wrote at the beginning of the chapter. How, if at all, has your definition changed?

Be prepared to share your thoughts in a small group and/or to the whole class.

SUMMARY

This chapter examined curriculum or the content of education in five dimensions: (1) intended; (2) enacted; (3) assessed; (4) learned; and (5) hidden. All of these curriculum dimensions are shaped by individual beliefs, values, external cultural politics, and policies. Effective instructional leaders recognize that written curriculum standards are subject to interpretation by classroom teachers when they teach the curriculum to their students. Exemplary instructional leaders (principals and teachers) work together to map curriculum guidelines, link instruction with assessments, and monitor explicit learning (outcomes) and the implicit hidden curriculum.

According to the ISLLC standards, curriculum is also characterized by rigor, relevance, and coherence. Rigor should be addressed in terms of texts, instruction, and outcomes as well as cognitive demands. Yet instructional leaders must balance students' interests, cultural funds of knowledge, and rigorous (tested) curriculum expectations. Curriculum coherence helps principals and teachers attain this balance by organizing the curriculum in ways that connect rigorous expectations with other ideas, students' interests, and cultural backgrounds. Curriculum content is also shaped by broader cultural politics and hegemony. In other words, instructional leaders must help teachers and others think about how policy and cultural political rhetoric affect curriculum content, what we consider legitimate knowledge, and what is hidden in the curriculum. As schools and communities become increasingly diverse, the new instructional leader must become more critical, conscious of children's funds of knowledge, and skilled in the kind of curriculum work needed to attain social justice. This chapter concluded with strategies or processes that help instructional leaders put curriculum rigor, relevance, and coherence into practice in all dimensions of curriculum work.

BIBLIOGRAPHY

Ainsworth, L. and Viegut, D. (2006). *Common formative assessments: How to connect standards-based instruction and assessment.* Thousand Oaks, CA: SAGE.

Anderson, G. (2001). Disciplining leaders: A critical discourse analysis of the ISLLC Examination and Performance Standards in educational administration. *International Journal of Leadership in Educational Administration, (4)*3, 199–216.

Apple, M. (1988). *Teachers and texts: A political economy of class and gender relations in education.* New York: Psychology Press.

Apple, M. (1996). *Cultural politics and education.* New York: Teachers College Press.

Apple, M. (2000). *Official knowledge: Democratic education in a conservative age.* New York: Routledge.

Apple, M. (2004). *Ideology and curriculum.* New York: Routledge.

Au, W. (2007). High-stakes testing and curricular control: A qualitative metasynthesis. *Educational Researcher, 36*(5), 258–267.

Au, W. (2008). *Unequal by design: High stakes testing and school organizations.* London: Metheun.

Ball, S. (1994). *Education reform: A critical and poststructural approach.* Buckingham, UK: Open University Press.

Beane, J. A. (1995). Introduction: What is a coherent curriculum? In J. A. Beane (Ed.). *Toward a coherent curriculum.* Alexandria, VA: Association for Supervision and Curriculum Development.

Bloom, B. (1956). *Taxonomy of educational objectives, handbook 1: The cognitive domain*. New York: David McKay.

Brazee, E. N. & Capelluti, J. (1995). *Dissolving boundaries: Toward an integrative curriculum*. Columbus, OH: National Middle States Association.

Cotton, K. & Savard, W. G. (1980). *The principal as instructional leader: Research on school effectiveness project*. Portland, OR: Northwest Regional Educational Laboratory.

Cuban, L. (1992). Managing dilemmas while building professional communities. *Educational Researcher, 21*(1), 4–11.

Daggett, W. (2005). *Achieving academic excellence through rigor and relevance*. Rexford, NJ: International Center for Leadership in Education.

Darling-Hammond, L. (2006). Constructing 21st-century teacher education. *Journal of Teacher Education, 57*(3), 300–314.

Darling-Hammond, L., Ancess, J., & Falk, B. (1995). *Authentic assessment in action: Studies of schools and students at work*. New York: Teachers College Press.

Dewey, J. (1956). *The child and the curriculum and the school and society*. Chicago, IL: University of Chicago Press.

Dewey, J. (2008/1916). *Democracy and education*. New York: Seven Treasures Publications.

Edmonds, R. (1979). Effective schools for the urban poor. *Educational Leadership, 37*, 15–24.

Eisner, E. W. (1970). Curriculum development: Sources for a foundation for the field of curriculum. *Curriculum Theory Network, 5*, 3–15.

Erickson, H. L. (Ed.). (2007). *Stirring the head, heart, and soul: Redefining curriculum, instruction, and concept-based learning*. Thousand Oaks, CA: Corwin.

Finn, J. & Voelkl, K. (1993). School characteristics related to student engagement. *Journal of Negro Education, 62*(3), 249–268.

Fenstermacher, G. (2006). *Rediscovering the student in democracy and education*. Albany, NY: SUNY Press.

Freire, P. (1993). *Pedagogy of the oppressed*. New York: Continuum.

Gay, G. (2000). *Culturally responsive teaching: Theory, research, & practice*. New York: Teachers College.

González, N., Moll, L., & Amanti, C. (2005). *Funds of knowledge: Theorizing practices in households, communities, and classrooms*. New York: Lawrence Erlbaum Associates, Inc.

Hayes-Jacobs, H. & Johnson, A. (2009). *The curriculum mapping planner*. Alexandria, VA: Association for Supervision & Curriculum Development.

Henderson J. & Gornik, R. (2006). *Transformative curriculum leadership* (3rd ed.). Upper Saddle River, NJ: Prentice-Hall.

Hirsch, E. D., Jr. (1996). *The schools we need and why we don't have them*. New York: Anchor Books.

hooks, b. (1994). *Teaching to transgress*. New York: Routledge.

Johnson, B. & Johnson (2005). *High stakes: Poverty, testing, and failure in America's schools*. Lanham, MD: Rowan & Littlefield.

Kliebard, H. (1992). *Forging the American curriculum*. New York: Routledge.

Liebling, C. R. (1997). *Achieving standards-based curriculum alignment through mindful teaching*. Arlington, VA: The New York Technical Assistance Center and The George Washington University Region III Comprehensive Center.

Ladson-Billings, B. (1992). Reading between the lines and beyond the pages: A culturally relevant approach to literacy teaching. *Theory Into Practice, 31*(4), 312–320.

Madaus, G., & Clarke, M. (2001). The adverse impact of high-stakes testing on minority students: Evidence from one hundred years of test data. In G. Orfield & M.L. Kornhaber (Eds.). *Raising standards or raising barriers?* (pp. 85–106). New York: Routledge.

McMahon, B. & Portelli, J. (2004). Engagement for what? Beyond popular discourses of student engagement. *Leadership and Policy in Schools, 3*(1), 59–76.

McNeil, L. (2005). *Contradictions of school reform: Educational costs of standardized testing.* New York: Routledge.

McNulty, R. J. & Quaglia, R. J. (2007). Rigor, relevance, and relationships. *School Administrator, 64*(8), 18–24.

Newmann, F., Wehlage, G., & Lamborn, S. (1992). The significance and sources of student engagement. In Fred Newman (Ed.). *Student engagement and achievement in American secondary schools* (pp. 11–39). New York: Teachers College Press.

Page, R. (2006). Curriculum matters. In David Hansen (Ed.). *John Dewey and our educational prospect: A critical engagement with Dewey's democracy and education.* Albany, NY: SUNY Press.

Pinar, W. (2004). *What is curriculum theory?* Mahwah, NJ: Lawrence Erlbaum.

Pinar, W. F., Reynolds, W. M., Slattery, P., & Taubman, P. M. (1995). *Understanding curriculum: An introduction to the study of historical and contemporary curriculum discourses.* New York: Peter Lang.

Porter, A. C. (2006). Curriculum assessment. *Handbook of complementary methods in education research,* 141–159.

Reeves, D. B. (2009). *Leading change in your school: How to conquer myths, build commitment, and get results.* Alexandria, VA: Association for Supervision & Curriculum Development.

Reynolds, T. (2012). Forensic analysis process. A paper presented at the Leadership development: Principal instructional leadership conference, Tucson, AZ.

Shor, I. (1992). *Empowering education: Critical teaching for social change.* Chicago, IL: University of Chicago Press.

Smith, W., Butler-Kisber, L., LaRocque, L., Portelli, J., Shields, C., Sparkes, C., & Vibert, A. (1998). *Student engagement in learning and life: National project report.* Montreal, Quebec: Office of Research on Educational Policy, McGill University.

Steinberg, L. (1992). Impact of parenting practices on adolescent achievement: Authoritative parenting, school involvement, and encouragement to succeed. *Child Development, 63*(5), 1266–1281.

Tyler, R. (1949). *Basic principles of curriculum and instruction.* Chicago, IL: University of Chicago Press.

Walker, D. & Soltis, J. (2004). *Curriculum and aims.* New York: Teachers College Press.

Webb, N. (1997). Determining alignment of expectations and assessments. Retrieved from http://archive.wceruw.org/nise/Publications/Briefs/Vol_1_No_2/

Whitty, G., Power, S., & Halpin, D. (1998). *Devolution and choice in education: The school, the state, and the market.* Buckingham, UK: Open University Press.

Ylimaki, R., (2011). *Critical curriculum leadership: A framework for progressive education.* New York: Routledge.

CHAPTER 4

Create a Personalized and Motivating Learning Environment for Students

Rose M. Ylimaki

KEY TOPICS

- Engagement and Learning
- Extrinsic and Intrinsic Motivation
- Motivating Student Learning Environments
- Teachers' Work Environments

According to the ISLLC Standard 2, instructional leaders create a personalized and motivating learning environment for students. Personalized and motivating learning environments are essential for learning to occur in classrooms and schools. This chapter asks aspiring instructional leaders to consider intrinsic as well as extrinsic dimensions of learning environments that support student and teacher engagement in learning. More specifically, this chapter will provide instructional leaders with understandings of the relationships among motivation, engagement, creativity, and learning. The chapter also includes a case study and learning activities to help aspiring leaders think through challenges or tensions that may arise as leaders work to change learning environments. To begin, I invite you to reflect on your own experiences as an adult learner in the opening reflection activity. Keep your reflection available to reconsider as you work through the next section of the chapter. Subsequent activities will ask you to relate your learning experiences to student learning.

The next section considers the conditions theorists (e.g. Cambourne, 1993) have identified as essential for engagement in the learning process.

EXTENDED REFLECTION 4.1

Your Learning Process

Think about a recent experience when you became so engrossed in learning something well that you forgot everything else going on around you. What motivated you to take on the new learning? Describe what you learned and the process that you followed to develop your skills. Compare your description with a partner. Together, identify the commonalities in the process and be prepared to share the process steps with the class.

ENGAGEMENT AND LEARNING

Engagement is an essential condition of student (and adult) learning, in part due to the relationship among engagement, enjoyment in the learning process, and motivation to seek present and future learning experiences. The next subsection further explores conditions of learning that support engagement.

Cambourne's Conditions of Learning

Brian Cambourne (1993) studied hundreds of children as they learned to talk and found that children seemed to master very complex language learning processes outside of the classroom but struggled with the school curriculum. He wondered what conditions were present outside the classroom that allowed students to be so successful. After observing hundreds of students in various additional learning settings, Cambourne identified a set of conditions that were always present when children learned to talk: immersion, demonstration, engagement, expectations, responsibility, approximation, use, and response. Each condition is described below. Literacy scholars (e.g. Frank Smith, Ken Goodman, Don Holdaway) later applied Cambourne's (1993) conditions to literacy education. The next several paragraphs describe each condition of learning using examples from literacy and math.

Immersion. According to Cambourne and Brown (2003), children must be immersed in literacy, surrounded by and interact with a variety of text, both in visual and aural forms. Classrooms are filled with a variety of print—posters, labels, charts, poems, songs, children's work, shared writing, and so forth. There are books of all kinds easily accessible. Throughout the day, children hear various texts read aloud by the teacher, noted authors, peers, and themselves. The print may be controlled by the teacher or selected by students. Print sources change regularly, but there is always a print-rich classroom environment to explore a variety of written language meaningfully and deeply.

Immersion is also a critically important component of mathematics learning in both aural and visual forms. Several of the visual forms overlap with existing print-rich environments. Classrooms are filled with large charts and graphs. Children's attempts to solve math problems are displayed. Teachers are mindful to use math vocabulary while immersing students in experiences that give children ample opportunity to derive meaning from these experiences.

Demonstration. Children and adults tend to learn best (whatever the activity or content) when they see the concept demonstrated by someone they trust. Demonstrations can be in the form of actions (listening to someone talk or read aloud) or artifacts (seeing the symbolic form of the word or looking at the book). When children are immersed in language and receive repeated demonstrations of how language works, they find patterns in language that lead to an understanding of its structure. That is, in order for patterns to emerge, children need to see demonstrations. Further, it is important that demonstrations of sub-skills occur in context. In the current testing environment, the pressures to teach isolated skills have caused many teachers concerns about their abilities to provide powerful demonstrations. Teachers must plan demonstrations carefully, making sure to include the skills and processes in demonstrations. In addition, teachers can provide demonstrations of these skills in individual and group conferences, including materials that simulate the testing environment.

Traditionally, math has been taught by demonstrations followed by practice. The teacher demonstrates how to solve a particular problem and then students practice in a set of assigned problems. Such a demonstration-practice process is not aligned with Cambourne's notion of demonstration. Mathematics demonstrations—where the teacher and students talk out loud to reveal their thinking—are powerful ways to help children engage in a task and begin to see patterns and structure in the language and meaning of mathematics.

Engagement. Learning will not take place without engagement (Cambourne, 1993). Engagement requires that the learner feels capable of learning what is being presented to him/her. In other words, the material must be attainable, presented in a context that is meaningful to the learner, and presented in a safe environment. Students can be motivated to achieve high test scores or good grades but not be engaged in their learning. As a result, they may do well on tests but soon forget much of what they "learned". In other words, children can be interested in a concept or skill but not be engaged in a way that will affect their learning. For instance, engagement in mathematics can be encouraged with shared problem-posing activities. During shared problem posing, learners and teachers interact to pose and subsequently solve problems. Teachers and children generate the problems to be solved and then explore ways to solve them. For example, the teacher could ask children to identify some questions people might ask about their class (or questions they might want to ask about another class or school). Early examples might include: *How many girls have long hair? How many children wear brown shoes?* As questions are generated, they are written on large chart paper. After questions are listed, children are encouraged to solve each one. Teachers can also provide a numerical answer and ask students to pose possible questions that could have generated that answer.

Expectations. Children are expected to learn how to talk, and they do. Children are expected to learn how to read, but many do not. Why? The successful acquisition of oral language occurs in a nurturing environment where significant others (adults, parents, siblings) display confidence that the learner can and will learn to talk, demonstrate that they like and value the learner, celebrate all the learners' attempts to talk (no matter how small they may be), and place a high value on talking. These criteria apply naturally to learning any contexts. Children learn best when the teacher displays a sincere value in the child, the concepts to be learned, and the ability of the child to learn the concept. The child trusts that the teacher's expectations are reasonable and that the value of the concept outweighs whatever risks may be involved in learning it. Any deviation from these criteria erodes the trust and negatively affects the learning.

Responsibility. A child who is learning to talk is exposed to a great deal of language, much of it well beyond his or her reach. As he/she attempts to make meaning from the surrounding demonstrations, he/she alone chooses to ignore any parts of the demonstration for which he/she is not ready as well as those parts that represent things he/she already knows. In this sense, the learner is partly responsible for what he/she will learn. Successful learners must be willing to make choices, and teachers must be willing to trust that the learners will choose appropriately.

A critical component of the whole process is the teacher's responsibility to provide the learner with an appropriate set of choices within well-designed demonstrations. A child's ability to make choices will be maximized if demonstrations include a variety of concepts and jumping-in points. When learning to talk or when engaged in shared writing experiences, children are immersed in concepts that are much more sophisticated than anyone expects them to learn at that time. Traditional mathematics instruction, however, is typically limited to a narrow set of concepts we hope children will master in a short time. Limiting mathematics demonstrations severely limits the learners' opportunities to take responsibility for their learning, especially if they do not possess the requisite prior knowledge to make sense of the lessons.

Approximation. A child's first attempt at using language is merely an approximation of the word(s) he is trying to say. When a child utters anything remotely similar to a word we know, we typically celebrate enthusiastically. Within the celebration, we usually also include the correct word, thus helping the child feel confident that his attempt was worth the risk and gently providing him with the correct word. The steps of learning language are similar to the steps of problem solving in mathematics. Once the learner becomes engaged (i.e., identifies the problem), he forms a hypothesis, tests it, receives feedback, and then either revises his/her hypothesis or moves on to the next concept (problem).

Too often children are not given positive responses to approximations in school. It does not take long for a child to realize that there are some mistakes he/she really cannot afford to make. If his/her written work is consistently returned to him/her with corrected spelling and punctuation and low grades on the top, he/she will likely decide not to write very often, thus beginning a downward spiral in his literacy development. Obviously, it is critical that children eventually use the conventions in both oral and written language, but what degree of perfection should be expected along the journey to those conventions?

The issue of approximation is especially challenging in mathematics instruction when there are definitely right and wrong answers. A six-year-old at the beginning stages of learning the meaning of multiplication is very likely at a much different stage than a ten-year-old who has shut down as a result of a history of continuous failure. Sensitive responses to these errors will prevent the six-year-old from losing confidence in his ability to learn and begin to rebuild the confidence of the ten-year-old who has chosen to record any answer just to have the work completed.

Use. There is a great deal of repetition involved in learning to talk. Some of the same demonstrations are repeated in the child's environment. Games, songs, and read-alouds contain repetitive phrases, rhythms, and rhymes. The child repeats sounds that are interesting and those that produce the responses he seeks. The child listens to those around him/her, talks when others are present, and talks to himself/herself when alone. The child begins to talk when he/she sees a purpose for talking.

Transferring the principle of use to the literacy classroom requires that teachers create environments where children not only explore and refine literacy concepts and skills at their own pace, but also have nearly unlimited opportunities to use them. This takes time. A great number of restrictions are placed on today's classrooms. The curriculum continues to grow while nothing ever seems to be removed. As a result, time is a precious commodity. Cambourne and Brown (2003) encourage teachers to provide children with settings in which they will find "an urgent need to read and write in order to achieve ends other than reading and writing" (p. 74). Transferring the use principle to the mathematics classroom requires that learners feel an urgent need to do mathematics for purposes other than to learn mathematics. Most textbooks include at least one practice page in each lesson. Although these pages provide the learner plenty of opportunity to practice mathematics, they usually do not provide the opportunity to use mathematics for a purpose other than to learn mathematics.

Response. An important requirement of language acquisition is response. A child learning to talk tries a word or phrase and looks to those he/she trusts for a response. Based on that response, he/she will revise his hypothesis and try again, or move on to another word or phrase. Cambourne (1993) notes that these four levels of response are not naturally transferable to literacy learning. Teachers are not physically able to evaluate every learning attempt of every child in a timely fashion, nor are they able to provide demonstrations for all approximations of all children. Rather, teachers must choose which attempts to address and demonstrate only those that they feel are the most critical to the child's learning at that time. Graded papers that show which problems were done incorrectly seldom provide insight into the nature of errors.

FIELDWORK 4.1

Compare the conditions that supported your learning process (identified earlier) with Cambourne's Conditions of Natural Learning. How did your list compare with Cambourne's conditions of learning? Rework your list in relation to Cambourne's conditions of learning.

MOTIVATION (EXTRINSIC AND INTRINSIC)

When psychologists write about motivation, they typically refer to the reasons that students are engaged in learning to a point that they are aroused to action (Booth, 2013). Two different kinds of reasons have primarily emerged: *intrinsic* and *extrinsic* reasons. When students act for extrinsic reasons, they anticipate some kind of tangible payoff, such as good grades, recognition, and so forth. These rewards are said to be extrinsic because they are unrelated to the action. In effect, the activity becomes a means to an end. By contrast, students are said to be intrinsically motivated when they engage in activities for their own sake. In this instance, the rewards reside in the actions themselves; that is, the actions are their own reinforcement. In the case of intrinsic motivation, the repetition of an action does not depend as much on some external inducement as on the satisfaction derived from overcoming a personal challenge, learning something new, or discovering things of personal interest. Intrinsically engaged students are more likely than extrinsically engaged students to employ deep-level, sophisticated study strategies in their work (Ames & Archer, 1988). It is important to note that offering tangible rewards sometimes actually increases learning, especially if the assignment is seen as a chore or boring. The issue is whether offering rewards focuses undue attention on the tangible payoffs, thereby decreasing students' appreciation of what they are learning. What motivated you during the learning process you described earlier? Did someone offer you a tangible (extrinsic) reward? Were you intrinsically motivated to take on this learning? Were you motivated by both types of motivation?

The goal of fostering a love of learning is complicated not only by offering or withholding tangible rewards, but also by the scarcity of these rewards. In many classrooms, teachers distribute rewards (e.g. good grades) unequally, with the greatest number of rewards going to the best performers or to the fastest learners. This assumption is based upon the false assumption that achievement is maximized when students compete for a limited number of rewards. Although this may maximize motivation, students are aroused for the wrong reasons—to win over others and to avoid losing—and these reasons eventually lead to failure and resentment (Covington, 1998). In this competitive context, grades stand as a mark of worthiness because it is widely assumed in our society that one is only as worthy as one's ability to achieve competitively.

Actually, students may attach an intrinsic meaning to grades. Students also indicate that they often manipulate academic circumstances to create a tolerable balance between grades and caring. Students are more likely to value what they are learning and to enjoy the process (a) when they are achieving their goals; (b) when the dominant reasons for learning are task-oriented reasons, not self-aggrandizing or failure-avoiding reasons; and (c) when what they are studying is of personal interest. In fact, the evidence suggests that a student's appreciation for what he or she is learning is far greater when the student is failing but interested in the task than when the same student is succeeding (grade-wise) but finds little enjoyment and interest in the subject-matter content.

Flow

When people are highly engaged and enjoy whatever they are doing, they report some characteristic experiential state that distinguishes the enjoyable moment from the rest of life. The same characteristics are reported in the context of enjoying chess, climbing mountains, playing with babies, reading books, or writing. When all the characteristics were present, Csikszentmihalyi (1990) called this state of consciousness a "flow experience", because many of the respondents said that when what they were doing was especially enjoyable it felt like being carried away by a current, like being in a flow. Brophy (1983) argued that the flow experience requires certain conditions. First, flow occurs when there is an appropriate match between the learner's knowledge and experiences and the ways in which learning tasks are presented. In other words, there is an appropriate challenge to the activity or lesson. What constitutes a challenge? This question is critical to motivation. The problem is that the same thing will be an attractive challenge to one person and a bore to another.

Clear goals are also critical to engage the flow experience. When we really enjoy what we do, the goal is clear. The goal may be something obvious like winning a game, reaching the top of a mountain, or completing a writing piece. It may be an ad hoc goal that the person formulates on the spur of the moment, like finishing a writing project by a certain time. Clear goals help learners determine how well they are doing in terms of the goal. Without a goal, there cannot be meaningful feedback, and without knowing whether learners are doing well or not, it is very difficult for them to maintain involvement. It is important to realize, however, that the goal is not sought for itself; it is sought only because it makes the activity possible. A climber does not climb in order to reach the top; he reaches the top in order to climb. Poets do not write so that they will have poems; they seek to create poems so that they can write (Csikszentmihalyi, 1990).

In a study of fifth-grade students, Csikszentmihalyi (1990) found evidence of the flow experience. Children described what they enjoyed most about playing the piano or swimming. When asked to describe what they enjoyed most about these activities, children most often said, "I can forget my problems." Yet in class, these same students claimed that they could seldom achieve such concentration; their minds were usually dwelling on other things. Csikszentmihalyi (1990) concluded that a vicious circle is set up: because students do not concentrate enough, extraneous thoughts enter consciousness, further undermining their concentration. Not surprisingly, little learning takes place under such conditions.

When these conditions of the flow experience are present, the activity becomes rewarding in itself. Even though initially one may have been forced to do it, or did it for some extrinsic reason like the promise of good grades, if during the activity one starts to experience flow, the activity becomes worth doing for its own sake. It is important to note that what people enjoy the most in their lives is almost never something passive. When reading or math is enjoyed, it is active reading or problem solving. In reading, for instance, the reader chooses a book, identifies with the characters, recreates visually the places and events described and so on. Flow requires the use of skills and depends on gradual increments of challenges and skills so that boredom or anxiety will not take over.

Standardized instructional programs have become popular in recent years as part of the accountability movement (Ylimaki, 2011). And while standardized instructional programs can make it easier to align instructional materials with standards and assessment requirements, such programs make it challenging for students to get involved in materials at the right level for them. According to Csikszentmihalyi (1990), "the task of educators is to *educare*, to 'lead out' which implies meeting youth goals, interests, and skills. Only after students become engaged in learning will they willingly follow our lead" (p. 125).

The nature of the response/feedback teachers give students also determines how easy or how difficult it will be for the latter to experience flow while learning. Amabile (1983) found four ways that a child's spontaneous interest in learning can be destroyed. One is for adults to attempt to control the child's performance as much as possible, by imposing strict rules, procedures, time constraints, and so forth. The more the child's attention is drawn to external rules, the more difficult it becomes to experience the intrinsic rewards of flow.

Booth (2013) agrees. Through extrinsic motivation, you can get people to do all kinds of things—regurgitating information on command, performing mental and physical tasks and so forth. You cannot compel someone to create or make a new, personally relevant connection or learn from experience—the fundamental acts of learning—through extrinsic motivators. Going further, Booth (2013) argues that learning can be transformed into understanding only with *intrinsic* motivation. Learners must make an internal shift; they must invest themselves to truly learn and understand. Here, Booth's (2013) argument reinforces the notion that meaningful learning requires students to be immersed in the enjoyment of the learning experience. It is important to note, however, that some learning activities may not have an immediate intrinsic value for all students. In such cases, teachers must provide engaging demonstrations, opportunity to use the new skills, and appropriate feedback within a motivating learning environment.

CREATING MOTIVATING LEARNING ENVIRONMENTS FOR STUDENTS

Instructional leaders must encourage their teachers to create motivating learning environments for students in classrooms. Physical and virtual learning environments contribute greatly to student motivation for lifelong learning. The next two sections describe characteristics of physical and virtual learning environments with particular examples for reading.

Physical, social, and instructional environments

More important than the physical space, the overall environment established in the classroom—the social and instructional components—add to or detract from students' motivation for learning. Experts in literacy education, for instance, widely recommend the establishment of a large classroom library to enhance the classroom literacy environment (e.g. Allington, 2011). Specifically, Allington (2011) recommends a classroom library with 500 or more books, evenly divided between various types of fiction and informational texts and evenly split between books that are on grade level and those that are slightly below.

In addition to the large quantity of books recommended for a classroom library, the display and organization of books also can enhance the engagement among readers. Allington (2011) offers a few organizational approaches to increase children's access and interest in books in a classroom library. He suggests creating displays of books with the covers visible rather than having only the spines showing as on traditional shelves. Displays should be changed often and may have a theme of current concepts or future study to enhance background knowledge and curiosity. Additional themes for displays may include author studies and genres.

Aside from book displays, Allington (2011) advises teachers to preview a small selection of books each day, offering what type of reader may enjoy the book, and allowing students to check them out. Perhaps teachers' most important job in enhancing reading motivation is to expose children to books within the library in order to show them the interesting possibilities. Students need books that will be of interest to them to motivate them to pick up a book (Allington, 2011). Gambrell (1996) further reports that "curiosity is acknowledge to be a driving force in motivation. The children in our study were curious about and more motivated to read books that were familiar" (p. 22).

Beyond quality, quantity, and display of reading materials, researchers also support various social and instructional structures. In a mixed methods study of teachers as readers, Cremin et al. (2009) concluded that a common reason why students were reading more after the study was "having more choice or control both over what they read and when, and having more or more preferable resources and more time to read" (p. 17). Students also seem to grow as motivated readers when allowed to share and evaluate literature in a social realm. "Opportunities for sharing and talking with others about books is an important factor in developing engaged, motivated readers and supports the contention that social interactions have a positive influence on reading achievement" (Gambrell, 1996, p. 22). Knowing the influence students can have on one another, educators will want to hone that influence in the classroom library. With striking similarity to Cambourne's (1993) Conditions of Learning, Gambrell (1996) offers the following insight about motivation and reading development:

> Motivation and reading development are fostered when children are immersed in a book-rich environment; exposed to many demonstrations of how books are used; engaged in interaction with others about books, given the responsibility for making decisions about what, when, and how they read; provided with opportunities to approximate literary activities; and supported by interactions with adults who have high expectations for their success.
>
> (p. 17)

Brophy (1983) argues that a learning environment can operate within students' motivational Zone of Proximal Development when teachers or other mentors enable students to appreciate the value of learning opportunities and connect them to students' personal lives. According to Brophy, teachers and mentors can include students' classroom teachers or well-designed technological activities. Game-like features help promote learning and motivation and are typically better at accomplishing these goals than are typical commercial games. Whereas many game-like activities can help enhance motivation and learning, some games, especially competitive ones or ones that activate students' anxieties, distract from learning and can frustrate learners. Virtual learning environments are further described below.

Virtual environments

According to Cambourne (1993), there is no learning without engagement, a situation that happens all too often in lecture-based classrooms. At the same time, engagement without learning, which frequently happens in today's digital environments, is not a healthy alternative. Some claim that online gaming is the answer to engaging and motivating students in their academic work. Yet, students can frequently be engaged in these virtual worlds without actually learning anything or being more academically motivated. How can motivation be incorporated into innovative instructional technology and virtual learning environments? For instance, Harvard's Transforming the

---

FIELDWORK 4.2

Observe students during a lesson. How did students respond to the demonstration? Were they actively involved? Did the number of students who were involved in the lesson increase or decrease during the course of the lesson? Describe the teachers' use of demonstration and feedback. What opportunities did students have to use and take responsibility for their learning? To what extent did students appear to be intrinsically motivated to learn and enter a flow experience? How, if it all, did the teacher use extrinsic motivation strategies?

Engagement of Students in Learning Algebra (TESLA) introduces students to the concepts to be learned in a two-day classroom math lesson using avatars' active involvement in an event (Booth, 2013).

Like most video games, the Harvard activities immerse students in a three-dimensional virtual environment where students are able to either take on the identity of a STEM professional and solve mathematical puzzles in an engaging manner or vicariously observe others solving these puzzles. In designing a game-like environment that was instructionally and motivationally sound, the researchers removed elements of commercial games that either undermine or detract from the learning and goals (e.g. competition, time-sensitive pressures, and overt performance goals). Preliminary findings suggest increased motivation among students who participated actively in the virtual learning environment.

ENGAGEMENT, MOTIVATION, AND TEACHERS' WORK ENVIRONMENTS

Teachers' work environments must also be conducive to adult learning in schools. Classic motivation theorists (e.g. Maslow, Herzberg) offer great insight into understanding teachers' motivation for learning and growth. The next three subsections review these classic theories of motivation as well as Daniel Pink's work on "drive" that helps instructional leaders understand teachers' needs to contribute to a broader purpose.

Maslow's Theory of Human Motivation

Maslow explains that human needs extend from the physiological (lowest) to self-actualization (highest). Maslow's theory of human motivation (1987) helps principals/instructional leaders understand why teachers respond or do not respond to work incentives. Further, Maslow's theory clarifies the meaning and significance that people (teachers) place on work. From Maslow's hierarchy of needs, instructional leaders may conclude that teachers and students want to feel physiologically safe and secure and have a sense of community with others. Further, a leader's (or teacher's) actions, dispositions, and language can communicate acceptance or rejection of people and their ideas. What other conclusions would you draw?

Herzberg's Theory of Motivation

Frederick Herzberg (1993) developed a theory of motivation that delineates the satisfaction workers derive from internal and external rewards. Herzberg classified rewards into two categories: hygiene factors (external factors that might motivate subordinates) and motivators (internal factors that motivate peak performance in subordinates). Hygiene factors include such factors as job security, salary, fringe benefits, the organizational climate, and physical conditions of the work environment. Herzberg (1993) believed that these factors could not alone motivate people to achieve their full potential. Herzberg believed that the internal motivators (achievement, professional, and personal growth, added responsibility, and recognition) enabled people to achieve greater personal and organizational results.

As adult learners, teachers need to feel safe and secure in their learning environment —free to try, reflect on, and then use new strategies and methods based on supportive feedback. Commensurate with Cambourne's (1993) Conditions of Learning, Brophy (1983) identified strategies to develop and sustain the learner over time:

- Give recognition for real effort because any time a teacher attempts to learn something; learning requires risk-taking and courage.
- Acknowledge the teacher's effort—make perseverance a valued disposition for the organization.
- Minimize mistakes while the teacher is struggling because learning takes mistakes.
- Demonstrate a confident and realistic expectancy that the teacher will learn in each learning task.
- Show faith in the teacher's capacity as a learner.
- Work with the teacher at the beginning of a difficult task.
- Reinforce the "process" of learning.

Learning is not a linear progression. There are often wide spaces, deep holes, and regressions in learning. When the principal provides teachers with authentic encouragement, he/she signals that the task of professional growth is important.

These strategies to sustain the teacher/learner over time are also consistent with Daniel Pink's work on what drives teachers as they gain experience in the profession.

Daniel Pink's Motivation and Drive

According to Daniel Pink (2010), teachers want to master quality instruction and contribute to a larger purpose. As teachers gain experience, they want to feel empowered to develop and grow, to give back and contribute to the school leadership. Empowerment and self-direction are strong motivators, particularly for teachers in mid- to late-career stages as they seek recognition for their expertise and contributions over time. As Pink (2010) noted, management leads to compliance, but only self-direction leads to engagement. Ideally, today's schools demand creative and conceptual capabilities more than compliance. Routine jobs require direction; non-routine, interesting work like teaching demands self-direction and engagement. Further, Pink drew on studies of business open-source projects and argued that mastery is its own reward. While people will work for a raise or to avoid sanctions, they will spend discretionary time working for free. Pink referred to this phenomenon as "enjoyment-based intrinsic motivation—namely, how creative a person feels when working on the project—is the strongest most pervasive driver" (2010, p. 27). Finally, Pink identified "the purpose motive" as the third driver for motivation. That is, people have the need to direct their own lives, to learn and create new things, and to do better by ourselves and our world. "That's what makes us human. And increasingly, it is our humanity that makes us effective" (Pink, 2010, p. 29). Gage and Berliner (1998) combined Herzberg and Maslow's work to support instructional leaders as they nurture an environment more responsive to the individual. Table 4.1 illustrates Gage and Berliner's framework with the addition of Daniel Pink's work on drive.

Across Herzberg, Maslow, and Pink's work on motivation, we see an emphasis on higher order needs, such as teachers' needs for knowledge, creativity, and the ability to contribute to a larger purpose. At the same time, these motivation theorists remind us that pay and safe work environments must be in place in order for higher order needs to be paramount in teachers' minds. Moreover, Pink argues that teachers' learning needs shift over the course of their experience.

Table 4.1 Motivation Framework

	Herzberg's Motivation Model	Maslow's Hierarchy of Needs	Pink's Work on Drive
Higher Order Needs			
Internal Motivators	• Job content • Achievement • Recognition • Growth • Advancement	• Need for knowledge • Need for understanding • Self-actualization	• Need to master quality instruction • Need to contribute to a larger purpose • Empowerment • Self-direction • Creativity on the job
Lower Order Needs			
Hygiene Factors	• Pay/salary • Fringe benefits • Type of supervision • Company policies and procedures • Status • Job security • Interpersonal relations		

FIELDWORK 4.3

Ask Teachers

Interview three teachers: (1) one teacher from early career with 1–5 years' experience; (2) one teacher from mid-career with 10–15 years' experience; and (3) one teacher from late career with 20 or more years' experience. Ask each teacher what motivates him/her in their work. Working with your class, compare the answers across the three groups.

LEADERSHIP STRATEGIES

How do instructional leaders put all of this background on student and teacher motivation into practice? Effective leaders actively motivate teachers throughout their careers. Motivated teachers have higher degrees of efficacy or confidence in their teaching skills than unmotivated teachers. In sum, effective instructional leaders need to:

Know:

- conditions that engage students in learning
- characteristics of intrinsic and extrinsic motivation
- conditions that contribute to flow in learning
- theories of student motivation
- theories of adult motivation and drive
- characteristics of motivating physical and virtual environments
- what constitutes challenge in the learning process.

Be able to:

- foster conditions of learning for students and adults
- recognize flow or the experiential state that distinguishes the enjoyable moment from the rest of life.
- create motivating learning environments for students
- create motivating work environments for teachers
- motivate teachers throughout all career stages.

CASE 4.1 GOOD STUDENT ENGAGEMENT . . . FOR WHAT?

Elementary principal Maria Gonzalez watched her new teacher's literacy lesson with nagging concern. Over the past forth-five minutes, she observed the teacher deliver a literacy lesson in how to use context cues to help understand the meaning of content (nonfiction) vocabulary. All of her teachers were using a new reading program series designed to increase rigor in terms of standards and the use of nonfiction texts at lower grade levels. Further, teachers throughout the school had recently adopted a "Response to Intervention" system whereby students were identified for early literacy support. Much of the intervention activities were designed around assessed literacy standards (e.g. fluency, phonemic awareness, comprehension).

In some respects, Maria was pleased with the teacher's lesson with a Big Book, a highlighter, post-it notes, with the children gathered around her on the floor. The lesson began with a review of the previous day's lesson as well as information on key content vocabulary. Students watched attentively in the first few minutes as the teacher demonstrated how to use context cues to decode unknown words. As the lesson progressed, interest waned. Some children were looking at the floor and in the space behind the teacher rather than the book. Yet some students were engrossed in the book and the read-aloud activity.

By the end of the lesson, only a few students were engaged in the lesson and reading aloud. At the same time, some children were clearly not engaged. They were not looking at the text, and clearly not excited about further reading. Few children were smiling or actively involved in reading the text. The teacher noticed and said, "I know you're getting tired. There will be stickers for those who stay focused through the rest of the lesson." Some additional students perked up and read aloud. And a few students were so engrossed in the book and reading aloud that they stayed in the rug area to re-read the book after the teacher ended the lesson and initiated student free time. Further, when Dr. Gonzalez walked through classrooms, she wondered if the environment was sufficiently engaging to motivate children toward lifelong literacy as well as achieve common core standards. There were books displayed from past lessons, and there was a chart of student writing displayed above the whiteboard. Dr. Gonzalez noted that much of the print had been on display for the past couple months. Dr. Gonzalez returned to her office to consider how she would support her new teacher to create a more motivating learning environment for all students in her classroom.

Questions

1. What would you think about this lesson if you were the principal/observer?
2. How did the teacher's lesson use extrinsic and intrinsic motivation? How can the classroom environment be more motivating and engaging for students?
3. How could the teacher create conditions that support a flow experience in literacy instruction for more students?
4. How can Dr. Gonzalez motivate the teacher to participate in professional development regarding student engagement in literacy?

EXTENDED REFLECTION 4.2

Design a visual model that represents your theory of learning, including the role of engagement and motivation. How might you apply your theory with students in classrooms? How might you apply your theory with teachers?

SUMMARY

This chapter examined motivation (extrinsic and intrinsic) in relation to engagement and learning in classrooms and schools. When psychologists write about motivation, they typically refer to the reasons that students are engaged in learning to a point that they are aroused to action. Students are driven to act for extrinsic reasons when they anticipate some kind of tangible payoff, such as good grades, recognition, and so forth. These rewards are said to be extrinsic because they are unrelated to the action. In effect, the activity becomes a means to an end. By contrast, students are said to be intrinsically motivated when they engage in activities for their own sake. According to Cambourne (1993), student motivation occurs when teachers foster conditions of learning in their classrooms: immersion, demonstration, engagement, expectations, responsibility, approximation, use, and response. When students are engaged in particularly enjoyable learning, they experience flow or an experiential state that distinguishes the enjoyable moment from the rest of life.

Instructional leaders must encourage their teachers to create motivating learning environments for students in classrooms. Physical and virtual learning environments contribute greatly to student motivation for lifelong learning. The physical space where teachers meet with their students, the classroom, can be arranged in a variety of ways, decorated to fit the taste of a particular taste, and maintained as far as cleanliness and organization. More important than the physical space, the overall environment established in the classroom—the social and instructional components—add to or detract from students' reading motivation. Some claim that online gaming is the answer to engaging and motivating students in their academic work. Yet, students can frequently be engaged in these virtual worlds without actually learning anything or being more academically motivated. Harvard's Transforming the Engagement of Students in Learning Algebra (TESLA) provides an example of how math lessons can be taught with avatars' within a digital learning environment.

Work environments must be conducive to adult (teacher) learning in schools. Classic motivation theorists (e.g. Maslow, Herzberg, Pink) offer great insight into why teachers respond as they do. As teachers gain experience, they want to feel empowered to develop and grow, to give back and contribute to the school leadership. This chapter concludes with a case study and strategies to help instructional leaders create a personalized and motivating learning environment for all learners.

REFERENCES

Allington, R. (2011). *What really matters for struggling readers: Designing research-based programs.* New York: Pearson.

Amabile, T. (1983). *The School Psychology of Creativity.* New York: Springer Verlag.

Ames, C. & Archer, J. (1988). Achievement goals in the classroom: Student learning strategies and motivation processes. *Journal of Educational Psychology, 80,* 260–267.

Booth, E. (2013). Rethinking motivation. *Educational Leadership*, February, 22–27.

Brophy, J. (1983). Conceptualizing student motivation. *Educational Psychologist, 18,* 200–215.

Cambourne, B. (1993). *The whole story: Natural learning and the acquisition of literacy in the classroom.* Auckland, New Zealand: Ashton-Scholastic.

Cambourne, B. & Brown, H. (2003). *Read and retell: A strategy for the whole language/natural classroom.* Portsmouth, NH: Heinemann.

Covington, M. V. (1998). *The will to learn: A guide for motivating young people.* New York: Cambridge University Press.

Cremin, T., Mottram, M., Collins, F., Powell, S., & Safford, K. (2009). Teachers as readers: Motivating communities of readers. *Literacy, 43*(1), 11–19.

Csikszentmihalyi, M. (1990). Literacy and intrinsic motivation. *Daedalus, 119*(2), 115–140.

Gage, N. L. & Berliner, D. (1998). *Educational psychology (6th edn.).* Boston, MA: Houghton Mifflin.

Gambrell, L. B. (1996). Creating classroom cultures that foster reading motivation. *The Reading Teacher, 50*(1), 14–25.

Herzberg, F. (1993). *Motivation to work.* New Brunswick, NJ: Transaction Publishers.

Maslow, A. (1987). *Motivation and personality* (revised ed.). New York: Harper & Row.

Pink, D. (2010). Gainful employment. *RSA Journal, 2*, 25–29.

Ylimaki, R. (2011). *Critical curriculum leadership: A framework for progressive education.* New York: Routledge.

CHAPTER 5

Supervise Instruction

Peter Burke and Henry St. Maurice

KEY TOPICS
___

- History of Supervision
- Approaches to Instructional Supervision
- Models of Instructional Supervision
- The Importance of Language

This chapter is about one aspect of ISLLC Standard 2, namely instructional supervision. Supervision is explicit in one of nine functions associated with ISLLC Standard 2 and implicit in the rest.

Supervision of instruction is both affected by and has effects on school cultures, curricula, learning, assessment, leadership, instruction, technology, and evaluation. In our view, every aspect of leadership is incorporated when a leader supervises a member of a learning organization in which they are engaged. The success or failure of supervision rides on apparently small interactions, because these interactions create a crucial space at which cultures are formed, maintained or changed. Throughout schools in myriad cultures, whether large or small, new or old, supervision is more complex and contested than it often appears at first glance.

EXTENDED REFLECTION 5.1

Before reading this chapter, write down your definition of supervision and the role of a leader in developing and implementing a system of instructional supervision. Keep your definition available and revise it as you read the chapter and participate in reflections and fieldwork experiences.

- responsible for supervision of teachers, students, + building
- should work collaboratively w/ teachers to est. a vision
- should be knowledgeable of curriculum framework
- set clear expectations + guidelines for staff

DEFINITIONS AND DISTINCTIONS

Instructional supervision is a process that is distinct from observation, which must precede it, and evaluation, which can follow it. A widely accepted definition of supervision is: one-to-one professional development (Glickman, Gordon, & Ross-Gordon, 2010). By professional development, we mean processes by which professional educators adapt their discourses and practices to affect student learning. Heideman (1990) identified five processes of professional development as follows: assessment, planning, implementation, evaluation, and empowerment (p. 4).

In the next two sections of this chapter, we will offer five approaches and two models, using a distinction made by Tracy (1998) to distinguish between specific theories of supervision, known as approaches, which are set in historical and political contexts, and models, which are more generic theories with which to inform present practice and generate future research (pp. 80–81).

APPROACHES AND MODELS OF INSTRUCTIONAL SUPERVISION

The following historical tour of schooling in the U.S. is adapted from a cross-cultural comparison (Gromyko & St. Maurice, 2000). It is presented to highlight changes in approaches, theories, and methods of instructional supervision. The five eras shown here span two centuries and are spaced approximately fifty years apart, an arbitrary and inexact sequence meant to illustrate broad trends (Table 5.1). At the same time, it is important to keep in mind that previous eras persist through later ones. As you read the following descriptions, consider how earlier eras still echo in supervision practice today.

The Chapel Era

Chapels are the archetypes or images of mass public schooling in primary subjects. By the 1840s, public, or common, schools were organized in the U.S., starting in the original thirteen colonies where reading instruction had long been mandatory on the grounds that religious instruction in Protestant sects depended on literacy (Kaestle, 1983). Common schools were promoted to bring together pupils of various backgrounds, and thus were intended to promote faith in democracy or, in the words of Mann (1849),

Table 5.1 Eras of Instructional Supervision in the U.S.

Era	Spaces	Means	Ends	Approach
Chapel, 1840	common	uniform	spiritual	pastoral
Factory, 1890	subdivided	coordinated	material	industrial
System, 1940	aggregated	ascriptive	social	managerial
Mall, 1990	variegated	discrete	individualized	clinical
Network, 2040	connected	confluent	global	developmental

to be "balance-wheels of the social machinery" (p. 42). In these places, epitomized as little red school houses, were gathered under one roof all members of local communities, and there were preached democratic and bourgeois, upper class virtues, using texts and instructional methods derived from the Protestant chapels that often stood adjacent to them. Fittingly, we call this era of schooling in the U.S. the Chapel Era.

Using a curriculum developed by state boards of education, and methods copied from religious education, common schools did not depend on professional educators. Until normal schools became prevalent in the 1850s, teachers in common schools were young men, who temporarily taught until employed elsewhere (Herbst, 1989; Ogren, 2005; Rury, 1989). They were supervised by so-called inspectors (Glanz, 1998, p. 47) who traveled a circuit, as did judges and prelates, and were empowered to correct or replace their charges (Blumberg, 1985; Kaestle, 1983; Mattingly, 1975). Standards and criteria for knowledge, skills, and dispositions were implicit and open to interpretation by an inspector. We call this approach to supervision "pastoral", connoting attention to each detail of every process, including its mission along with facilities—curriculum— to instruction. Pastoral supervisors assume complete command of instruction, as a shepherd does over a flock or a prelate over many parishes.

The Factory Era

As the U.S. became increasingly industrialized at the end of the nineteenth century, a new model of schooling formed, bringing with it another approach to supervision (Glanz, 1998). The chapel school remained predominant in rural areas and in religious schools, especially those serving enclaves of immigrants. By the 1890s, however, urban reformers were calling for public schools that enrolled more children for longer terms that offered attainments more suited to an industrial economy (Cremin, 1961). Professional educators, trained in normal schools and newly founded graduate schools, formed professional associations and conducted research aimed at bringing scientific methods to curriculum (Kliebard, 2003) and methods of instruction (Callahan, 1962). In two decades, sweeping changes were implemented: schools were organized by age-grades, curriculum was divided into subjects in departments, assessment was rigorous and quantified; instruction was subdivided into units and days regimented by clocks and bells (Tyack, 1974). In the Factory Era, supervisors evaluated teaching practice in rigid categories: preparation, presentation, association, generalization, or application (Dunkel, 1969; Kliebard, 2003).

During the Factory Era, the teacher workforce comprised a majority of females from working-class backgrounds, supervised by male, middle-class supervisors, thereby duplicating the work structures of factories and offices (Rury, 1989). Superintendents, whose duties explicitly included supervision, delegated those duties to assistants in centralized bureaucracies. These positions, comparable to supervisors and foremen in businesses and industries, did not emerge without strife and conflict (Painter, 1989). A movement for social efficiency and scientific management was dubbed "Taylorism" after popular advocate Frederick Winslow Taylor (Hughes, 2004; Kanigel, 2005; Taylor, 1913). Taylorism was enthusiastically adopted in education (e.g. Dewey & Dewey, 1915; Dutton & Snedden, 1908; Tichi, 1987), despite resistance by teachers (Glanz, 1998).

During this era, approaches to supervision may be simply described as "industrial" (Flinders, 1998). When school enrollments stabilized after immigration was restricted in 1924 (Cremin, 1988), supervisors acquired additional roles, but until then, their duties were limited to regulating production. An anonymous author (1929) captured the industrial approach in a poem quoted by Glanz (1998):

> With keenly peering eyes and snooping nose,
> From room to room the Snoopervisor goes.
> He notes each slip, each fault with lofty frown,
> And on his rating card he writes it down;
> His duty done, when he has brought to light,
> The things that teachers do that are not right . . .
>
> (p. 54)

There is no more apt description of the industrial approach to supervision. The emblem of Taylorism was and remains a rating card in the hand of a minatory male who "notes each slip" and avoids direct communication with his ostensibly female subject.

The System Era

By the 1940s, most schools in the U.S. were organized as factories. Educators' discourses and practices, including instructional supervision, were widely disseminated in texts and training programs (Glanz, 1998). By this time, schools were further organized into systems that differentiated among groups of pupils, just as smaller factories were consolidated into integrated systems of production and distribution. Scientific management now was used to command supply chains and distribution grids, as well as to analyze data to command and control these enterprises. Likewise, schools were using system-wide data to ascribe pupils' needs and skills, group them accordingly, then assign them, with or without their knowledge and consent, to programs or sometimes even separate schools with tracked curricula that were specialized for career outcomes or special needs.

System schools, while retaining the spiritual and material ends of their predecessors, extended those purposes into maintaining workforces in complex industrial societies (Smyth, 1998). Supervisors approached these extensive purposes as managers with delimited responsibilities, such as subject areas or special needs. One consequence of this specialized *managerial* approach was to deepen class, race, and gender divisions among supervisors and teachers. Managerial approaches thereby maintained the same hierarchical evaluative responsibilities as pastoral and industrial ones, but with added specializations.

With the passage of the National Defense Education Act of 1958, federal policy and funding supported greater expansion of school systems and further specialization of educators, especially in mathematical and scientific subjects deemed crucial to waging the Cold War (Kliebard, 2003; Ravitch, 2001). Also, supervisory duties more explicitly included monitoring political beliefs (Urban, 2010), making even more manifest the purposes of system schools for socialization. The Snoopervisor now had national security items on his rating card. After ten decades spanning three eras, schools had become integrated into every aspect of social life (Menand, 2010). Every citizen now knew their academic calendar, how pupils progressed through levels, were assigned to tracks and assessed with numbers or letters that resemble industrial process controls or financial ratings (Lemann, 2000). Supervisors were explicitly charged with ensuring that school systems met national and local goals for citizenship and employment. The next changes in schools and instructional supervision began in the courts, ushering in a new era by 1990.

The Mall Era

In 1954, The US Supreme Court ruled that racially segregated schools violated the equal-protection clause of the Fourteenth Amendment to the Constitution. This ruling, known as *Brown v. Board of Education* (347 U.S. 483, 1954), came after decades of struggle culminating in a strategy of training a so-called *talented tenth* elite to challenge school systems that suppressed minority groups (Banks, 2006; Franklin & Higginbotham, 2010). The decision resulted in huge changes in school systems throughout the nation (Ogletree, 2004). Among a host of consequences, including judicial and military intervention in school governance, the Court's decision led to rulings and laws that gave individual citizens more standing to appeal for access to education based on ability (Education for All Handicapped Children Act of 1975), socioeconomic status (Elementary and Secondary Education Act of 1965) or gender (Title IX of the Education Amendments of 1972), in addition to race or ethnicity.

In response to laws and policies empowering students and families to make choices, schools gradually became sites of consumption or malls (Newmann & Wehlage, 1995; Powell, Farrar, & Cohen, 1985). Curricula and instructional methods offered individual-ized means to discrete ends, such as certificates for technical education. Discourses and practices such as regimentation remained from preceding eras, and often were in overt conflict with individual needs, however in the Mall Era, by 1990 every pupil and family in schools had access to choices unknown in previous eras.

Among many changes in schools in the mall era were *clinical* approaches to supervision developed in consultation with psychologists (Cogan, 1973; Goldhammer, 1969; Hunter, 1983). Dialogue and discussion were added to the repertoire of supervisory methods, joining but not displacing pastoral attention to detail, industrial collection of data and managerial analyses. Local, state and federal policies were combined with growing powers of teachers' associations for negotiating contracts with protocols for advancement, professional development supervision, evaluation (Mitchell & Kerchner, 1983), and certification (Hazi, 2002). In most contracts, clinical supervision was the specified method, but it was not as fully implemented as its proponents recommended (Glanz, 1998). In short, clinical supervision promised more participa-tion to individuals being supervised, but in practice did not accord them more power (St. Maurice, 1987).

The Network Era

In this historical overview, we do not infer that exact boundaries can be set between eras; discourses and practices flow into each other, like eddies in a stream. In the flow of time, nonetheless, certain laws and court decisions serve as markers. The mall era continues in these times, as do remnants of preceding chapel, factory, and system eras. Two dates, however, mark a fresh current in schools. In May of 1980, the U.S. Department of Education opened, consolidating many growing Federal education agencies at the level of the Presidential Cabinet. Within three years, a report entitled *A Nation at Risk* (U.S. Department of Education, 1983) led to heightened national attention on schools, precipitating a movement for nationally uniform and markedly high standards for student achievement, teacher quality, and school performance. After a tidal wave of media attention and political actions in summit conferences and sweeping laws, new and high standards were promulgated for teaching and learning. They called for concrete results in more graduates prepared to excel in fast-moving and highly competitive global economies (Tyack & Cuban, 1995). The ISLLC Standards were a direct result of actions taken by five Presidents and their Secretaries of Education, along with chief state school officers (Council of Chief State School Officers, 1996, 2008a). The movement to set universally high standards for schools in the U.S. was justified on the grounds that the nation needed to emphasize the production, distribution, and consumption of knowledge as well as goods and services. Knowledge itself was a commodity, the management of which required advanced educational attainment by all citizens (Bell, 1974; Drucker, 1969; Luttwak, 2000; Ozga et al., 2006; Turner, 2006).

A second date that marks a new era for schools came in February of 1991, when the first World Wide Web address was published (Cailliau & Gillies, 2000). Knowledge, in its quantity, distribution, and accessibility, since became more attenuated more rapidly than at any time since 1840s (Mumford, 1934; Standage, 1998; Starr, 2005). The Network Era has been a time of great changes in all aspects of human life, including schools (Taylor, 2002; Turner, 2006). Vast quantities of information are more readily available to anyone with a connected device, so schooling is now in cyberspace on 24/7 schedules, not just in physical space on workday schedules (Collins & Halverson, 2009). Distance education had once been a substitute for school attendance; it now became part of every school system, from the most rural ones to those in the hearts of great cities. The means and ends of schooling are now more confluent and instantaneously global, even beyond the planet. Pupils in schools can watch astronauts in space, gaze with them beyond the Earth's solar system, and even have conversations with them. Transactions that formerly were accessible to only a few specialists now are routine for millions.

It is still too soon to know all the effects of the Network Era on education, but combined with centralized governance encoded in standards, some certain consequences for instructional supervision are large-scale, high-stakes assessments mandated by Federal and state policies. These assessments of performance are administered and distributed across networks, resulting in comparisons and competitions among pupils, teachers, schools, states, and nations. Educators, their leaders, communities, policy-makers, and media now have access to more data and more sophisticated analyses than were dreamt possible by the first inspectors riding circuits nearly two centuries ago. The approach to supervision that most typifies the network era is called "developmental" (Glatthorn, 1984; Glickman, 1981). Developmental approaches are built on pastoral, industrial, managerial, and clinical approaches. Their hallmarks are measurable stages of professional development, as well as scales of knowledge, skills, and dispositions in educators' discourses and practices. These data are analyzed alongside standardized results of their pupils' achievement tests.

Via networks that connect supervisors with researchers, practitioners, and policy-makers, educators can easily combine their knowledge in detailed frameworks of instruction (Halverson, 2005; Halverson & Dikkers, 2008; Kane & Cantrell, 2010; Marzano, Danielson, & Reeve, 2011). Graduated licensing and induction programs connect educators in action research, portfolio development, and analyses of assessment data (Burke & Krey, 2005; Glanz & Sullivan, 2005; Hammerness, Darling-Hammond, & Bransford, 2005). In short, individualization of teaching, learning, and supervision that occurred in the mall era has become turbocharged with information in the network era.

SUMMARY OF APPROACHES TO SUPERVISION

One implication that can be drawn from this brief history of five eras of schooling, each with specific approaches to instructional supervision, is that supervision must be approached as a complex endeavor laden with meanings infused over twenty decades of mass public schooling in the U.S. A supervisory transaction is far from simple. From the moment that a supervisor and teacher make an appointment to carry out this professional function and contractual responsibility, they enter a symbolic place that has traces of a chapel's common spaces, a factory's regimented spaces, a system's assigned spaces, a mall's discrete spaces, and a network's cyber-spaces.

FIELDWORK 5.1

What are some effects that approaches and methods of instructional supervisions have on practices? One way to know is to ask practitioners. Who was the first instructional supervisor that you worked with? Who was the most recent? Match the above approaches and methods with their practices. If possible, interview one or the other. If not, ask colleagues for their recollections. Most educators welcome contacts from colleagues, however great the time and space that separate them. Another way to know is to reflect on school settings as they change. In many schools, remnants of the five eras described above can be seen. What are places where everyone gathers, as they did in the chapel era? What routines show evidence of the factory era? Try your own archaeological exploration of schooling.

MODELS OF SUPERVISION

Throughout the decades, educational leaders, along with leaders in business, military, legal, medical or religious professions, have disseminated their discourses and practices in thousands of textbooks, articles, and training packets. This chapter offers two theoretical models of supervisory discourses and practices. We propose to name the following two models *democracy* and *republic*, common nouns defined by James Madison in 1787 as follows:

> a pure Democracy, by which I mean, a Society, consisting of a small number of citizens, who assemble and administer the Government in person . . . A Republic, by which I mean a Government in which [a] scheme of representation takes place . . .
>
> (Bailyn, 1993, p. 408)

Here it is important to note that Madison's terms are not meant to denote contemporary political parties. On one hand, a democratic model of supervision is run by majority rule, with each participant holding an equal franchise to vote, then to act on or to seek redress from majority decisions. On the other hand, a republican model of supervision is conducted by representatives, whose powers may be checked and balanced, but who nevertheless may on certain occasions and in certain functions act without majority approval. A republican model, therefore, involves an unequal division of responsibility in assessing needs, planning activities, implementing methods, evaluating them, and empowering change agents (Heideman, 1990).

A prophet of democracy, Dewey (1980/1916), stated,

> A democracy is more than a form of government; it is primarily a mode of associated living, of conjoint communicated experience. The extension in space of the number of individuals who participate in an interest so that each has to refer his own action to that of others, and to consider the action of others to give point and direction to his own . . .
>
> (p. 258)

Dewey implies that individuals must refer their interests to those of others in the same community. A republic, on the other hand, may encompass many communities, or in the terms used by Madison (1993/1787), *factions*.

A democratic model of supervision may, therefore, be said to involve small groups, and proceed by consensus. A republican model involves representatives of larger groups making similar decisions. In any organization, both models of supervision can coexist, in that small-group consensus might be ways to some decisions, and large-group representation might be means to some ends. It is important to note that the scale or size of the group does not determine the model of supervision. For example, schools were small in the chapel era of schooling, but representatives such as inspectors and superintendents, decided every detail of supervisory practice. In contrast, supervision in large school systems may be delegated to small, independent groups in buildings, units or departments. These committees may well operate more democratically than their systems would seem to allow. However, industrial and managerial approaches usually presumed hierarchical authority under law and policy. Clinical and developmental approaches need not be hierarchical, and could foster mutual supervision among peers, as has often been advocated, if not always implemented (e.g. Glanz & Sullivan, 2005; Glickman, Gordon, & Ross-Gordon, 2010; Waite, 2000).

In the Network Era, supervisors have access to data and analytical tools that have potential uses in either model of supervision. Identical data could be collected, analyzed, and reported by a supervisor who acts as a representative of a large school or district, or one who acts as a peer within a small school community. In brief, a supervisor's approach could be any of the five approaches described above, and still be located in either model (Democracy or Republic).

To show differences between these two models of supervision, consider two supervisors, whom we'll call R and D. Supervisor R has been designated by a superintendent and holds a leadership role as an administrator. Now consider Supervisor D, a teacher in a faculty role in the same system, in a school that has site-based supervisory responsibility. Supervision processes for both supervisors are stipulated in a contract that has been negotiated by union leaders elected by a teachers' association, ratified by majority votes of association members and by an elected school board. Furthermore, the contract meets state statutes governing state-supported education, and guidelines for eligibility to receive federal funds. Both supervisors must collect, analyze and report data about teaching and learning with an instrument that takes a developmental approach and is aligned with ISLLC and state standards (e.g. Danielson, 2007; Halverson, 2005). Both supervisors know the teachers, the curriculum, the learners and the school environment. Both have been trained to use detailed checklists of observable and measurable activities, scored with and rubrics (e.g. Figure 5.1). Both meet a teacher in a fifteen minute pre-conference at which they each plan a supervisory visit. Both supervisors then observe the same teacher teaching the same lesson for at least one hour. Afterward, each will analyze data, discuss it with the teacher, and complete a report that will be signed and filed. What differences can be attributed to the models of supervision?

Both supervisors have the teacher's rapport and trust as their supervisory transaction is planned, but their models entail very different degrees of two qualities, which we will call *reciprocity* and *tolerance*.

In democracy as defined by Dewey (1980/1916), interactions are two-way streets. Blumberg (1980) defined reciprocity as a "contract . . . for exchange, socialization and accommodation" (Ch. 15, passim), and asserts that, "The psychological contract is rarely fulfilled" (p. 182). The psychological and professional contract that grants site-based supervision to Supervisor D's unit ostensibly requires that teachers exchange supervision with each other. Supervisor D makes a formal supervisory visit to a teacher knowing that the teacher is ready and able to turn the table tomorrow. Supervisor R, within a republic as defined by Madison (1993/1787), is not under any similar contracts. In such cases where educational leaders are evaluated by educators whom they are charged to lead, one-on-one supervision is rarely reciprocal, as indicated in many studies (Goldsberry, 1998; Carrington, 2004). Instruments similar to Danielson's

Domain 1: Planning and Preparation	Domain 3: Instruction
1a: Demonstrating knowledge of content and pedagogy 1b: Demonstrating knowledge of students 1c: Setting instructional outcomes 1d: Demonstrating knowledge of resources 1e: Designing coherent instruction 1f: Designing student assessments	3a: Communicating with students 3b: Using questioning and discussion techniques 3c: Engaging students in learning 3d: Using assessment in instruction 3e: Demonstrating flexibility and responsiveness
Domain 2: Classroom Environment	**Domain 4: Professional Responsibilities**
2a: Creating an environment of respect and rapport 2b: Establishing a culture for learning 2c: Managing classroom procedures 2d: Managing student behavior 2e: Organizing physical space	4a: Reflecting on teaching 4b: Maintaining accurate records 4c: Communicating with families 4d: Participating in a professional community 4e: Growing and developing professionally 4f: Showing professionalism

Figure 5.1 Four Domains of the Framework for Teaching (Danielson, 2007)

framework for teaching have been developed to assess leaders' knowledge and skills as supervisors (e.g. Halverson, 2005), and could be used in this hypothetical instance. Teachers could use rubrics to evaluate their administrators, but certainly not in supervisory transactions that include one-hour observations. Assuming that Supervisor R were assigned to visit twenty teachers, then their reciprocal visits would involve twenty times the workload of Supervisor D and colleagues.

Reciprocity is common in many other professional development transactions: there are examples of college or university supervisors engaging in reciprocal action research with student teachers, (Gore, 1991; Mills, 2010; Munro, 1991); peer review, coaching, or mentoring is usually reciprocal among teachers, although not across bargaining units under most contracts and laws (Clark & Erickson, 2003; Little, 1990; Smith & Ingersoll, 2004). Although peer reviews and coaching sessions are valuable, we define supervision in this chapter as one-on-one professional development. Supervisor R is on a one-way street and cannot exchange identical supervisory practice with teachers under supervision.

Tolerance

Another difference between models of supervision can be called *tolerance*, which we define here as limits on discourses and practices that are evident in the social norms or rules binding social interactions (Dewey, 1980/1916; Foucault, 1988; Putnam, 2000). According to Mosher and Purpel (1972), tolerance keeps the focus on the present evaluation of teacher performance rather than changes in the organization and other aspects of the teacher's work. Tolerance in developmental supervision is described by Cutcliffe, Hyrkas, & Fowler (2010) as a "balance between challenges and confirmation . . ." (p. 248). In supervision, tolerance may or not be reciprocal, depending on the approach and model.

SUMMARY OF APPROACHES AND MODELS OF SUPERVISION

In the preceding sections, we have presented five approaches and two models as theoretical bases upon which instructional leaders build their discourses and practices of supervision. These are descriptions of theories, not prescriptions for discourses and practices. To summarize this section, we propose to array the approaches and models described so far on a matrix whose axes are tolerance and reciprocity (Figure 5.2).

On this matrix, models are located to show that a democratic model of supervision may have relatively higher tolerance and higher reciprocity than a republican model. Approaches to supervision are then placed in relation to their potential for tolerance and reciprocity. The developmental approach is shown as more highly related to reciprocity and tolerance, while a clinical approach is deemed more related to tolerance but less related with reciprocity. Pastoral, industrial, and managerial approaches are deemed to have relatively lower potential for reciprocity and tolerance.

Readers are invited to use this matrix to locate theoretical approaches and models of supervision in their organizations, or to conduct empirical research with these variables. Knowing these distinctions, and their historical and political contexts, is preliminary to asking, how do leaders supervise?

Supervisee becomes an active participant in supervisory process

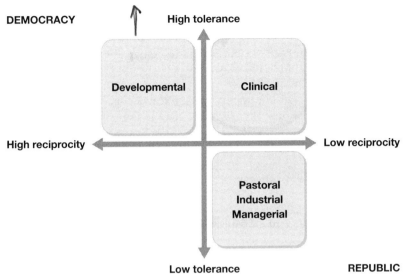

Figure 5.2 Matrix of Approaches and Models

FIELDWORK 5.2

Use the matrix to locate models of supervision that you have experienced. Ask colleagues to do the same. Where would you locate your own preferred model?

somewhere in between developmental + clinical

METHODS OF INSTRUCTIONAL SUPERVISION

Consider the following examples that illustrate the importance of language or rhetoric in various methods of instructional supervision. It is important to note that supervisory rhetoric and practices are congruent with cultural and political situations in contemporary schools. In other words, these methods depend on the contexts in which leaders operate. They are not prescriptions that apply to all situations. Various methods have been inherent in the rhetoric or language of supervision for nearly a century as exemplified by an anonymous author's (1929) stanza about the Snoopervisor:

> The Supervisor enters quietly.
> "What do you need? How can I help today?
> John let me show you. Mary, try this way."
> He aims to help, encourage and suggest,
> That teachers, pupils, all may do their best.
>   (in Glanz, 1998, p. 54)

1. Entry: "The Supervisor enters quietly . . ."

The first function of ISLLC Standard 2 is to "nurture and sustain a culture of collaboration, trust, learning, and high expectations" (Council of Chief State School Officers, 2008b). These functions all indicate that the first step for supervisors is to determine the terms of supervision. For example, a clinical approach to supervision calls for a pre-conference, at which the supervisor and teacher agree on ground rules such as data to be collected and analyzed, along with the date and time for the actual visit. Clinical and developmental approaches stress gaining entry by communicating respect if not reciprocity. Clinical supervisors, versed in commonplaces of medical practice, "enter quietly," by appointment as arranged in advance, whereas Snoopervisors "peer" unbidden and unannounced (Spears, 1941, p. 382, as cited in Iwanicki, 1998, p. 156).

2. Questions: "What do you need? How can I help today?"

In classical rhetoric (Crowley & Hawhee, 2004), discourse is shaped in at least three parts: an opening statement of what will be said, a full statement including challenges and confirmations, and a summary restatement. In clinical and development approaches to instructional supervision, however, such statements are not considered sufficiently persuasive. In addition, supervisors are instructed to open with open-ended questions such as, "What do you need? How can I help?" that are purposely non-directive (Rogers, 1951) and are designed to build trust. Clinical and developmental approaches were devised to counter supervisory methods that often subjected teachers to humiliation and dismissal, especially in eras before contractual protections (Apple, 1988 pp. 73–74; Blumberg, 1985; Mosher & Purpel, 1972; St. Maurice, 1987). But, when a supervisor has already located a topic and collected data, initial questions may be perceived as one-sided (Black, 1992). How does a supervisor communicate data about supervision?

Information is never neutral, however reliable and valid. Data can be dangerous if mishandled. It can be collected, analyzed, and presented in ways that undermine trust and rapport in any relationship, especially those involving hierarchical power relations (White, 1989). At some point, supervisors must introduce their data, followed by discussion, and ending with a summary/review.

3. Persuasion: "John, let me show you. Mary, try this way."

At this point in a supervisory transaction, persuasion takes place. The anonymous author's supervisor, apparently taking a managerial approach, offers to demonstrate a recommended change. Whether the same sentences are directed to two pupils or two teachers, the supervisor is seeking to persuade an audience to do something. The anonymous author drew on that long tradition in suggesting demonstration as an ideal supervisor's preferred means of persuasion. More recent models (e.g. Danielson, 2007) suggest the importance of modeling or demonstrating some aspect of a lesson that needs additional support.

4. Value: "He aims to help, encourage and suggest . . ."

Assuming a supervisor and teacher reach agreement on the instructional aspect in need of professional development, the next function of supervision is evaluation (Heideman,

1990), a term distinctly separate from observation and supervision, although usually inseparable (Iwanicki, 1998). Any approach to supervision leads to the forming of value judgments, and any model of supervision requires an eventual determination of the worth of discourses and practices to the enterprise in which they occur (Miles & Baroody, 2011; Stronge, 2006). A crucial difference in most cases, however, is that value judgments in supervision extend beyond the supervisory transaction into the realm of politics. As Stronge (2006) stated, "[a] major obstacle to effective teacher evaluation systems can be in the influence of politics . . . groups involved in the process represent . . . both external and internal stakeholders . . ." (p. 11). The aims of the anonymous author's supervisor are confounded by the multiple purposes of evaluation. For example, recent proposals for using student test data to evaluate teachers apply formulas for so-called "value added" (Whitehurst et al., 2010). They define reform as a result of personnel decisions that follow normative scales for ranking teachers, as if they were competing. Educators have replied such proposals are impractical (Manna, 2010) and erroneous. Kennedy (2010) claimed that policy makers make a "fundamental attribution error [of] overestimating the influence of personal characteristics on behavior and underestimating the influence of the situation itself" (p. 591):

> Many current policies seem to presume that teaching practices follow directly from such enduring personal characteristics as credentials, knowledge, or perhaps dispositions and personality traits. For example, the notion that we should hold teachers accountable for student outcomes presumes that those outcomes are largely in teachers' hands and overlooks the role of the textbook, the physical space, and other resources. It even overlooks whether children actually attend school every day.
>
> (Kennedy, 2010, p. 592)

In summary, evaluation is literally rooted in values. However, evaluations are often detached in space and time from the situations in which supervisors and teachers conduct their supervisory transactions. We propose that leaders who would base their discourses and practices on ISLLC standards remain aware of the multiple purposes of and influences on supervision and evaluation. Evaluation is an elusive practice influenced and shaped by the broader culture, politics, and policies.

5. Power: "That teachers, pupils, all may do their best."

A key function of supervision or any professional development is empowerment (Heideman, 1990). Foucault (1988) offers a relevant definition of power:

> Technologies of power . . . determine the conduct of individuals and submit them to certain ends or domination, an objectivizing of the subject; . . . certain modes of training and modification of individuals, not only in the obvious sense of acquiring certain skills, but also in the sense of acquiring certain attitudes.
>
> (p. 18)

Foucault's (1988) description of power is complicated, but the main point is that power is defuse and circulating in any social interactions. In other words, power is not simply top-down from formal leaders/supervisors to teachers. Rather, power gets produced during social interactions, such as those actions aimed at changing teachers' discourses and practices. At the same time, supervisory interactions do empower teachers to change their own practices as they change students' skills and attitudes.

To demonstrate a rhetorical analysis of power in instructional supervision, we will take the last word in the anonymous author's poem, "best". An apparently simple word, it is evidence of multi-directional power, and is a fulcrum on which persuasion can move audiences to change their discourses and practices. The superlative form of the adjective *good*, *best* connotes an upper limit of possibility. Given a choice of doing well, better or best, who wouldn't choose the latter? Acknowledging the power imbued in that word, our response is a question, "Says who?" Although the phrase *best practice* has become rampant (e.g. over 15 million hits on Google, including a link to "buzzwords" in Wikipedia), it usually denotes comparatively better norms of practice that are temporary and changeable, but not permanently superior. Even in the absence of clinical trials and quantitative, comparative studies, the rhetorical force of best practice persists (e.g. Daniels, Zemelman & Hyde, 2005; National Education Association, 2011; Stronge, 2006). Along with *reform* and *improvement*, *best* is a "terministic screen" (Burke, 1969) upon which various meanings may be projected. Those who would claim that there is one best way to teach, or one best curriculum to be taught, ignore lessons that can be found in any history of education, and that are evident every day as educators make practical choices which they are persuaded will better serve the interests of their pupils and communities.

FIELDWORK 5.3

Try a rhetorical analysis of an actual supervisor. Listen to the language he/she uses in supervisory practices. How does his/her language relate to their methods of entry, questions, persuasion, values, and power? Compare their language and practices to the cases below.

CASE 5.1 ELEMENTARY SCHOOL

Shabazz is a rural elementary school that has one teacher for each of the grades kindergarten through grade 6. Students leave Shabazz Elementary to enter a grades 7–12 middle and high school in the rural district. Shabazz Elementary is located on one of three municipalities in the school district, a village of 220 residents. Students come to the school by foot or by bus and the enrollment is 127 students K–6, with an average class size of eighteen students. The principal of the school has the responsibility for two additional elementary schools in the district, so her time in the building is limited. In order to provide continuity for the building the sixth-grade teacher has been designated as lead teacher for the school.

The faculty at the school, with one exception, has been teaching at the school for more than fifteen years together as a unit. The one exception is the fourth-grade teacher who was just hired to replace a retirement. The new teacher came directly from her teacher preparation and is in her first year of teaching. Her clinical practice was completed at a large suburban elementary school close to the campus where she received her degree. The experienced teachers in the school were part of the hiring process for this new teacher, and as a group they had positive feelings and expectations for her success.

The state department of education in the state where Shabazz Elementary School was located had a policy mandate that all new teachers be provided a mentor teacher by the hiring school district. The state regulation defined the role of mentor as:

> "Mentor" means an educator who is trained to provide support and assistance to initial educators and who will have input into the confidential formative assessment of the initial educator and who is not to be considered as part of the formal employment evaluation process.

In essence, the mentor's role combined the aspects of both supervision and professional development for the new teacher.

For this beginning teacher at Shabazz Elementary School, the teacher-leader who was the sixth grade teacher was assigned the role of mentor. The first step in the mentoring experience was for the lead teacher and the neophyte to schedule a series of meetings for the purpose of discussing the new teacher's progress, and to create structures for the new teacher's success (i.e., planning). This planning began prior to the opening of school in the fall, and included the third grade teacher who had taught the students who were to be in the new teacher's class. The two experienced teachers provided the beginner, in a triad, with an overview of the school curriculum, an induction to the textbooks and other instructional materials available to her, and support in preparing her classroom for the students.

Part of the plan was for the lead teacher to visit the new teacher's classroom on a regular schedule, and to teach together as a team on pre-prepared lessons (implementing). The lead teacher felt that it was important for the students to see the two of them as equals in the delivery of the lessons (dyad), rather than seeing the two in a hierarchical relationship. While in the classroom, of course, the lead teacher was able to identify characteristics, specialty knowledge, or performance items that may be targets for improvement for the beginner, or *assessing*. The judgments made by the lead teacher (evaluating) would become the topics of the mentoring sessions that were scheduled on a regular basis after school for the two of them (i.e., a dyad).

State policy also required continued professional development for all teachers to keep license current. Part of the role of the mentor was to help the new teacher identify areas of strength and areas that might need improvement. This supervisory task resulted, as the policy dictated, in formative assessment for the new teacher, and the opportunity to determine what professional growth plans could be made. The new teacher professional growth plan was not dictated by the mentor, rather it was designed by the neophyte based on the dyad sharing that took place, or *empowering*.

In this case, the participants were equals in the profession. The planned structure of induction for the new teacher came by way of state policy, and ended with positive learning goals for the new teacher in this rural elementary school. Professional educators, working as a team, can fulfill the mandates and provide the opportunity for improvement to occur.

CASE 5.2 HIGH SCHOOL

César Chavez High School is an urban high school of 2100 students, one of five high schools in the district. It is composed of grades 9 through 12, and the entering ninth grade class is usually over 600 students, but the senior graduating class is most often between 520 and 550 students. Nearly 10 percent of each class is lost through students dropping out. The pupil services area at César Chavez High School is staffed with six counselors, three school psychologists, and one school social worker. The school administration has a head principal, two associate principals, and two assistant principals. The assistant principals are tasked with oversight of student attendance, co- and extra-curricular activities, building maintenance, and scheduling. The associate principals have responsibility for supervision and professional development for the school, in partnership with the principal. One of the associate principals has, as part of load, the responsibility for oversight of the pupil services area.

There is a leadership team at César Chavez High School that includes all of the principals, the director of guidance, and teacher representatives elected from the teaching staff. The primary goal of the leadership team was to reduce the number of dropouts and, therefore, increase the high school graduation rate at their school. The leadership team had been studying a variety of options to help meet this goal, and one promising alternative was a relatively new technique that was brought to the team by the director of guidance. That technique was called Response to Intervention (RtI).

The director of guidance explained that RtI was an assessment and intervention system for schools. School personnel identify students who have poor learning outcomes early in their schooling, monitor their progress throughout school, and provide evidence-based interventions when warranted. RtI at the high school level is a tiered approach to student support (Duffy, 2011). Students who come to the high school with poor academic records are identified and monitored for success. When students show signs of academic failure, specific remediation is provided within the regular classroom. Targeted interventions are provided to those students who are not successful in tier one, and their progress in academics is monitored frequently and more direct interventions are planned, often with the classroom teacher receiving support from other professional educators in the building. The third tier is a multi-disciplinary team review, with parent or guardian consent, to determine eligibility for special education services.

At César Chavez High School the associate principal with responsibility for the pupil services area and the director of guidance form a dyad to plan and implement a set of second tier interventions for students deemed at risk of failure. The success of intervention at the second tier requires the cooperation of several professional staff members. The associate principal and guidance director together create a list of students in need of intervention, and a list of teachers and other professionals who need to be involved in *planning*. The guidance director agrees to recruit the needed staff members, and the associate principal volunteers to find the necessary resources to put the plan in place.

Together the director and associate principal design appropriate interventions for students at-risk, and teacher tutors are assigned specific students with whom they will meet to provide academic support in *implementing*. Since the foundation of RtI is data-driven decisions, the students are assessed for improvement, and alternative interventions prepared for *assessing*. The classroom teachers and the volunteer interventionists keep careful records of the students' progress, and provide the reports to the director/associate.

The guidance director and associate principal review the teacher reports for *evaluating*, in order to make determinations for future interventions, or for third tier action. The administrator tasked with the oversight responsibility of the pupil services area and the director of guidance work together accomplish the supervisory responsibility through the empowerment of the director for the purpose of student retention and success.

These two cases provide a brief picture of real-world implementations of concepts planning, implementing, assessing, evaluating, and empowering supervision. Any process is only as strong as the individual members engaged in supervision to link it to professional development and, eventually, student success. Student success should be the basic objective of all professional educators and of all programs and processes in the schools.

FIELDWORK 5.4

Use the above section to help you describe three different schools or agencies. What are some differences and commonalities of instruction supervision in each setting? What can you learn from these differences and commonalities to inform your own practice as an instructional leader?

STRATEGIES FOR LEADERS

How do instructional leaders put all of this background on supervision into practice? This section provides guidance for what today's instructional leaders need to know and be able to do as well as two illustrative examples. Instructional leaders need to:

Know:

- district expectations for supervision
- potential for past supervision models to affect current practice
- various approaches to supervision
- various models of supervision
- the importance of language in supervisory practice.

Be able to:

- create a school culture conducive to supervision
- use various approaches to instructional leadership
- build trust and relationships with teachers
- use constructive language in feedback.

PROVIDING FEEDBACK

Lynnette Brunderman

Providing feedback is critical to the growth and development of all educational professionals. Yet beyond the feedback provided by the instructional supervisor, it is imperative that teachers and leaders learn to reflect on their own experiences and decisions as they journey toward building expertise. In the journey toward becoming expert, skills are refined and enhanced. Some of these include the ability to understand others' perspectives, adjust to the learning styles of those around you, communicate in ways that allow others to understand, anticipate issues, prioritize, and be flexible and comfortable with uncertainty. "Self-evaluation leads to scrutiny, discussion and analysis of these expert processes. Reflection allows people to learn from their experiences, and administrative skills are acquired through a combination of theory and practice" (Martin, 2005).

Therefore, after observing a lesson, and prior to meeting with the teacher, ask the teacher to reflect on the lesson and be prepared to talk about the lesson when you meet. Questions to prompt them are:

- As you reflect on your lesson, in what ways were students productively engaged?
- Did the students learn what you wanted them to learn? How do you know—or how and when will you know?
- Did you modify and adjust your lesson as you taught it? On what did you base your decisions?
- If you could reteach this lesson again to the same students, what, if anything, would you do differently? Why?

Additionally, the art of questioning is important to the success of the supervisor. Table 5.2 illustrates essential questioning techniques.

Table 5.2 Six Characteristics of Effective Questions

Effective questions are	They sound like this:	Not like this:
Open ended	Tell me about your teaching experience. What do you think about . . .?	Where did you teach? Do you believe in . . .?
Invitational	It would be great to hear about . . . Would you consider . . .?	Why on Earth would you . . .? Why don't you . . .?
Specific	How often does she . . .? What does it look like when . . .?	Does she . . . much? What will happen if . . .?
Evocative/persuasive	What might this mean? Let's speculate about . . .	What does this mean? What will happen if . . .?
Positively or neutrally biased	What might you learn from this? Tell me what you were thinking.	What's up with . . .? What did you think would happen?
Challenge assessments	What evidence do you have that . . .? How could that be interpreted differently?	What is wrong with . . .? What's your feeling about . . .?

SUMMARY

In this chapter, we have presented approaches, models, methods, and examples of instructional supervision as practiced in the U.S. over the past two centuries. In our definition, supervision is professional development conducted along with observations, and leading to informal and formal evaluations. We treat supervision as a nexus where historical, cultural, political, psychological, and philosophical issues inform educators' language and practices. Supervisory interactions occur within limits of space and time, in social contexts and personal experiences. Within those narrow frames, however, supervision opens a wide range of negotiations and choices, informed by the cultures and politics in each classroom and school, as well as broader politics of education in the 21st century.

We hope to leave readers ready and eager to reflect on and discuss their discourses and practices as leaders in education. A guiding question for supervision might be: how can educational leaders supervise instruction that ensures equitable and excellent education for all? Our responses come from our experiences as supervisors and leaders. More complete and important responses will come from you as leaders, as you plan, implement, assess, evaluate, and empower yourselves and educators whom you supervise in the cultures you inhabit and the organizations that you lead.

BIBLIOGRAPHY

Apple, M. (1988). *Teachers and texts: A political economy of class and gender relations in education.* New York: Psychology Press.

Bailyn, B. (Ed.). (1993). *The debate on the Constitution, part one.* New York: Library of America.

Banks, J. (2006). *Race, culture, and education.* New York: Routledge

Becker, G. (1993). *Human capital: A theoretical and empirical analysis, with special reference to education* (3rd ed.). Chicago, IL: University of Chicago Press.

Bell, D. (1974). *The coming of post-industrial society.* London: Heinemann.

Black, E. (1992). *Rhetorical questions: Studies of public discourse.* Chicago, IL: University of Chicago Press.

Blasé, J. & Blasé, J. (2004). *Handbook of instructional leadership* (2nd ed.). Thousand Oaks, CA: Corwin.

Blumberg, A. (1980). *Supervisors and teachers: A private cold war* (2nd ed.). Berkeley, CA: McCutchan.

Blumberg, A. (1985). Where we came from: Notes on supervision in the 1840s. *Journal of Curriculum and Supervision, 1*(1), 56–65.

Blumberg, A. & Jonas, S. (1987). Permitting access: The teacher's control over supervision. *Educational Leadership, 44*(8), 58–62.

Brown v. Board of Education, 347 U.S. 483 (1954).

Burke, K. (1969). *A rhetoric of motives.* Berkeley, CA: University of California Press.

Burke, P. & Krey, R. (2005). *Supervision: A guide to instructional leadership.* Springfield, IL: C.C. Thomas.

Cailliau, R. & Gillies, J. (2000). *How the Web was born: The story of the World Wide Web.* Oxford, UK: Oxford University Press.

Callahan, R. (1962). *Education and the cult of efficiency.* Chicago, IL: University of Chicago Press.

Carrington, G. (2004). Supervision as a reciprocal learning process. *Educational Psychology in Practice, 20*(1), 31–42.

Carruthers, M. (1990). *The book of memory: A study of memory in medieval culture.* Cambridge, UK: Cambridge University Press.

Clark, T. & Erickson, G. (Eds.). (2003). *Teacher inquiry: Living the research in everyday practice.* London: Routledge.

Cogan, M. (1973). *Clinical supervision.* Boston, MA: Houghton Mifflin.

Coleman, B. (2004). Pragmatism's insult: The growing interdisciplinary challenge to American harassment jurisprudence. *Employment Rights & Employment Policy Journal, 8*(2), 239–314.

Collins, A. & Halverson, R. (2009). *Rethinking education in the age of technology.* New York: Teachers College Press.

Cook, P. & St. Maurice, H. (2006). A genealogy of standards. In S. Gordon (Ed.). *Standards for Instructional Supervision.* Larchmont, NY: Eye on Education.

Council of Chief State School Officers. (1996). *Interstate School Leaders Licensure Consortium: Standards for school leaders.* Washington, DC: Council of Chief State School Officers.

Council of Chief State School Officers. (2008a). *Interstate School Leaders Licensure Consortium.* Washington, DC: Council of Chief State School Officers. Retrieved from http://bit.ly/MW3IGI

Council of Chief State School Officers. (2008b). *Educational leadership policy standards.* Washington, DC: Council of Chief State School Officers.

Cremin, L. (1961). *The transformation of the school: Progressivism in American education, 1876–1957.* New York: Knopf.

Cremin, L. (1988). *American education: The metropolitan experience, 1876–1980.* New York: Harper & Row.

Crowley, S. & Hawhee, D. (2004). *Ancient rhetorics for contemporary students.* New York: Pearson Education.

Cusick, P. (1991). *The egalitarian ideal and the American high school* (2nd ed.). New York: Teachers College Press.

Cutcliffe, J., Hyrkas, K., & Fowler, J. (2010). *Handbook of clinical supervision: Fundamental international themes.* London: Taylor & Francis.

Daniels, H., Zemelman, S., & Hyde, A. (2005). *Best practice: Today's standards for teaching and learning in America's schools.* Portsmouth, NH: Heinemann.

Danielson, C. (2007). *Enhancing professional practice: A framework for teaching.* Alexandria, VA: Association for Supervision & Curriculum Development.

DeSimone, L. (2009). Improving impact studies of teachers' professional development: Toward better conceptualizations and measures. *Educational Researcher, 38*(April), 181–199.

Dewey, J. (1980/1916). Democracy and education. In J. Boydston (Ed.). *John Dewey: The middle works* (vol. 9). Carbondale and Edwardsville, IL: Southern Illinois University Press.

Dewey, J. & Dewey, E. (1915). *Schools of to-morrow.* New York: Dutton.

Drucker, P. (1969). *The age of discontinuity: Guidelines to our changing society.* New York: Harper and Row.

Duffy, H. (2011). *Meeting the needs of significantly struggling learners in high school: A look at approaches to tiered intervention.* Washington, DC: American Institutes for Research.

Duncan, A. (2010). *Secretary Duncan on teacher evaluation and rewarding excellence.* Washington, DC: US Department of Education.

Dunkel, H. (1969). Herbartianism comes to America: Part II. *History of Education Quarterly, 9*(3), 376–390.

Dutton, S. & Snedden, D. (1908). *The administration of public education in the United States.* New York: Macmillan.

Edelfeldt, R. & Raths, J. (1999). *A brief history of standards in teacher education.* Washington, DC: Association of Teacher Educators.

Encyclopædia Britannica. (2011). Herbartianism. Retrieved from www.britannica.com/EBchecked/topic/262691/Herbartianism

Farkas, G. (2000). Teaching low-income children to read at grade level. *Contemporary Sociology, 29*(1), 53–62.

Flinders, D. (1998). Industrial dimensions of supervision. In G. Firth & E. Pajak (Eds.). *Handbook of research on school supervision* (pp. 1123–1148). New York: Macmillan.

Foucault, M. (1988). Technologies of the self. In L. Martin, H. Gutman and P. Hutton (Eds.). *Technologies of the self.* Amherst, MA: University of Massachusetts Press.

Franklin, J. & Higginbotham, F. (2010). *From slavery to freedom.* New York: McGraw-Hill.

Garver, E. (1994). *Aristotle's rhetoric.* Chicago, IL: University of Chicago Press.

Gates Foundation (2010). Measures of effective teaching. Retrieved from www.gatesfoundation.org/united-states/pages/measures-of-effective-teaching-fact-sheet.aspx

Glanz, J. (1998). Histories, antecedents and legacies of school supervision. In G. Firth & E. Pajak (Eds.). *Handbook of Research on School Supervision* (pp. 39–79). New York: Macmillan.

Glanz, J. & Sullivan, S. (2005). *Supervision that improves teaching: Strategies and techniques.* Thousand Oaks, CA: Corwin Press.

Glass, G. (1978). Standards and criteria. *Journal of Educational Measurement, 15,* 237–262.

Glatthorn, A. (1984). *Differentiated supervision.* Alexandria, VA: Association for Supervision & Curriculum Development.

Glickman, C. (1981). *Developmental supervision.* Alexandria, VA: Association for Supervision & Curriculum Development.

Glickman, C., Gordon, S., & Ross-Gordon, J. (2010). *Supervision and instructional leadership: A developmental approach* (8th ed.). New York: Pearson.

Goldhammer, R. (1969). *Clinical supervision: Special methods for the supervision of teachers.* New York: Holt, Rinehart and Winston.

Goldsberry, L. (1998). Teacher involvement in supervision. In G. Firth & E. Pajak (Eds.). *Handbook of Research on School Supervision* (pp. 428–462). New York: Macmillan.

Gordon, S. (Ed.). (2006). *Standards for instructional supervision.* Larchmont, NY: Eye on Education.

Gordon, S. & Nicely, Jr., R. (1998). Supervision and staff development. In G. Firth & E. Pajak (Eds.). *Handbook of research on school supervision* (pp. 801–841). New York: Macmillan.

Gore, J. (1991). Action research and the supervision of student teachers. In K. Zeichner & B. Tabachnick (Eds.). *Encouraging reflective practice in teacher education.* London & Philadelphia, PA: Falmer Press.

Gould, S. (1997). Evolution: The pleasures of pluralism. *The New York Review of Books, 44*(11), 47–52.

Gromyko, Y. & St. Maurice, H. (2000). Constructions of community: Aspects of cultural historical study of school curriculum. *Discourse: Studies in the Cultural Politics of Education, 21*(2), 193–204.

Groopman, J. (2010). Health care: Who knows "best"? *New York Review, 57*(2). Retrieved from www.nybooks.com/articles/archives/2010/feb/11/health-care-who-knows-best/?pagination=false

Halverson, R. (2005). *School leadership rubrics.* Madison, WI: Wisconsin Education Research Center.

Halverson, R. & Dikkers, S. (2008). *Formative leadership for learning: Leveraging empirical studies of educational leadership for formative tools.* Madison, WI: Wisconsin Center for Education Research.

Hammerness, K., Darling-Hammond, L., & Bransford, J. (2005). How teachers learn and develop. In L. Darling-Hammond & J. Bransford (Eds.). *Preparing teachers for a changing world* (pp. 358–389). San Francisco, CA: Jossey-Bass.

Hammersley, M. & Atkinson, P. (2007). *Ethnography: Principles in practice*. London: Taylor & Francis.

Hargreaves, A. & Fullan, M. (2012). *Professional capital: Transforming teaching in every school*. New York: Teachers College Press.

Hazi, H. (2002). The status of supervisory certification in the 50 states. Paper presented at the annual meeting of the American Educational Research Association, New Orleans, April 2002.

Heideman, C. (1990). Introduction. In P. Burke, C. Heideman, & R. Heideman (Eds.). *Preparing for staff development*. London: Falmer Press.

Herbart, J. (1898). *The application of psychology to the science of education* (B. Mulliner, Trans.). Boston, MA: Scribner's.

Herbst, J. (1989). *And sadly teach: Teacher education and professionalization in American culture*. Madison, WI: University of Wisconsin Press.

Hofstadter, R. (1955). *The age of reform: From Bryan to F.D.R.* New York: Knopf.

Holland, P. (1998). Processes and techniques in supervision. In G. Firth & E. Pajak (Eds.). *Handbook of research on school supervision* (pp. 397–408). New York: Macmillan.

Hughes, T. (2004). *American genesis: A century of invention and technological enthusiasm, 1870–1970* (2nd ed.). Chicago, IL: University of Chicago Press.

Hunter, M. (1983). *Mastery teaching*. El Segundo, CA: TIP Publications.

Iwanicki, E. (1998). Evaluation in supervision. In G. Firth & E. Pajak (Eds.). *Handbook of research on school supervision* (pp. 138–175). New York: Macmillan.

Joseph, M. (2002). *The trivium: The liberal arts of logic, grammar, and rhetoric*. Philadelphia, PA: Paul Dry.

Kaestle, C. (1983). *Pillars of the republic: Common schools and American society, 1780–1860*. New York: Hill & Wang.

Kane, T. & Cantrell, S. (2010). Learning about teaching: Initial findings from the Measures of Effective Teaching Project. Retrieved from http://bit.ly/X1utJU

Kanigel, R. (2005). *The one best way: Frederick Winslow Taylor and the enigma of efficiency*. Cambridge, MA: MIT Press.

Karier, C. (1982). Supervision in historical perspective. In T. Sergiovanni (Ed.). *Supervision of teaching* (pp. 2–15). Alexandria, VA: Association for Supervision & Curriculum Development.

Kennedy, G. (Ed. & Trans.). (1991). *Aristotle, on rhetoric: A theory of civic discourse*. New York: Oxford University Press.

Kennedy, M. (2008). Sorting out teacher quality. *Phi Delta Kappan, 90*(1), 59–61.

Kennedy, M. (2010). Attribution error and the quest for teacher quality. *Educational Researcher, 39*(8), 591–598.

Kliebard, H. (2003). *The struggle for the American curriculum 1893–1958* (3rd ed.). London: Routledge Falmer.

Larson, M. (1977). *The rise of professionalism*. Berkeley, CA: University of California Press.

Lasch, C. (1991). *The true and only heaven: Progress and its critics*. New York: W. W. Norton.

Leithwood, K., Seashore Louis, K., Anderson, S., & Wahlstrom, K. (2004). *Executive summary: How leadership influences student learning*. New York: The Wallace Foundation.

Leff, M. (1983). The topics of argumentative invention in Latin rhetorical theory from Cicero to Boethius. *Rhetorica, I*(1), 23–44.

Lemann, N. (2000). *The big test: The secret history of the American meritocracy*. New York: Macmillan.

Lindner, R. (1999). *The fifty-minute hour: A collection of true psychoanalytic tales*. New York: Other Press.

Little, J. (1990). The mentor phenomenon and the social organization of teaching. In C. Cazden (Ed.). *Review of Research in Education* (pp. 97–351). Washington, DC: American Educational Research Association.

Luttwak, E. (2000). *Turbo-capitalism*. New York: Harper.

Madison, J. (1993/1787). "To break and control the violence of faction," Federalist Paper X. In B. Bailyn (Ed.). *The debate on the Constitution: Part one*. New York: Library of America.

Mann, H. (1849). *Twelfth annual report to the Massachusetts Board of Education*. Boston, MA: Dutton & Wentworth.

Manna, P. (2010). *Collision course: Federal education policy meets state and local realities*. Washington, DC: CQ Press.

Marshall, K. (2009). *Rethinking teacher supervision and evaluation*. San Francisco, CA: Jossey-Bass.

Martin, M. (2005). Reflection in teacher education: How can it be supported? *Educational Action Research*, *13*(4), 525–542.

Marzano, R., Danielson, C., & Reeve, D. (2011). *iObservation: Advancing professional growth*. York, PA: Learning Sciences International.

Mattingly, P. (1975). *The classless profession: American schoolmen in the nineteenth century*. New York: NYU Press.

Menand, L. (2010). *The marketplace of ideas: Reform and resistance in the American university*. New York: W. W. Norton.

Miles, K. & Baroody, S. (2011). *Moving beyond test scores*. Watertown, MA: Education Resource Strategies.

Mills, G. (2010). *Action research: A guide for the teacher researcher* (4th ed.). New York: Merrill/Prentice Hall.

Mitchell, C. & Kerchner, J. (1983). Teacher unions. In L. Shulman & G. Sykes (Eds.). *Handbook of teaching & policy*. New York: Longman.

Mosher, R. & Purpel, D. (1972). *Supervision: The reluctant profession*. Boston, MA: Houghton Mifflin.

Mumford, L. (1934). *Technics and civilization*. New York: Harcourt, Brace.

Munro, P. (1991). Supervision: What's imposition got to do with it?, *Journal of Curriculum and Supervision* 7(1), 77–89.

National Education Association. (2011). *Best practices in education*. Retrieved from www.nea.org/tools/17073.htm

Nelson, J., Megill, A., & McCloskey, D. (1988). *The rhetoric of human sciences: Language and argument in scholarship and public affairs*. Madison, WI: University of Wisconsin Press.

Newmann, F. & Wehlage, G. (1995). *Successful school restructuring: A report to the public and educators*. Madison WI: National Center on Restructuring & Organizing Schools.

Ogletree, C. (2004). *All deliberate speed: Reflections on the first half-century of Brown v. Board of Education*. New York: W.W. Norton.

Ogren, C. (2005). *The American state normal school: An instrument of great good*. New York: Macmillan.

Ozga, J., Seddon, T., & Popkewitz, T. (Eds.). (2006). *Education research and policy: Steering the knowledge-based economy. World Year Book, 2006*. London: Taylor and Francis.

Painter, N. (1989). *Standing at Armageddon: The United States, 1877–1919*. New York: W. W. Norton.

Popkewitz, T. (1991). *A political sociology of educational reform: Power/knowledge in teaching, teacher education and research*. New York: Teachers College Press.

Powell, A., Farrar, E., & Cohen, D. (1985). *The shopping mall high school: Winners and losers in the educational marketplace*. Boston, MA: Houghton Mifflin.

Putnam, R. (2000). *Bowling alone: The collapse and revival of American community*. New York: Simon & Schuster.

RAND Corporation (2012). Measuring teacher effectiveness. Santa Monica, CA: The RAND Corporation. Retrieved from www.rand.org/education/projects/measuring-teacher-effectiveness.html

Ravitch, D. (2001). Introduction. In S. Mondale & S. Patton (Eds.). *School: The story of American public education*. Boston, NY: Beacon.

Reese, W. (1999). *The origins of the American high school*. New Haven, CT: Yale University Press.

Rogers, C. (1951). *Client-centered therapy: Its current practice, implications and theory*. London: Constable.

Rury, J. (1989). Who became teachers? The social characteristics of teachers in American history. In D. Warren (Ed.). *American teachers: Histories of a profession at work* (pp. 9–48). Washington, DC: American Educational Research Association.

St. Maurice, H. (1987). Clinical supervision and power: Regimes of instructional management. In T. Popkewitz (Ed.). *Critical studies in teacher education* (pp. 242–264). Philadelphia, PA: Falmer Press.

St. Maurice, H. (1991). A Guide to commonplaces: On the use of loci in educators' discourse. *Journal of Curriculum Studies, 23*(1), 41–53.

Sergiovanni, T. & Starratt, R. (2007). *Supervision: A redefinition* (7th ed.). New York: McGraw-Hill.

Shapiro, R. & Blumberg, A. (1998). Social dimensions of supervision. In G. Firth & E. Pajak (Eds.). *Handbook of research on school supervision* (pp.1055–1084). New York: Macmillan.

Slick, S. (1998). A University supervisor negotiates territory and status. *Journal of Teacher Education, 49*(4), 304–315.

Smith, T. & Ingersoll, R. (2004). What are the effects of induction and mentoring on beginning teacher turnover? *American Educational Research Journal, 41*(3), 681–714.

Smyth, J. (1998). Economic forces and supervision. In G. Firth & E. Pajak (Eds.). *Handbook of Research on School Supervision*. New York: Macmillan.

Soder, R. (2001). *The language of leadership*. San Francisco, CA: Jossey-Bass.

Standage, T. (1998). *The Victorian Internet: The remarkable story of the telegraph and the nineteenth century's on-line pioneers*. New York: Walker & Company.

Starr, P. (2004). *The creation of the media: Political origins of modern communications*. New York: Basic.

Stoelinga, S. (2010). Pressuring teachers to leave: Honest talk about how principals use harassing supervision. *Phi Delta Kappan, 92*(4), 57–61.

Stronge, J. (Ed.). (2006). *Evaluating teaching* (2nd ed.). Thousand Oaks, CA: Corwin.

Stumbo, C. & McWalters, P. (2010). Measuring effectiveness: What will it take? *Educational Leadership, 68*(10), 10–15.

Smyth, J. (1998). Economic forces affecting supervision. In G. Firth & E. Pajak (Eds.). *Handbook of Research on School Supervision* (pp. 1178–1183). New York: Macmillan.

Taylor, F. (1913). *The principles of scientific management*. New York: Harper.

Taylor, M. (2002). *The moment of complexity: Emerging network culture*. Chicago, IL: University of Chicago Press.

Tichi, C. (1987). *Shifting gears: Technology, literature, culture in modernist America*. Chapel Hill, NC: University of North Carolina Press.

Tracy, S. (1998). Models and approaches. In G. Firth & E. Pajak (Eds.). *Handbook of Research on School Supervision* (pp. 80–108). New York: Macmillan.

Turner, F. (2006). *From counterculture to cyberculture*. Chicago, IL: University of Chicago Press.

Tyack, D. (1974). *The one best system: A history of American urban education*. Cambridge, MA: Harvard University Press.

Tyack, D. & Cuban, L. (1995). *Tinkering toward utopia: A century of public school reform*. Cambridge, MA: Harvard University Press.

Tyack, D. & Hansot, E. (1986). *Managers of virtue: Public school leadership in America*, 1820–1980. New York: Basic.

U.S. Congress. (1965). Elementary and Secondary Education Act of 1965, 79 Stat. 27, 20 USC, ch. 70.

U.S. Congress. (1975). Education for All Handicapped Children Act of 1975, 20 USC 1401 et seq.

U.S. Congress. (1972). Title IX of the Education Amendments of 1972, 20 USC, § 1681.

U.S. Department of Education. (1983). *A Nation at risk: The imperative for educational reform: A report to the nation and the Secretary of Education United States Department of Education by The National Commission on Excellence in Education.* Washington, DC: Department of Education.

Urban, W. (2010). *More than science and Sputnik: The National Defense Education Act of 1958.* Tuscaloosa, AL: University of Alabama Press.

Waite, D. (2000). Identity, authority, and the heart of supervision. *International Journal of Educational Reform, 9*(4), 282–291.

Waters, T., Marzano, R. J., & McNulty, B. (2003*). Balanced leadership: What 30 years of research tells us about the effect of leadership on pupil achievement.* Denver, CO: Mid-continent Research for Education and Learning (McREL).

Wei, R., Darling-Hammond, L., & Adamson, F. (2010). *Professional development in the United States: Trends and challenges.* Dallas, TX: National Staff Development Council.

The White House, Office of the Press Secretary. (2010). *Fact Sheet: The race to the top.* Retrieved from www.whitehouse.gov/the-press-office/fact-sheet-race-to-top

White, J. B. (1989). *Heracles' bow: Essays on the rhetoric and poetics of the law.* Madison, WI: University of Wisconsin Press.

Whitehurst, G., Glazerman, S., Goldhaber, D., Loeb, S., Raudenbush, S., & Staiger, D. (2010). *Evaluating teachers: The important role of value-added.* Washington, DC: Brookings Institution.

Williams, R. (1985). *Keywords: A vocabulary of culture and society.* New York: Oxford University Press.

Yates, F. (1966). *The art of memory.* Chicago, IL: University of Chicago Press

Zeichner, K. (2005). Becoming a teacher educator. *Teaching and Teacher Education, 21*, 117–124.

Zepeda, S. (2002). *Instructional supervision: Applying tools and concepts.* Larchmont, NY: Eye on Education.

CHAPTER 6

Develop Assessment and Accountability Systems to Monitor Student Progress

Rose M. Ylimaki

KEY TOPICS

- Accountability Levels and Issues
- A Comprehensive Assessment System
- Summative and Formative Assessments
- Assessment-Curriculum Connections

According to the ISLLC Standard 2, effective instructional leaders develop assessment and accountability systems to monitor student progress. Today's instructional leaders face accountability pressures at all levels. Principals/instructional leaders must be able to implement and monitor various summative and formative assessments, align assessments with curriculum and instruction, and lead difficult conversations regarding achievement gaps. In other words, principals/instructional leaders must have the assessment literacy (knowledge and skills) to enhance learning opportunities and close achievement gaps. This chapter presents leadership for effective accountability and assessment systems (formative and summative) that improve teaching and learning for all students.

EXTENDED REFLECTION 6.1

Define accountability. Describe your current assessment system, including summative and formative assessments. Be prepared to share your thoughts with your colleagues. Refer to your answers as you read the chapter.

ACCOUNTABILITY LEVELS: DIRECT AND INDIRECT INFLUENCES

As a landmark of education reform in the United States, the No Child Left Behind (NCLB) Act of 2001 uses accountability to leverage policy implementation. Some studies have indicated direct positive effects of NCLB on leveraging much-needed improvements for students in persistently underperforming schools (e.g. Skrla et al., 2004). Findings from other studies disagree. For instance, analyses of state test score trends revealed the marginal effects of NCLB accountability policy on student achievement gaps and graduation-rates between racial and socioeconomic groups of students (Lee, 2006; Orfield, Losen, & Balfanz, 2006). Still other studies have raised concerns about the effects of NCLB policy on the narrowing of teaching practices, curriculum (e.g. Daly, 2009; Ylimaki, 2011), and on local leaders' decision-making practices to a focus on standardized testing data (e.g. Duke et al., 2003; Luizzi, 2006). Thus, studies of NCLB accountability indicate direct influences on student achievement overall, marginal direct influences on closing racial/ethnic achievement gaps, and some unintended (indirect) influences on narrowing the curriculum and teacher decision-making strategies. Direct and indirect influences of accountability are further described in the next two sections.

DIRECT INFLUENCES

Federal and State

The federal NCLB Act of 2001 and related state testing mandates use accountability as a direct lever of policy implementation. In particular, the No Child Left Behind Act articulates consequences for failure to make adequate yearly progress on state tests toward a goal of 100 percent proficiency by the year 2014. As this chapter is written, thirty-two states have filed for waivers regarding the 2014 goal. Regardless of the 100 percent waivers, if schools do not make adequate *yearly* progress on state-administered standardized tests over a series of years, their leaders and teachers face severe consequences, including conversion to charter school status, staff restructuring, and reconstitution. In a similar vein, Race to the Top rewards schools for attaining "labels" of high performance. School performance indicators may also impact principals in other ways, including particularly administrator and teacher evaluations. For instance, Arizona mandated that districts base 33–50 percent of principal evaluations on student academic growth or student outcomes on state tests (Arizona Revised Statutes § 15–203(A) (38)).

Common Core Curriculum also uses accountability as a lever for increased rigor and post-secondary preparation. As this chapter is written, forty-five states have adopted the Common Core Standards, and each state must develop an accountability system to ensure that each child has access to a "high quality education" and post-secondary options. According to the Common Core Standards initiative, schools must accomplish these goals by: (1) driving school and district performance towards college and career readiness; (2) distinguishing among students performances in order to provide supports and interventions to students most in need; and (3) providing timely and transparent data to promote action at all levels; and (4) fostering continuous improvement throughout the system. PARCC assessments will also directly influence district and school use of resources within each of these recommended processes. If PARCC assessments require students to be proficient in particular strategies and in using technology to demonstrate their proficiency, how are districts likely to respond? Districts are likely to expend resources on technology and professional development aimed at these tested strategies.

Local District

Closely related, instructional leaders are often directly influenced and held accountable for many local district accountability policies or implantation mandates. For example, many districts mandate the use of locally developed benchmark assessments or commercial tests, such as Galileo, that have predictive value for state test performance. That is, quarterly benchmarks are aligned with state test items, and student benchmark performance predicts how well students will perform on the yearly state assessments. The logic is as follows: if students struggle on particular benchmark items, they are likely to struggle on the state assessments. Benchmark assessment results, then, provide teachers with critical information to guide instruction for the remainder of the school year. Many districts hold principals and teachers accountable for benchmark assessment results, with rewards that include performance pay tied to teacher evaluation systems and even merit pay. As a result, some studies have noted a narrowing of curriculum and teacher decision-making focus to the benchmark and state assessment results (e.g. Johnson & Johnson, 2005; Ylimaki, 2011). Today's instructional leaders must be careful to avoid narrowing the curriculum to standardized test items.

INDIRECT INFLUENCES

School and district leaders are also influenced and held accountable in indirect ways. For instance, local/regional newspapers and organizations often publish state assessment results that indirectly put leaders under tremendous pressure to improve performance. Such reports frequently rank districts and schools according to their performance on assessments with top-performing districts/schools at the top and low-performing ones at or near the bottom. When a district and/or school performs at or near the bottom of such a ranked list over a series of years, local school boards, parents, and other community members often see their local schools (and leaders) as deficient. As a result, instructional leaders may change their priorities to focus on tests. And while a focus on high test performance is not bad in and of itself, the related narrowing of curriculum and decisions is problematic for educating the whole child (e.g. Johnson & Johnson, 2005; Ylimaki, 2011).

Consider the following questions:

- How often have your professional learning communities (PLCs) focused on standardized test data analysis?
- How much time do your PLCs spend on formative assessments aligned with standardized test improvement?

Now think about these questions:

- How often have your PLCs focused on community/civic engagement or service learning?
- How often do you and your colleagues talk about students' funds of knowledge and background information as assets for the curriculum?
- How often do your PLCs talk about improving the arts and humanities?

Answers to these questions point to the need for a comprehensive assessment system aligned to curriculum, instruction, and learning for the whole child.

FIELDWORK 6.1

Ask a Principal about Accountability Pressures

Ask a principal about the different types of accountability he/she faces. Prompt him or her to talk about national accountability sources (NCLB, Race to the Top, Common Core assessments), state accountability (testing mandates, principal/teacher evaluation systems), and local sources (newspaper rankings, community, school board, benchmark assessments). Then ask the principal how he/she manages these accountability pressures.

Finally, ask him/her how the accountability pressures have reduced or even eliminated other goals (e.g. service learning, the arts). Be prepared to share your responses with the class.

A COMPREHENSIVE ASSESSMENT SYSTEM AND ITS COMPONENTS

Effective instructional leaders use formative and summative assessment measures, as essential components of a comprehensive accountability system that connects assessments, instruction, and curriculum for the whole child within local communities and beyond. We can divide an assessment system into two broad categories of assessments: summative and formative. Essentially, summative assessments provide information about what students have learned at a particular point in time, and formative assessments provide feedback about what students are learning during an instructional time. Teachers use formative assessment feedback to modify their instruction in ways that help all children learn more during subsequent instruction.

Summative Assessments

Summative assessment (an assessment *of* learning) typically documents how much learning has occurred at a particular point in time. Overall, the purpose of summative assessment is to measure the level of student, school, or program success. Today's instructional leaders must know how to analyze summative assessment data and use that data to analyze program effectiveness and develop plans for school or curriculum improvement (see Chapter 10 for suggestions). At the same time, leaders must recognize summative assessments as part of an overall comprehensive assessment system.

Summative assessments are most often given periodically to determine at a particular point in time what students know and do not know. Commonsensically, the term "summative assessment" is often associated with large-scale standardized tests, such as state assessments, but summative assessments are also used in district and classroom programs. In this sense, the key is to think of summative assessments as a way to measure student learning at a *particular* point in time. Summative assessments provide important information that can only help in evaluating specific points in the learning process. Because summative assessments of learning are spread out over time and occur after the instruction occurs (from a few weeks to a year), they are useful to evaluate the effectiveness of programs and access to a quality education. In the wake of NCLB and related accountability policies, instructional leaders must examine summative data for evidence of equitable opportunities for learning as well as academic achievement.

Equity audits and assessment processes. Skrla et al. (2004) developed an equity audit process to help school leaders and other school members systematically examine summative data, looking for equity of learning opportunities in their schools. More specifically, Skrla et al. (2004) posited twelve indicators grouped into three categories for equity audits—namely, teacher quality equity, programmatic equity, and achievement equity. High quality teachers are key determinants of students' opportunities to be academically successful (Skrla et al., 2004). Yet students of color and students form low income backgrounds often have non-certified teachers and or teachers with less experience and training. According to Skrla et al. (2004), if children of color and children living in poverty get lower quality teachers than their Anglo peers from middle and upper class neighborhoods, we cannot expect equitable achievement. Furthermore, if the inequity in teacher quality is distributed across a school or district, the result is likely to be a systemic inequity in achievement. Similar quality patterns can exist within schools. In your school, do the more experienced teachers teach advanced placement courses? Do least experienced teachers teach intervention classes?

Equity in the quality of programs is just as important as teacher quality (Skrla et al., 2004). Skrla and colleagues recommend an audit of four key indicators of program quality:

1. special education
2. gifted and talented education
3. bilingual education
4. student discipline.

Historically, students of color and students from low-income backgrounds are over-represented in special education and under-represented in gifted/talented programs. In the equity audit, the indicator for quality in special education and gifted talented programs is whether all student groups are represented in reasonably proportionate percentages. With regards to bilingual education, the question is whether students are being well served and not simply segregated from the kind of quality instruction necessary to make academic progress. Students who are routinely and consistently removed

---

FIELDWORK 6.2

Work with your principal, PLC, and/or grade level team to conduct an equity audit, looking at data regarding teacher quality, programmatic quality, bilingual education, and discipline. Add the resulting data to your Data Wall. Interview your PLC members to gain an understanding of their perceptions about the resulting equity data. Work with your team to develop plans to attain more equitable academic achievement in your school.

---

from classes for discipline are also denied equal access to learning. In combination, teacher quality equity and programmatic equity contribute to achievement equity.

Equity audits require deep trust among staff members and instructional leaders who can facilitate difficult conversations with regards to race, whiteness, language, and poverty. Moreover, today's instructional leaders must have strategies and analytical tools to help school members get beyond deficit views and blaming external factors for achievement gaps. See Chapter 2 for additional culturally responsive assessment strategies that help school members move beyond deficit views of traditionally marginalized students. Summative data provides instructional leaders with many understandings about what students have learned as well as their opportunities for learning (teacher quality and programmatic quality. Yet summative assessments happen too far away from instruction and other school practices to make instructional adjustments or interventions *during* the learning process. For that, we need formative assessments.

Formative Assessments

Formative assessments (assessments *for* learning) provide information or feedback to modify teaching and learning activities. According to Heritage, Kim, Vendlinski, and Herman (2009), formative assessment is "a systematic process to continuously gather evidence and provide feedback about learning while instruction is underway" (p. 24). Popham (2003) adds that formative assessment is a planned process; it does not happen accidentally. Teachers who regularly utilize formative assessments are better able to: (1) determine what curriculum content students already know and to what degree *during* the instructional process; (2) decide what minor modifications or major changes in instruction they need to make so that all students can succeed in upcoming instruction and on subsequent assessments; (3) create appropriate lessons and activities for groups of learners or individual students; and (4) inform students about their current progress in order to help them set goals for improvement.

Common Formative Assessments

Ainsworth and Viegut (2006) recommend common formative assessments designed by teams of teachers and then administered to students by each participating teacher periodically throughout the academic school year. In particular, common formative assessments assess student understanding of particular curriculum standards that the grade-level or department educators are currently focusing on in their individual classrooms. Teachers collaboratively score the assessments, analyze the results, and discuss ways to achieve improvements in student learning on the next common formative assessment they will administer. In this way, assessment informs decision-making during the instructional process. If the common formative assessments are aligned to the large-scale assessments in terms of what students will need to know and be able to do on those assessments, the formative assessment results will provide valuable information regarding what students already know and what they yet need to learn in order to do well on summative assessments. Using formative assessment results, educators can adjust instruction to better prepare students for success on the large-scale, summative assessments. Further, educators can use formative assessments to understand each child's learning approach, background knowledge, and any misconceptions that may negatively affect their comprehension of material.

Instructional leaders/principals play a vital role in implementing common formative assessment processes in their schools. They must look for creative ways to change daily teaching schedules to promote to promote collaborative curriculum development, instructional planning, and analysis of student progress. By freeing participating teachers to meet in appropriate teams, administrators/instructional leaders provide teachers with the support necessary to plan and align curriculum, instruction, and assessments. In sum, whether to regard an assessment as either formative or summative depends on the assessment's purpose and how it is to be used.

Summative and formative assessments are integral to a comprehensive assessment system. Further, instructional leaders/principals and teachers need to consider what they regularly assess, what they do not regularly assess, and for what purpose. With many schools under tremendous pressure to quickly raise standardized test scores, teachers and principals may prioritize tested standards in terms of instruction and formative assessments to the exclusion of promoting civic responsibility, inclusion, and social justice.

The next several subsections describe a comprehensive assessment system (summative and formative) with components that inform a multi-dimensional curriculum (described

---

FIELDWORK 6.3

Formative or Summative?

Decide if the following assessment examples are formative or summative:

1. The assessment is a final measure of how students performed on constructed response items on multiple measures taught during the quarter.
2. The teacher uses the results from a unit test to inform instruction for the same students during the next unit of study.
3. A teacher provides students with the opportunity to revise and then improve their performance on a particular assessment during the evaluation process.
4. Students complete their revisions and the final evaluation is determined.

Be prepared to share your responses.

in Chapter 3) and consider the issues identified in equity audits. When instructional leaders connect a comprehensive assessment to a multi-dimensional curriculum, they have the potential to avoid a narrow curriculum and limited decision-making identified in the research on NCLB (e.g. Johnson & Johnson, 2005; Ylimaki, 2011).

The entire process begins with the policy-related curriculum (now common core) as well as students' funds of knowledge and then continues through each successive practice. Common formative (school-based) assessments should be intentionally aligned to all of these standards. Previously in many states, teachers needed to power or prioritize long lists of discrete state standards. The Common Core Standards are relatively brief and relatively equal in importance; common core standards work better in their totality than as individual standards. In this prioritization process, the Common Core Standards are the power standards (Shanahan, 2012).

Teachers then align classroom performance assessments to both the Common Core Standards and to the school-based common formative assessments. School-based common formative assessments are deliberately aligned to the formative and summative district benchmark assessments (typically administered quarterly) and end-of-course or end-of-year summative assessments. Last, district benchmark assessments and the end-of-course assessments are deliberately aligned to the annual state assessments. In this model, curriculum standards (academic core including students' funds of knowledge, humanities, and social goals) are aligned with daily practice.

Teachers work together to gain deep, collective understandings about what children need to learn in relation to their backgrounds/funds of knowledge. Next, teachers determine big ideas and essential questions to focus instruction and assessment for each standard. In so doing, teachers cross-reference students' funds of knowledge and Common Core Standards with state assessment data and state assessment requirements. In this part of the process, teachers examine state assessment data to see where students are scoring low and to identify in the state test requirements those standards that receive the greatest emphasis. Teachers consider how students' funds of knowledge may be assets for learning these standards. Teachers then make any instructional modifications as needed and continue the cycle. These sequential steps are described in the next several sub-sections.

Develop a Common Understanding of Standards-based Curriculum

Because the Common Core Standards are minimal in number and recursive in nature, instructional leaders should provide teachers with a full K–12 set of the core standards rather than a set per grade level. With many previous state standards, standards were much more linear and discrete, and thus grade level standards made sense.

In these instances, asking teachers to prioritize or "power" grade level standards made sense. The point is that leaders must examine standards and adjust any alignment or prioritization processes in relation to the needs of particular standards. In any case, teachers should develop deep, collective understandings of standards prior to the development of formative assessments. After teachers conduct a thorough review of the Common Core Standards or whatever standards are mandated, teachers need to consider interdisciplinary application, students' funds of knowledge, and broader social goals.

Develop Big Ideas and Essential Questions

Teachers determine the "Big Ideas" inherent in the Common Core standard and relevant social goals for their schools and communities. Big Ideas are statements of understanding that students derive from study of particular standards. These Big Ideas often occur to students during the "ah-ha" moments of the learning process, particularly when teachers guide students to draw conclusions and make connections among curriculum standards and needs for an equitable and just democratic society. Wiggins and McTighe (1998) describe Big Ideas as enduring understandings, "the important understandings that we want students to get inside of and retain after they've forgotten many of the details" (p. 10).

The value of developing big ideas is in the collaborative process among teachers. As educators analyze the standards, they get to know exactly what the standards require them to teach and the students to learn. Many teacher teams reorganize the information into a graphic organizer that makes sense to all teacher participants. The standards become less daunting, and the educator is better able to consider how best to teach the concepts and skills that now become much clearer. Beyond recall of new information (knowledge), students learn to make inferences and gain insights between new information, prior understandings, and skills that students will need to use throughout their lives. Moreover, students learn to access and draw on their background experiences or funds of knowledge in order to gain these new insights and understandings.

Formulate Essential Questions Matched to the Big Ideas

"Essential questions represent the essence of what you believe students should examine and know in the short time they have with a teacher" (Hayes-Jacobs, 1997, p. 26). Essential questions serve as instructional filters (Ainsworth & Viegut, 2006) for selecting the most appropriate lessons and activities to advance student understanding of the concepts and skills. The goal is for students to be able to respond to Essential Questions with the Big Ideas stated in their own words at the conclusion of an instructional unit. Identification of Big Ideas and Essential Questions lays the foundation for developing classroom and common assessments. In the following example, teachers matched Essential Questions to corresponding Big Ideas (in parentheses).

ESSENTIAL QUESTIONS AND CORRESPONDING BIG IDEAS (GRADE 5 MATH)

1. *Why do we need to know and be able to use text structure?* (Understanding how to use text structure is a way to comprehend the main idea of a text and is a necessary reading skill applicable to all expository text.)
2. *Why learn how to graphically organize text structure?* (Graphic organizers provide shortcuts for accessing various text structures.)
3. *How can we apply text organizational skills in writing?* (Graphic organizers can be used to guide the pre-writing phase of writing an expository text.)

Collaboratively Design Common Formative Pre- and Post-Assessments

After teachers develop big ideas/essential questions, they work in teams to collaboratively design a common formative pre- and post-assessment matched directly to those concepts, skills, and "Big Ideas" in the standards. Assessment questions and items need to be written so as to address each of concepts inherent in the Common Core. Items also need to match the specific level of rigor of the identified standard. (See information about level of rigor in Chapter 3). For example, if the standard requires students to analyze or evaluate, assessment items need to reflect that higher level of cognition and rigor.

In order to assess student proficiency of Common Core Standards, teachers will need to develop selected response type of common formative assessments as well as a constructed response type of common formative assessment in which students write their own responses to the Essential Questions. The Big Ideas—stated in the students' own words—along with supporting details derived from the standards should appear in the students' written responses. Combining two types of assessments (selected- and constructed-response) provides teachers with a multiple-measure assessment of students' understandings. Teachers may analyze constructive responses of expository text and other writing forms to assess students' funds of knowledge in relation to the learned curriculum (see Chapters 2 and 3). Because teachers know in advance the students' funds of knowledge as well as core concepts, skills, and understandings students will be required to demonstrate on the common formative pre- and post-assessments, each individual teacher on the team can plan and teach the instructional unit that is aligned with the curriculum and assessments used to evaluate students' learning progress.

Administer and Score Common Formative (Pre-) Assessments

Teachers administer common formative assessments individually and then score them with colleagues in a collaborative setting, particularly for constructed responses. Collaborative scoring of constructed-response assessments requires timely professional development. Teachers will need a conceptual and procedural framework for scoring common formative assessments, including a rationale and process for scoring assessments. To begin, teachers consider their purposes for the common formative assessment—what they most wanted to find out about their students' learning—before deciding which type of assessment would best meet their needs. Questions might revolve around:

- what *understandings and/or funds of knowledge* the students have with regard to using particular Common Core Standards
- what *application* of the concepts and skills embedded in those standards the students can demonstrate
- what kind of *integration* of understanding the students have gained (i.e., whether or not students can articulate the Big Ideas in their own words and then support those Big Ideas with details from the standard concepts and skills).

For example, teachers may answer the above questions to decide that the best type of assessment to meet these multiple purposes has to be a constructed-response assessment, such as an extended response writing assessment. After administration of the assessment in individual classrooms, teachers then meet to score the assessments. Students can also learn to self-assess their work against a set of established scoring guide criteria. Such self-assessment enables students to identify where their strengths lie and where they need to improve: "Engaging in self-assessment prior to receiving feedback . . . shifts the primary responsibility for improving the work to the student, where it belongs" (Stiggins et al., 2004, p. 195). Many teachers prefer to wait until they have more experience with their own evaluation of common formative assessments before they involve students. Teachers who do involve their students in the evaluation of assessments using the scoring guide the students help create will benefit from these efforts, including providing students with greater ownership of the learning process.

Administer and Score Common Formative (Post-) Assessments for Use by Data Teams

The collaborative scoring process described below will provide participating teachers with the degree of reliable and valid feedback on student performance they need to "inform" their future instruction. The sequence of eight steps to collaboratively score constructed-response student papers is as follows (Ainsworth & Viegut, 2006):

1. Discuss the definition of key terms.
2. Review criteria in task-specific or generic rubric created by team that will be used to score papers. Clarify and revise any subjective criteria to ensure consensus of understanding among members.
3. Read through student assessments and select exemplars/"anchor" papers/constructed responses and "range finder" papers to use during group scoring practice.
4. Conduct a group scoring *practice* to evaluate selected student papers representing a range of student responses. The practice session should include the following activities.
5. Begin with actual scoring of student papers using the rubric while referencing "anchor" and "range finder" papers.
6. Double-score or conduct a "read behind" scoring of each student paper to ensure inter-rater reliability.
7. Resolve adjacent or discrepant scoring disagreements by having a third evaluator score the paper in question.
8. Record rubric scores on a student roster for each class of students.

Analyze Post-Assessment Results in Data Teams

Compare pre- to post-assessment results, reflect on the process, and make plans for further improvement during the next instructional cycle. The term "data team" is defined as a grade-level, cross-grade level, or department team of educators composed of teachers who all teach the same content standards to their students, and who meet regularly for the express purpose of analyzing common assessment data. Data teams often include educators from the areas of special education, English language acquisition, and performing arts.

The data team process is a practical method that school systems throughout the nation are using to make their data meaningful in terms of improving instruction and

Subject Area:	Persuasive Writing	Grade: 3–4–5

Standards Addressed: Letter writing–parts of a letter
Voice and audience; Persuasive language; Research/
Data collection and analysis; Fact and opinions

Targeted Grade

Level Benchmarks: 3–4–5th
Letter Writing–parts of a letter
Voice and audience; Data collection and analysis; Fact and
opinions; Persuasive language–being persuasive

Description of

The Task: Collect research and data about activities provided by the city
parks and recreation, write a persuasive letter to parks and
recreation and city council showing activities student chose
and reasons for choices; Persuade city parks and recreation
to include activities more students chose

Community-Based Setting: Community parks and recreation

Collaboration: Activities wanted by most students and benefits of those
activities; Partner to other communities on activities and
persuasive writing

Formative Assessments Used: Letter writing–parts of letter; Research and data collection;
Data analysis; Voice and audience for persuasive letter

Scoring Guide/Rubric: PAGE UNIFIED – PINON SCHOOL

Rubric Guidance

	1 Needs Additional Support Now	2 Moving Towards the Standard	3 Meets the Standard	4 Exceeds the Standard
Evidence I Would Accept			Persuasive letter used in formal format showing research and data to support decision.	Oral presentation with technology smart boards power points to defend the letters and points of interest. Move to written publishing and defense of argument.

Figure 6.1 Common Formative Assessment and Rubric

student achievement. Data team processes frequently feature the following five steps, but the steps are very recursive and interactive. The data team process enables teacher teams to collaboratively identify in student work the strengths or characteristics of proficiency as well as the learning challenges of non-proficiency. Once the analysis is complete, the team establishes a very specific goal for student improvement on the next common assessment and selects the most effective instructional strategies to meet that goal.

- **Step 1: Chart the data.** Record the number and percentages of students who met or exceeded the established proficiency score on the common formative *pre*-assessment and do the same for those who did not. Record data regarding teacher quality (experience, certification if appropriate) and programmatic quality (percentages of students in special education, gifted/talented, time in bilingual education and in discipline).
- **Step 2: Analyze the results.** Identify strengths in proficient student papers and areas of need in non-proficient student papers. Identify proportional percentages for traditionally marginalized students in special education and gifted/talented as well as time spent in bilingual education and discipline programs.
- **Step 3: Set goal.** Write a specifically worded goal statement based on the common pre-assessment results and equity audit results that represent achievable student improvements on the common *post*-assessment and equity improvements.
- **Step 4: Select effective teaching strategies.** Select the most effective instructional strategies (experience-based and research-based) to achieve identified goal.
- **Step 5: Determine the results indicators.** Decide how to gauge the effectiveness of the team's selected instructional strategies and other processes designed to increase equity in learning opportunities.

Each step is further described below.

Step one. The first step of the data team process is to record on a group chart each teacher's student assessment results derived from the common formative pre-assessment. For example, if all the participating teachers agreed to score the common pre-formative assessment using a percentage scale and decided prior to administration of the assessment that the "cut" score for student proficiency would be 80 percent, then each teacher first separates all the student papers into two broad groups—those that scored 80 percent or higher (proficient and above) and those that scored below 80 percent (non-proficient). Each teacher records on a student roster the number and percentage of students who scored in each of these two categories and submits the student roster to a team member who prepares a group chart with all participant teachers' scores. In order to examine students' learning needs more specifically during the data team meeting, the teachers often sort all of their own proficient student papers into "proficient" or "above proficient" percentage bands (i.e., 80–89 percent and 90–100 percent, respectively). Teachers then sort the non-proficient papers into "almost proficient" or "beginning proficient" percentage bands (i.e., 70–79 percent and below 70 percent, respectively). Because these scores are derived from a common pre-assessment administered before any instruction takes place, in all likelihood, there will be many students scoring below 70 percent. Each teacher records the student data on an individual class roster and submits this data to the person designated to chart the data for the entire team. Teachers may decide to use a rubric rather than a percentage scale to evaluate student proficiency record the number and percentage of students in each class who scored at or above the rubric "cut" score and those who did not. As a group, teachers then record data regarding teacher quality (experience, certification if appropriate) and programmatic quality (percentages of students in special education, gifted/talented, time in bilingual education and in discipline).

Step two. Data team time is devoted to analysis of student learning needs (strengths/funds of knowledge or assets and learning challenges) and equity issues based in the data. If the participating teachers designed and administered a *selected-response* type of common formative assessment using a percentage scale, they first review their sorted student papers by levels of proficiency. Next, teachers dialogue to determine student learning strengths, challenges, and uses of funds of knowledge as revealed in the student responses. In analyzing selected responses, educators will need to determine which particular items the students marked correctly and which particular items they marked incorrectly. The teachers can then conduct an *item analysis* of each of the assessment items to pinpoint the concepts and skills students are understanding and not understanding. Teachers will prepare a T-chart of strengths and challenges based on their findings and rank-order the challenges according to the greatest need.

Finally, teachers need to examine *written student work* as opposed to completed multiple-choice answer sheets. This can only be accomplished if the common formative assessment includes constructed response types of items. For example, if teachers gave a common formative assessment that asked students to draw on their background knowledge and apply that knowledge to a curriculum standard, teachers may be able to assess students' funds of knowledge, any misconceptions, and the degree to which the student uses his/her background knowledge to comprehend the standard and content.

After determining students' funds of knowledge/background knowledge, strengths, and greatest areas of student need—by ordering the challenges to proficiency in the list above—data team members are ready to set goals for the post-assessment results. Further, after identifying proportional percentages for traditionally marginalized students in special education/gifted and talented programs as well as time spent in bilingual education and discipline programs, data team members are ready to set goals for improving equity in a systemic way.

Step three. Data team members use the assessment results to set appropriate goals for students. Many team members struggle with goal setting in terms of percentages, often arbitrarily setting a certain percentage number as a goal. In the example above, imagine that the *pre*-assessment data only showed 15 percent of students scoring at the proficient and above levels. Since the data team will write a *post*-assessment goal based on a short instructional cycle of typically a month in duration, many team members hesitate to set high goals (i.e., 100 percent of students will attain proficiency). Dramatic gains in student learning are possible if participating teachers' focus on the concepts and skills from the specific standards on which the common formative assessments are based and if all teachers (regular and special area teachers) work together to help children learn those concepts and skills.

By referring back to the Step 1 chart created by the data team, the members use their actual student data to write a realistic goal statement. With student papers already sorted into developmental categories, the teachers can project with more accuracy, the number and percentage of students likely to achieve proficiency and above on the common formative *post*-assessment. Conzemius and O'Neil (2001) developed a system for writing goals called SMART goals, which are specific, measurable, achievable, relevant, and timely. For example:

> The percentage of Grade 4 students scoring at proficiency and above in math multiple-step story problems will increase from 17% to 88% by April 30 (4 weeks) as measured by a grade-level developed common formative post-assessment that each participating teacher will administer to students on April 30.

> The percentage of Grade 10 students of color with out-of-class or in-school discipline will decrease to a proportional level from 60% to 23% by April 30 (12 weeks) as measured by a school-wide calculation of data on April 30.

SMART goals do not include the *how* or instructional strategies that individual teachers will use to achieve those results. Instructional strategies are determined in the next step.

Step four. After the data team sets the short-term SMART goals for the current instructional cycle or grading period, the participating teachers will generate a list of possible instructional or systemic change strategies to meet it. The teachers (regular and special) might choose to begin by reflecting upon their own professional experience and identifying research-based strategies that have proven effective. The data team conducts a search of research-based instructional or systemic change strategies in order to identify and select the most appropriate techniques to meet the goal they have set. After strategies have been selected, data team members review the list and decide upon the two or three that they think will have the greatest impact on improving student learning (or equity to learning) relative to the specific purpose—the rank-ordered challenges that were identified in Step 2. All of the teachers then agree to use each of the selected strategies during the instructional cycle or grading period. If teachers are not experienced with using one or more of the strategies, instructional leaders/principals and coaches will need to provide mentoring or coaching along with professional development about the strategy during faculty meetings and or PLC meetings.

Step five. The final step in the data team process is to decide what evidence the team will need to determine if the instructional strategy they selected in Step 4 proved effective. Specifically, the team is interested in determining the positive indicators that will give them the evidence that their selected strategies accomplished their purpose. Data teams then write a "Results Indicator" statement to represent the effectiveness of their selected strategies. Returning to the reading/writing example, the results indicator statements might be written as follows:

> Students who scored in the non-proficient range on the common formative pre-assessment will score in the proficient range on the post-assessment. The students will be able to:

- correctly use graphic representation to illustrate text structure in a given expository text
- arrive at a correct identification of the text structure

- incorporate text structure vocabulary and structure to develop an original writing piece
- communicate their understanding of the process they used in order to use text structure for comprehension and how they used that structure in their own writing.

When the five steps are completed, the data team creates an action plan to guide the instructional improvement process. The data team leader then shares this action plan with the principal along with a summary of the team's progress as recorded on the data team's five-step documents. This action plan can be as brief or as detailed as the school members would like but should address:

- instructional strategies used
- resources, materials and additional collaboration time needed
- rigor required
- instructional differentiation
- informal coaching and classroom support visits needed and when these classroom visits will be conducted
- sources for help if teachers encounter problems with implementation of the strategies
- strategies to eliminate systemic inequities in the school (teacher experience, program quality, bilingual education, and discipline)
- additional help or support needed from administrators.

Post-Assessment Data Team Meetings

After the common formative *post*-assessments are administered and scored at the end of the month, the data from each participating member of the team must again be charted prior to the data team meeting. The actual number and percentage of students who scored in each of the proficient and non-proficient categories on the common formative post-assessment are calculated and recorded for each educator on the team. The teachers then compare their pre-assessment results with the post-assessment results and later represent their gains on a data wall display. In this context, a data wall is not only a graphical representation of student achievement gains as measured by pre- and post-common formative assessment data collected during an instructional cycle but also a representation of how students' funds of knowledge are reflected in the curriculum. According to Ainsworth and Viegut (2006), the data wall is a three-part display that includes the group's identifying information, the student data results, the analysis of that data, the team-determined goal, and the results indicators are continually changing to reflect the current emphasis of instruction and provide a visible means of assessing growth from one instructional cycle to the next. Naturally, faculties celebrate gains in student learning evident on the data walls. At the same time, data walls provide visible evidence of challenges to improving student learning for individual students and subgroups. NCLB specifically requires schools to report student progress according to subgroups in an attempt to close achievement gaps according to race, gender, and SES.

When teachers attain (SMART) achievement goals and have evidence that they attained equitable student achievement among various subgroups (e.g. gender, race/ethnicity) in culturally responsive ways, then teachers, administrators, students and parents have reason to celebrate. If, however, this is not the case, team members must be able to discuss these challenges openly. Instructional leaders can use the following questions to guide this discussion:

- Did we use the identified strategies effectively and in culturally responsive ways?
- Did we use the identified strategies with sufficient frequency?
- Did we differentiate the identified strategies to meet diverse learning needs of students who are not yet proficient?
- Did we use the identified strategies to eliminate systemic inequities for traditionally marginalized students?
- Do we need further assistance or practice in how to use the identified instructional or systemic change strategies?
- Do we need to abandon the strategy and use others that might be more effective?
- How are our students doing overall and why do we think they performed the way they did?
- What are we going to do about intervening for students who are not proficient?
- How will we accelerate instruction for students who continue to excel so that we keep them motivated and progressing according to their own learning needs?
- Which instructional or systemic change strategies produced the greatest results?
- What other modifications do we want to make in our work collaboratively designing, administering, scoring, and analyzing common formative assessments?

Using these conversations and reflections, teachers then determine when to plan the next administration of a common formative assessment. They will repeat each of the steps in the data team process and plan for greater improvements in equity and student learning.

FIELDWORK 6.4

Observe a data team in your school or a nearby school. What aspects of the data team process described above did you observe? What else did the team do? How, if at all, did the team use common formative assessments? What other kinds of assessment data did the group use (e.g. students' funds of knowledge, equity audit, state assessment/summative data)?

STRATEGIES FOR LEADERS

How do instructional leaders put all of this information on accountability, assessment, and equity into practice? This section provides guidance for what today's instructional leaders need to know and be able to do as well as analytical tools and strategies for practice. Instructional leaders need to:

Know:

- requirements for rigor in text and instructional strategies
- requirements of assessments
- options for formative assessments
- options for summative assessment
- students' funds of knowledge and assets.

Be able to:

- help teachers develop deep understandings of curriculum standards
- align curriculum with assessments and instructional approaches
- monitor student progress on summative and formative assessments
- provide time for collaborative work on data, assessments, and culturally responsive instructional strategies
- disaggregate data by subgroups
- conduct equity audits
- lead difficult conversations about achievement equity and gaps.

How might you use these strategies in relation to the case study below?

CASE 6.1 IMPRESSIVE TEACHING BUT UNIMPRESSIVE SCHOOL LABEL

Middle School principal Isabel Sanchez stared at the state assessment results. Her school had improved in all academic areas, but the improvements were not enough to move out of a "C" rating. Dr. Sanchez is principal of a school in a barrio with tremendous pride in the Mexican-American culture, with many citizens of Mexican descent as well as immigrants (documented and undocumented). The school also has a high percentage of English language learners and children living in poverty. She knew that the ratings would be published in the local newspaper in the morning and that her teachers would be very disappointed. At the same time, Dr. Sanchez had worked very hard to develop a data-driven culture focused on continuous improvement. She hoped the teachers would see the ratings as a challenge, and she would not have long to wait. When the scores were released, Dr. Sanchez called a special faculty meeting so that she could discuss the results with her staff in person.

Dr. Sanchez watched her teachers' positive reactions as she presented increases for each grade level. Then she said, "Well, all of these improvements show our hard work is paying off, but we have farther to go. The state still gave us a 'C' rating." Cindy, one of her best veteran teachers, spoke up first, "Well, okay, so we have to work harder." Meg, one of her new teachers, said, "I think most of my kids did their best. I don't want to sound like I'm making an excuse, but the bar is very high, and many of the students did not have background experiences in the topics featured in the reading passages. What did I miss in the common formative assessments?" Jose responded with a bit more skepticism, "I think the tests are doing what they are supposed to do. They are telling us where we stand as a school and a district. The formative assessments gave us good information to help the kids develop from where they are. You're right. It's a steep climb with some of those nonfiction passages." Dr. Sanchez responded, "I have to say I'm pleased with the way all of you are trying to use these results to improve your practices."

Over the past year, the school had prioritized their standards and developed common formative assessments. A data team, along with the principal, analyzed the results with teachers. In the last quarter, Cindy and some other teachers developed an intervention system for students who were struggling with the common formative assessments and district benchmarks. Dr. Sanchez made a mental note to talk with Cindy and the other intervention teachers about the content of this program.

The next morning, Dr. Sanchez stopped by the "intervention" room to observe Cindy and a couple other teachers and assistants working with students on non-fiction reading, writing, and math. She was immediately struck by the rigor of the reading material and dialogue. In the discussion, students were questioning underlying assumptions in the text and making connections across texts as well as their personal experiences. During the course of the lesson, the students talked about the big idea in their own words. Students naturally completed a formative assessment in which they mapped the text structure of each text and made comparisons across the readings. Overall, Dr. Sanchez told the teachers she was impressed and that, with more time, she believed their efforts would yield results on the state assessments.

At the same time, Dr. Sanchez wondered if she and the teachers were missing something beyond time. She reflected on all the assessment and alignment activities from the past year. Teachers worked collaboratively to develop and score common formative assessments, all of which were aligned with the state tests and the state standards. What were they missing? Why was the school coasting?

Questions

1. What were they missing?
2. Why was the school coasting?
3. How did Dr. Sanchez and the teachers use formative and summative assessments to meet accountability requirements and improve student learning? What else could they have done?
4. How do the principal's and teachers' assessment practices consider the needs of the students and community that are not as obvious in the state assessment data?

EXTENDED REFLECTION 6.2

Revisit your definition of accountability that you wrote at the beginning of the chapter. How, if at all, has your definition changed? How, if at all, would you like to change your school's assessment system based upon what you learned in this chapter?

Be prepared to share your thoughts in a small group.

SUMMARY

This chapter examined accountability and a comprehensive assessment system, including summative and formative assessments. Recent major policies (e.g. NCLB) indicate direct influences of accountability on student achievement overall, marginal direct influences on closing racial/ethnic achievement gaps, and some unintended (indirect) influences on narrowing the curriculum and teacher decision-making strategies. In order to meet accountability demands at all levels, today's instructional leaders must use formative and summative assessment measures as essential components of a comprehensive accountability system that connects assessments, instruction, and curriculum for increasingly diverse students.

Thus, this chapter divided an assessment system into two broad categories of assessments: summative and formative. Essentially, summative assessments provide information about what students have learned at a particular point in time, and formative assessments provide feedback about what students are learning during an instructional time. NCLB and related accountability policies require instructional leaders to examine appropriate data for evidence of equitable opportunities for learning and academic achievement. Drawing on Skrla et al.'s (2004) reconception of equity audits, this chapter provides instructional leaders with strategies to examine data with regard to teacher quality, programmatic quality, and overall academic opportunity. This chapter provides guidance for assessing students' funds of knowledge as resources for the curriculum. As schools and communities become increasingly diverse, curriculum rigor and accountability has increased. The new instructional leader must integrate their assessment literacy skills with understandings of equity and intercultural education to develop and sustain a comprehensive assessment system aimed at improved teaching and learning for all students.

REFERENCES

Ainsworth, L. & Viegut, D. (2006). *Common formative assessments: How to connect standards-based instruction and assessment*. Thousand Oaks, CA: SAGE.

Arizona State Legislature. (2011). Arizona Revised Statutes § 15–203(A) (38).

Conzemius, A. & O'Neil, J. (2001). *Building shared responsibility for student learning*. Alexandria, VA: Association for Supervision and Curriculum Development.

Daly, A. (2009). Rigid response in an age of accountability. *Educational Administration Quarterly*, *45*(2), 168–216.

Duke, D., Grogan, M., Tucker, P., & Heinecke, W. (2003). *Educational leadership in an age of accountability: The Virginia experience*. Albany, NY: SUNY Press.

Hayes-Jacobs, H. (1997). *Mapping the big picture: Integrating curriculum and assessment K–12*. Alexandria, VA: Association for Supervision and Curriculum Development.

Heritage, M., Kim, J., Vendlinski, T., & Herman, J. (2009). From evidence to action: A seamless process in formative assessment? *Educational Measurement Issues and Practices*, *28*(3), 24–31.

Johnson, B. & Johnson, D. (2005). *High stakes: Poverty, testing, and failure in American schools* (2nd ed.). Lanham, MD: Rowan & Littlefield Publishers.

Lee, J. (2006). *Tracking achievement gaps and assessing the impact of NCLB on the gaps: An in-depth look into national and state reading and math outcome trends*. Cambridge, MA: Civil Rights Project at Harvard University.

Luizzi, B. D. (2006). *Accountability and the principalship: The influence of No Child Left Behind on middle school principals in Connecticut.* (Doctoral dissertation). New York: Teachers College, Columbia University. Retrieved July 24, 2009 from http://proquest.umi.com/pqdlink?Ver=1&Exp=07-23-2014&FMT=7&DID=1203564851&RQT=309

Orfield, G., Losen, D., & Balfanz, R. (2006). *Confronting the graduation rate crisis in Texas.* Cambridge, MA: The Civil Rights Project at Harvard University. Retrieved August 23, 2009 from www.civilrightsproject.ucla.edu/research/dropouts_gen.php

Popham, W. J. (2003). *Test better, teach better: The instructional role of assessment.* Alexandria, VA: Association for Supervision and Curriculum Development.

Shanahan, P. (2012). *Shanahan on literacy.* Retrieved December 15, 2012 from www.shanahanon literacy.com/2012/07/common-core-or-guided-reading.html

Skrla, L., Scheurich, J., Garcia, J., & Nolly, G. (2004). Equity audits: A practical leadership tool for developing equitable and excellent schools. *Educational Administration Quarterly, 40*(1), 133–161.

Stiggins, R., Arter, J., Chappuis, J., & Chappuis, S. (2004). *Classroom assessment for student learning: Doing it right—using it well.* Portland, OR: Assessment Training Institute.

U.S. Congress. (2001). No Child Left Behind Act. Retrieved September 28, 2003 from www.ed.gov/nclb/landing.jhtml

Wiggins, G. & McTighe, J. (1998). *Understanding by design.* Alexandria, VA: Association for Supervision and Curriculum Development.

Ylimaki, R. (2011). *Critical curriculum leadership: A framework for progressive education.* New York: Routledge.

CHAPTER 7

Develop the Instructional Leadership Capacity of Staff

Catherine Hackney and James Henderson

KEY TOPICS

- Leadership for a Deepening Democracy
- Partnerships that Develop Staff Capacity
- Building Staff Capacity through an Inquiry-Based Curriculum Conversation

---

EXTENDED REFLECTION 7.1

- What drives you to be a leader? Do you have an image of a leader that inspires your professional development?
- What do you believe are the purposes of education?
- What does capacity building mean to you?
- What creating capabilities should school leaders consider?

Consider your responses to these questions as you read the chapter. Be prepared to share your reflections with the class.

According to ISLLC Standard 2, instructional leaders develop leadership capacity of staff. In this chapter, we propose that *capacity* is best conceived of as leading for a deepening democracy (LDD). Leading for a deepening democracy is a moral, ethical, and aesthetic art. It is grounded in the principles and ideals of democracy and an individual and social consciousness. The individual and the organization learn together through critical reflective inquiry about problems and then commit to public actions that solve these problems. Further, because LDD is founded on the principles and ideals

[handwritten margin note: Capacity is the staff's ability to take on leadership roles w/in the building; capacity is built through inquiry, reflection, + commitment to solve problems.]

of democracy, it is *tempered by humility*, which leaves us open to what others can teach us; it increases everyone's capacity to practice collaborative learning, problem-solving, and deliberative decision-making. It advances the elevation of others who share in the leadership.

Yet a democratic notion of leadership capacity is not always prevalent in today's schools surrounded by corporate models of leadership. Michelle Rhee, who is the former Chancellor of Washington, D.C., Public Schools and currently directs the "Student's First" movement, was recently in Cleveland and addressed the search for a new CEO of the Cleveland Municipal Schools (the Cleveland Municipal School District is under mayoral control). She offered advice on what the next CEO should possess:

- a clear and strong vision for what is possible and the "fire in the belly" to make it happen (Rhee, as cited by Starzyk, 2011, para. 3)
- the ability to manage people through change
- the strong backing from politicians in charge.

Many readers and listeners likely applauded her advice as necessary to straighten-out the beleaguered Cleveland schools. Of course a leader needs a strong vision and fire in the belly and the ability to manage people. As we read her remarks, though, we wondered about the her use of vision. How would it be developed? Would it be shared or imposed? Would invested and involved others be included in the process? Who would be the author(s)? Her leadership tenure in D.C., which was commonly known to be unilateral and coercive, contributed to my skepticism, as did the work of the former CEO, who created a reform plan that included closing scores of schools and the spending of 30+ million taxpayer dollars without a teacher or union representative at the decision-making table.

School leaders need a "fire in the belly" but not to advance a political and economic agenda of privatization and greater standardization, diminishment of collaborative local control, or the deskilling of the teaching profession. Rather, school leaders need a "fire in the belly" to promote capacity for a deepening democracy in schools and communities. In order to promote a capacity for a deepening democracy, we envision:

- leadership that is collaborative and equitable and honors pluralism
- leadership that promotes individual and collective inquiry
- leadership that advances professional efficacy
- leadership that is deliberative and dialectical
- leadership that is propelled toward public advocacy.

PROBLEMS WITH MANAGERIAL PARADIGMS

As discussed in Chapter 3, Rhee's thinking resonates with much of the public today. Michael Apple (2004) has written extensively about how dominant groups have circulated a particular set of discourses (e.g. "managerial vision" and "standardization") that have affected our common sense about good leadership and good schools. In other words, our nation is stuck in what Hargreaves and Shirley (2009) label as The Second Way of school reform. This Way's stronghold has reinforced the managerial paradigmatic approach to leadership—rational, technical "training," essentialist positions, power-over hierarchies, and professional constriction through a never-ending line of imposed standards and standardization. Since *A Nation at Risk* was published in 1983, this nation has been burdened with standardization and the restriction of possibilities. School leaders are required to implement curriculum standards, maintain high performance on state tests, and take administrative certification tests on professional standards like the ISLLC standards. School leaders clearly need to manage a building safely, work with the community, and create a climate conducive to student learning. Yet as Ryan (2010) has written, such leadership standards are too focused on the individual and "not consistent with democratic ideals" (p. 347). Rather, we argue that "the democratic leader must be careful not to lose sight of . . . the human vision of a caring learning community" (Noddings, 1984, p. 19).

BEYOND MANAGERIAL PARADIGMS

Over the past 20–30 years, feminism and other critical theories have positively affected our worldviews and perspectives on leading toward a deepening democracy. The movement to deconstruct what had been—to dismantle positivism,[1] behaviorism, and managerialism—acknowledged the value of lived experience and opened up possibilities of the imagination. Critical theories explicitly consider perspectives and lived experiences of those who have been oppressed in society because of gender, class, race/ethnicity, disability, sexual orientation, and intersections thereof. Furthermore, the experiences of those traditionally marginalized by gender, race, and class became validated and contributed to a re-visioning of leadership beyond the traditional, managerial model. Dominant groups establish the norm or who is normal and who is not. Critical theories, then, offered a lens through which normalizing, standardizing, essentializing, and positioning could be reexamined and challenged. As Foster (1986) explained, critical theory seeks social change and justice for those who have been traditionally oppressed or marginalized. Injustices and inequities that were uncovered enlightened us with deeper social awareness and called us to action and advocacy. Drawing on such critical theories, became more open to the altruism of transforming leadership as developed by Burns (1978) and realized the instrumentalist dangers of transactional leadership. These historical movements and theories also jarred the leadership world into disequilibrium.

Leading for "deepening democracy" demands such disequilibrium or fire in the belly. Transforming leadership from the utilitarian and functional to the noble and humble demands a constant rub or challenge to the status quo. It is not for the light-hearted or those comfortable with the status quo, conformity, compliance, and content with smooth sailing. Just as Saturn, instituted to revolutionize the traditional management paradigm of General Motors, became sucked into the larger machine and lost its identity, such is the likely end of school leaders without fire in the belly. As Lugg (2011) writes:

> The more reflective, social justice-minded leaders need to navigate around these demands by corporate oligarchs and devise strategies that appear facially compliant with the legal and policy demands, while securing real educative spaces within their buildings. What I am asking educational leaders to do is to engage in political subversion.
> (p. 373)

FIELDWORK 7.1

Interview a principal or teacher leader about what their perceptions of inequities in the community. Questions might include:

- What kinds of inequities have you noticed in the community?
- How, if at all, have you worked with staff members to change such inequities?
- Have you encountered resistance to these changes? Give examples.
- How did you handle that resistance?

LEADING FOR A DEEPENING DEMOCRACY

Leading for a deepening democracy is a moral, ethical, and aesthetic art. It is grounded in the principles and ideals of democracy and an individual and social consciousness. It is artistry described by Foster (1986) "to develop, challenge, and liberate human souls" (p. 18). As Ryan (2010) so aptly stated, it is leadership that is "heterarchical" (p. 347) rather than hierarchical. It values the lived experience; it validates the marginalized; it supports an individual's control over her personal and professional life. It is fluid, frameless, model-less and transcends individuals and groups. LDD is reminiscent of the Bodhisattvan wisdom whose aesthetic virtues are generosity, discipline, and patience (Ylimaki & McClain, 2009).

Our LDD conception of leadership includes simultaneously individuals and organizations as collections of individuals. Sometimes the individual informs the organization; sometimes the organization informs the individual. The individual and the organization learn together through critical reflective inquiry, identify problems, and commit to public action to correct solve them. LDD is *propelled by an emerging social awareness* of a vision that is just, equitable, democratic.

Of course such action requires courage, often to engage in Lugg's (2011) recommendation for political subversion. A way to think about courage is that it is not necessarily event-linked. Courage is really a way of life. It makes its home within us in a quiet voice. It bubbles under the surface patiently, fed by confidence, self-assurance, and a growing social awareness. As the French origins of the term suggest, courage is a discerning heart and spirit. LDD is *supported by such courage*.

Because LDD is founded on the principles and ideals of democracy, it is *tempered by humility*. Humility involves three connected dimensions: self-awareness, openness, and deep inspiration. In other words, curriculum leaders must have strong self-awareness, openness to learning from others, and an inspiration from democratic curriculum aims. As Walker and Soltis (2004) explained, some educators believe that education should prepare individuals for life after schooling; some educators feel that education is the key to creating societal change. Traditionalists believe that classical studies should form the basis of one's education while educators who favor a progressive curriculum think that education should be tailored to fit the needs of each individual student.

Furthering the curriculum debate is the argument over curriculum aims versus curriculum objectives. For decades, policymakers and educators have relied on Tyler's

Rationale (1949) for developing curriculum: objectives, goals, instructional processes, and evaluation processes. Here curriculum objectives are the tangible, measurable goals of the curriculum. For example, a curriculum objective would be for students to master 95 percent of the math division problems presented, or another curriculum objective could be for students to write a story. Therefore, curriculum objectives should be seen as products produced or targets achieved by students.

Beyond objectives or targets, Walker and Soltis (2004) wrote about the importance of curriculum aims. According to Walker and Soltis, curriculum aims, "are not aims to be achieved so much as values to be transmitted through the process of educating in a certain way" (p. 18). Curriculum aims are the ideals and values that motivate educators and guide what they do. For example, if educators value tolerance and want to impart that same value to their students, then those educators' curriculum will have activities focused on acknowledging and appreciating differences. Curriculum aims "envision desirable states for individuals and societies that seem approachable or achievable through education" (Walker & Soltis, 2004, p. 12). Curriculum aims are what the curriculum is designed or structured to do.

Moreover, without a clear sense of self, and what St. Thomas Aquinas called "keeping oneself within one's own bounds", it is difficult to lead curriculum aims with humility. Because humility leaves us open to what others can teach us, it increases everyone's capacity to practice collaborative learning, problem-solving, and deliberative decision-making. It advances the elevation of others who share in the leadership. In other words, curriculum leaders must cultivate inspired curriculum aims with and through others.

As public advocates, those who practice LDD commit to educate and inspire the public toward the principles and ideals on which the leadership rests. In the beautiful book of his essays and speeches, *On Becoming a Servant Leader* (Frick & Spears, 1996), Robert Greenleaf promoted leading in the service of others. To become a servant leaders, one who is generous in spirit, a leader must be attuned to the needs of others and willingly assume the responsibility of addressing those needs. That leader is less concerned with his/her need for recognition and advancement, and more concerned with protecting the heart of the community.

Greenleaf wrote that *somebody* needs to dream the big dream and help society—the family, the church, the school, the city, the nation, business, and perhaps the world—realize what can be possible. We would amend this statement only by substituting *somebody* with a *collective somebody*, a body collaborate willing to examine what is, realize

EXTENDED REFLECTION 7.2

- Self-awareness—How do I build my capacities to cultivate lead learning humility?
- Openness—How do I work on creating capacities for open-minded deliberations?
- Inspiration—How can I create my capabilities to articulate inspired curriculum aims?

what should not be, and advocate for what should be for a deepening of democracy in our schools and communities. LDD is manifested through a generosity of spirit, which cares less about rights and privileges and more about responsibility. LDD is wise and noble because of its commitment to inquiry, attention to injustice and inequity, its commitment to inclusive collaboration, and active public advocacy.

A PROFESSIONAL INTEGRITY CHALLENGE

As the LDD project developed, we have learned that educators who are concerned that their day-to-day curriculum lacks integrity are the most open and receptive to the alternative conception of curriculum leadership. These are educators who have the desire to practice Dewey's (1989/1939) vision that, "democracy . . . is a way of personal life and one which provides a moral standard for personal conduct" (p. 101).[2] In more concrete terms, these educators want to "walk the talk" of their organization's democratic mission statements and related documents (Henderson, 2010). They want to *be* the change that they seek.

Toward a Warm-Hearted and Open-Minded Curriculum Leadership

The curriculum leadership that we have been advancing is both *warm-hearted* in the spirit of Noddings' (1984) ethic of care and *open-minded* in the spirit of a Socratic love of wisdom. Noddings (2002) writes that, "As Dewey filled out his moral theory, he moved rapidly to problem solving—surely one aim of communication. As we fill out an ethic of care, we concentrate on the needs and responses required to maintain caring relations" (p. 22). Near the end of his highly productive scholarly career, Dewey thought that "transaction" was, perhaps, the better organizing term for what he meant by "experience" (Dewey & Bentley, 1949; Ryan, in press). The curriculum leadership that we have been conceptualizing is grounded in *caring transactions* with its four "components" of relational self-reflection, open-ended dialogue, interpersonal attention, and personal confirmation (Noddings, 2002, pp. 15–21).

- Relational self-reflection (modeling)—Educators are concerned with the growth of people as carers and cared-fors.
- Dialogue—Leaders engage people in dialogue about caring. As we try to care, we are helped in our efforts by the feedback we get from recipients of our care.
- Practice—The experiences in which we immerse ourselves tend to produce a "mentality". If we want to produce people who will care for one another, then it makes sense to give students/teachers practice in caring and reflection on that practice.
- Confirmation—Confirmation is an act of affirming and encouraging the best in others. When we confirm someone, we identify a better self and encourage its development.

Caring and compassion are also connected to wisdom in that we come to realize we are all in continuous development. Caring helps us be open-minded to what others teach us. When we practice a love of wisdom, we choose to live with an open-minded sense of doubt, as insightfully described by Davidson (1998):

> *Wisdom* is knowing how little you know. Ignorance is the beginning of wisdom, Socrates cautioned us. Zen practitioners call it "beginner's mind," which is truly open and fresh, willing to remain innocent and receptive to life, not attached to our knowledge. It is the willingness to be empty, and thus open to learning and growing. This is the source of creativity and innovation, the key to continuous improvement . . .
>
> (pp. 36–37)

Elliot Eisner (2002) writes:

> The curriculum is essential to any educational enterprise . . . When policymakers and educational theorists define curriculum for a school or a classroom, they are also defining the forms of thinking that are likely to be promoted in the school. They are, in effect, laying out an agenda for the development of the mind.
>
> (p. 148)

Eisner refers to more than just intellectual capacity in his definition of curriculum; he promotes the development of the soul, of the individual, and of an artist. He continues:

> I would urge teachers to use standards as an opportunity for discussion, as considerations for curriculum development, but not as prescriptions for processes or even goals. What goals or aims are appropriate for students is not best defined solely by policymakers who are not in contact with the students schools are intended to serve.
>
> (p. 177)

Curriculum decisions including "outcomes" are best made using "curriculum wisdom" (Henderson & Kesson, 2004). It is not an easy task to go against the grain. This goal requires tremendous self-knowledge, confidence, and the willingness to take those first steps toward the greater good.

Curriculum wisdom, then, goes beyond subject matter to integrate subject matter learning into democratic self and social learning (Henderson & Gornik, 2007). It denotes curriculum decision-making that is focused on the cultivation of enduring values that stand the test of time. Westbrook (1991) explained how Dewey articulated his love of democratic wisdom in an essay Dewey wrote in 1919, entitled "Philosophy and Democracy":

> Dewey argued [that] . . . philosophy was not "in any sense whatever a form of knowledge" but rather "a form of desire, of effort at action—a love, namely of wisdom." Wisdom was not "systematic and proved knowledge of fact and truth, but a conviction about moral values, a sense for the better kind of life to be led".
>
> (p. 145)

A love of democratic wisdom is as much about a way of *being* as it is about a way of *acting* (Aoki, 2005; Wang, 2004). Nancy (2010) writes, "If democracy has a sense, it would

---

FIELDWORK 7.2

Cultivating Curriculum Wisdom for Building Capacity

1. Identify leaders who you think have a curriculum wisdom perspective. Have a conversation with that leader.
2. Identify where there opportunities to leverage or initiate the study and practice of curriculum wisdom.
3. As a leader, how can you provide the study and practice of inspired curriculum aims?

Be prepared to share your responses with the class.

---

be that of . . . a desire—of a will, an awaiting, a thought—where what is expressed and recognized is a true possibility of being *all together, all and each one among all*" (p. 14, emphasis added). The practice of a democratic "eros" in education involves both the arts of embodiment (*way of being*) and enactment (*way of acting*). As Nancy (2010) notes, "democracy is first of all a metaphysics and only afterwards a politics" (p. 34).

AN INQUIRY-BASED CURRICULUM CONVERSATION

An enduring strength of Tyler's (1949) rationale is the fact that it is informed by the pragmatic problem solving cycle as succinctly outlined by Dewey (1933/1910). The conception of this cycle, which traces back to the beginning of the modern era in Europe and, particularly, to Descartes' (1960/1637) ground-breaking "discourse on method", has the following logic:

- frame the problem
- create a hypothesis on how to potentially resolve this problem
- act on this hypothesis
- reflect on the results of your actions with reference to underlying assumptions and consequences in public, peer reviewed venues
- make the necessary adjustments in problem definition(s) and action(s)
- recursively continue through this learning-through-experience cycle.

The constructive alternative to Tyler's rationale that we have conceptualized can be summarized as *the engagement in a complicated inquiry-based curriculum conversation that inspires a way of being and a way of acting*. The overarching purpose of this conversation is to "walk the talk" of one's democratic educational ideals in the context of curriculum and teaching problem solving. Seven inquiries provide prompts for this dialogical undertaking. Though these inquiries have emerged over years of collaborative research as central to curriculum conversations on the topic of *democracy-in-education*, other relevant inquiries can be added at any point in the process. Logically speaking, the seven inquiries are simply key elements in an open set of possibilities. Finally, the inquiry prompts have been selected to inform all pragmatic phases, from the initial framing of the problem to its possible reframing. However, there is not a precise one-to-one correspondence between the phases and the inquiry prompts. Any attempt to provide such literal, technical precision would undermine the "dialogical play" (Gadamer, 1975) that lies at the heart of the conversation. A sophisticated, humanizing process would be reduced to a step-by-step protocol; a limited technical rationality would supplant a holistic, curriculum "mindfulness" (Langer & Moldoveanu, 2000). This possibility is, of course, always the ghost in the modernist "machine" that we educators have inherited and goes to the heart of the "crisis of modernity" as described by Ryan (in press):

> We [must] think about the still unresolved crisis of modernity: the conjoined need for humane science and an experimental view of values. We can't work together, of course, until we begin to *see* together—not some preconceived *what*, some universal good, but a common *how* that is experimental, inclusive, and pluralistic.

The seven inquiry prompts are based on specific interpretations of critiquing, envisioning, deliberating, negotiating, self-examining, collegial learning, and public inspiring. Though there is no precise sequence to these prompts, we will use my above brief overview of problem solving pragmatics as a guide to introduce each one. We begin with *critiquing*. This is a multi-perspective analysis of how curriculum and teaching problems are framed. Three interrelated paradigms serve as the referent for this critical work: (1) standardized management (SM), with its focus on the problem of improving standardized test performances as enforced by high-stakes, accountability mandates; (2) constructivist best practice (CBP), with its focus on facilitating performances of understanding linked to one or more academic or vocational disciplines/traditions; and (3) curriculum wisdom (CW), with its focus on facilitating performances of understanding linked to the academic or vocational disciplines/traditions and by interpretations of "democracy" as a moral basis of living (Henderson & Gornik, 2007). This critical work is informed by Apple's (2006) and Ylimaki's (2011) comprehensive case-based analyses of how "right-wing" discourse-practices perpetuate SM hegemonic dominance and, hence, constrain and/or suppress democratic being and acting. Schwab's (1969) related notions of "arts of the practical" and "arts of the eclectic" are also central to this critical work since the question of which paradigm should be used to frame educational problems is best handled on a case-by-case basis and since CBP performances build on a certain amount of standardized learning and CW performances are holistic extensions of CBP learning. As Chehayl (2010) notes, this eclectic approach enables educators to address the challenges of facilitating students' 21st century learning. A key *critiquing* prompt would be: how should educators in information-age societies with democratic ideals frame student learning problems?

Envisioning involves "aims-talk" (Noddings, 2009) on what it means to educate for "deep democracy" (Green, 1999) and "experience-talk" (Adair Breault & Breault, 2005; Dewey, 1998/1938) on the experiential implications and applications of this exercise in moral imagination (Fesmire, 2003). What do students need to experience in classroom and other educational settings so that they can demonstrate a deepening understanding of one or more of the academic/vocational disciplines integrated with the personal and social joys/responsibilities of democratic living? *Deliberating* involves collaborative decision-making informed by an awareness of the interrelated nature of designing, planning, teaching, evaluating, and organizing actions in curriculum and teaching work. How can educators address the "ecological" nature of curriculum work in a context of case-by-case deliberations (Eisner, 1994)? *Negotiating* addresses the politics of cross-paradigm decision-making. In most educational settings today, it is not easy to practice the practical and eclectic arts with reference to the SM, CBP, and CW paradigms. Attempts to engage in this professional fluidity confront a complex mixture of adult developmental, political, and structural obstacles (Henderson & Kesson, 2004). How can these obstacles be negotiated?

Self-examining addresses the personal journey and ethical fidelity features of this curriculum and teaching work. If educators are not undergoing their own disciplined journeys of understanding, they will not be in a position to teach for the holistic understanding advanced by the CW paradigm. Furthermore, if they are not working on embodying a deepening democracy, they will not be in a position to inspire other colleagues and the general public, which are the final two inquiries in this open set. *Self-examining* addresses such questions as: Am I experiencing a shift in my personal beliefs about what constitutes quality education; how am I attuning to and interpreting the spirit of democratic education; are my actions congruent with my changing beliefs; do I have stories I can share about my journey of understanding; and as I work with students, colleagues and other curriculum stakeholders, do I model the deepening democracy that I espouse?

Collegial learning focuses on how to work effectively as a "lead learner" (Barth, 2008) on these inquiries. The lead-learning challenge is to inspire, organize, and nurture informal and/or formal practitioner inquiry communities (Cochran-Smith & Lytle, 2009) dedicated to the study and practice of this curriculum conversation. How can I reach out to one or more of my colleagues and invite them to join me in this dialogical engagement? *Public inspiring* focuses on explaining and celebrating this professional learning in civic venues. Educators must cultivate a "public" that understands and supports the practitioner inquiry communities (Henderson & Kesson, 2001). By linking the professional learning to students' 21st century learning, can I reach out to a broad range of curriculum stakeholders, including students' parents, school board members, and influential community leaders?

Educators who are committed to work on developing their capacities to practice this set of disciplined curriculum inquiries are addressing the challenge of *embodying and enacting a deepening democracy in education* in a comprehensive, pragmatic manner. With reference to the democratic mission statements of educational organizations, these inspired educators serve as vivid exemplars of professional integrity. They help set a tone of ethical fidelity in their educational settings, and they exemplify the power of practicing an internal discipline in the face of disempowering, external disciplinary systems. With reference to Nodding's (1984) ethic of care, by "confirming" their own professional capacities, they are in a position to confirm their colleagues' "best" democratic teaching selves. They are prepared to practice a democratic "generative leadership" (Klimek, Ritzehein, & Sullivan, 2008) as caring lead-learners.

SEVEN INQUIRY PROMPTS

- **Critiquing prompt**—How should educators in information-age societies with democratic ideals frame student learning problems?
- **Envisioning prompt**—What do students need to experience in classroom and other educational settings so that they can demonstrate a deepening understanding of one or more of the academic/vocational disciplines integrated with the personal and social joys/responsibilities of democratic living?
- **Deliberating prompt**—How can educators address the "ecological" nature of curriculum work in a context of case-by-case deliberations (Eisner, 1994)?
- **Negotiating prompt**—How can these obstacles be negotiated?
- **Self-examining prompts**—Am I experiencing a shift in my personal beliefs about what constitutes quality education; how am I attuning to and interpreting the spirit of democratic education; are my actions congruent with my changing beliefs; do I have stories I can share about my journey of understanding; and as I work with students, colleagues and other curriculum stakeholders, do I model the deepening democracy that I espouse?
- **Collegial learning prompt**—How can I reach out to one or more of my colleagues and invite them to join me in this dialogical engagement?
- **Public inspiring prompt**—By linking the professional learning to students' 21st century learning, can I reach out to a broad range of curriculum stakeholders, including students' parents, school board members, and influential community leaders?

THE HEART OF THE MATTER

In a recent publication, Darling-Hammond (2010) cites Drucker (1994) and Wagner (2008) as she lists what workers will need in the 21st century to find professional and personal success. They include the capacities to:

- design, evaluate, and manage one's own work so that it continually improves
- frame, investigate, and solve problems using a wide range of tools and resources
- collaborate strategically with others
- communicate effectively in many forms
- find, analyze, and use information for many purposes
- develop new products and ideas.

(Darling-Hammond, 2010, p. 2)

Implicit with these capacities are self-awareness, imagination, creative thinking, reflective inquiry, collegiality, deliberation, negotiation, and inspiration. And governing all of these transactions is the challenge of practicing a democratic ethical fidelity.

However, developing these capacities within the context of the present social and political climate in our country, presents a problem for children as well as adults.

Constrained by the standardization movement, which has bred a culture of conformity, compliance, competition, and fear, education and professional development has revolved around "meeting the standards" most efficiently. Standards, very often used as an evaluation tool, are not only imposed upon those who have not shared in their development, but are devoid of reference to collegial learning, promotion of thought and inquiry, inspiration of the public, or ethical fidelity. As currently written, the ISLLC standards do not explicitly advance leading for deepening democracy or collegial problem-solving and decision-making. Beyond the standard focus on positional authority, aspiring leaders need to develop curriculum wisdom with and through others.

CASE 7.1 A NEW TEACHER LEADER ENDORSEMENT PROGRAM

To address the challenges of practicing democratic fidelity and facilitating 21st century learning, we have developed an unlikely partnership that draws on our backgrounds in leadership and curriculum studies. We have designed a Kent State University (KSU) Teacher Leader Endorsement Program (TLEP) that has been formally endorsed by the state of Ohio's Board of Regents (OBR). Like other OBR-endorsed TLEPs, KSU's program introduces teachers to the state of Ohio's new Teacher Leader Standards in a context of leadership study and clinical practice activities. However, KSU's TLEP has a particular signature feature. Our teacher leader candidates are presented with the challenge of embodying and enacting a deepening understanding of democracy while engaged in site-specific professional leadership activities. Through a cohort-based sequence of four graduate courses, they study the seven inquiry prompts, practice working as lead learners for inquiry-based curriculum conversations, read educational leadership literature that informs the relevance of this dialogical engagement, study Ohio's Teacher Leader Standards (OTLS), and design and enact specific projects that infuse complicated curriculum conversations into teacher leadership activities. Each of these curricular steps is documented in a performance-based, e-portfolio system.

We initiated our first TLEP cohort in June, 2011, and we plan to report on the results of our collaborative venture in future publications. We are excited about our work together. We feel it is time to integrate leadership and curriculum studies in the creation of a new field of curriculum leadership, and we resonate with Ylimaki's (2011) call to action:

> The need to create a new curriculum leadership field comes upon realizing that the well-meaning instructional leadership rhetoric is betrayed not only by its emphasis on professional (data-driven) procedures but also by its failure to link leadership with broader cultural political movements and critical theories required to make inclusion and democratic education a reality.
>
> (p. 179)

We are deeply concerned that, without the practice of a visionary curriculum leadership, education will continue to be positioned as a semi-professional field ensnared in managerial paradigms and superficial, literal-minded *reform de jour* faddism. Education will never become the pivotal professional art that democratic societies require. Cynicism, alienation, burn-out, rapid turn-over and professional game playing will continue to prevail. Though there will always be instances of caring, wisdom-oriented, democratic teaching-learning transactions in education, such illustrations will serve as spotty, infrequent inspirational anecdotes, not well-respected and sustained professional norms. We believe that, over time, dynamic educational leaders can gradually overcome this sad, limited fate. So, it is with this faith that we strive to prepare future teacher leaders who will work with administrative leaders and other positional leaders to inspire, initiate, and sustain complicated curriculum conversations in the context of relevant reflective inquiry activities.

As a principal in the early 1990s, Cathy tells the story of being challenged to appoint teachers to serve as mentors for new district hires. Jim elected to tap a group of masterful teachers who intuitively understood the importance of complicated curriculum conversations in education. All of these teachers practiced a love of democratic wisdom and, consequently, were not central players in the district's power-over leadership and machinations. The "old guard" of administrators and teachers raised very loud and vocal complaints about the selection of untraditional mentors. We often think about those days and realize that if we had had access to a pool of teachers, such as those we are preparing, who were formally *educated* as democratic professional leaders and who were *sanctioned* with a state endorsement, complaints from the "old guard" would have had a hollow ring.

Now, through our TLEP, we have the opportunity to prepare dynamic teachers as curriculum leaders with the capacity to lead for a deepening democracy. Because they will be strong advocates for ethical fidelity, sophisticated problem solving and 21st century student learning, they will ensure that democratic ideals will prevail in schools through the years to come.

STRATEGIES FOR LEADERS

How do curriculum/instructional leaders put all of this background on building staff capacity into practice? This section provides guidance for what today's instructional leaders need to know and be able to do as well as example strategies for practice. Curriculum/instructional leaders need to:

Know:

- yourself—beliefs, worldviews, grounding purposes
- background behind managerial paradigms
- critical theories and perspectives on how to get beyond managerial paradigms
- democratic perspectives on capacity.

Have:

- humility
- vision of a caring learning community

- warm heart
- open mind
- fire in the belly.

Be able to:

- lead for deepening democracy
- lead staff through critical reflective inquiry
- learn from what others can teach us.

EXTENDED REFLECTION 7.3

Now return to the reflection you started at the beginning of the chapter. Answer the questions again. How have your understandings changed based upon what you read and thought about?

- What drives you to be a leader? Do you now have an image of a leader to inspire your professional development?
- What do you believe are the purposes of education?
- What does capacity mean to you now?

Be prepared to share your reflections with the class.

SUMMARY

School leaders must have a "fire in the belly" to promote capacity for a deepening democracy in schools and communities. By making time and space for deep democracy, leaders build staff capacity for seeking and attaining inspired curriculum aims. In this chapter, we redefined *capacity* as leading for a deepening democracy (LDD) grounded in the principles and ideals of democracy as well as an individual and social consciousness. We conceptualized LDD as not only founded on the principles and ideals of democracy but also *tempered by humility*. Humility involves three connected dimensions: self-awareness, openness, and deep inspiration. As such, today's curriculum leadership must be warm- hearted, open-minded, and wise. Curriculum wisdom goes beyond subject matter to integrate subject matter learning into democratic self and social learning (Henderson & Gornik, 2007). It denotes curriculum decision-making that is focused on the cultivation of capacities, enduring values, and inspired curriculum aims that stand the test of time.

NOTES

1   Positivism suggests that every rationally justifiable assertion can be scientifically verified.
2   For a more detailed discussion of Badiou's ethics as inspired by Dewey's see Kesson and Henderson (2010).

REFERENCES

Adair Breault, D. & Breault, R. (Eds.). (2005). *Experiencing Dewey: Insights for today's classroom*. Indianapolis, IN: Kappa Delta Pi.

Aoki, T. (2005). *Curriculum in a new key: The collected works of Ted T. Aoki*. Mahwah, NJ: Lawrence Erlbaum Associates.

Apple, M. W. (2004). *Ideology and Curriculum*. New York: Routledge.

Apple, M. W. (2006). *Educating the "right" way: Markets, standards, God, and inequality* (2nd ed.). New York: Routledge.

Barth, R. S. (2008). Foreword. In G. A. Donaldson, *How leaders learn: Cultivating capacities for school improvement* (pp. ix–xi). New York: Teachers College Press.

Burns, J. M. (1978). *Leadership*. New York: Perennial.

Chehayl, L. K. (2010). A 21st-century conversation: Preparing today's students for tomorrow's success. *Journal of Curriculum & Pedagogy, 7*(2), 97–102.

Cochran-Smith, M. & Lytle, S. L. (2009). *Inquiry as stance: Practitioner research for the next generation*. New York: Teachers College Press

Darling-Hammond, L. (2010). *The flat world and education: How America's commitment to equity will determine our future*. New York: Teacher's College Press.

Davidson, L. (1998). *Wisdom at work: The awakening of consciousness in the workplace*. Burdett, NY: Larson Publications.

Descartes, R. (1960/1637). *Discourse on method* (L. Lafleur, Trans.). New York: Macmillan.

Dewey, J. (1933/1910). *How we think: A restatement of the relation of reflective thinking to the educative process*. Boston, MA: D. C. Heath and Company.

Dewey, J. (1989/1939). *Freedom and culture*. Buffalo, NY: Prometheus.

Dewey, J. (1998/1938). *Experience and education*. West Lafayette, IN: Kappa Delta Pi.

Dewey, J. & Bentley, A. F. (1949). *Knowing and the known*. Boston, MA: Beacon Press.

Drucker, P. F. (1994). The age of social transformation. *Atlantic Monthly, 274*, 53–80.

Eisner, E. W. (1994). *The educational imagination: On the design and evaluation of school programs* (3rd ed.). New York: Macmillan.

Eisner, E. W. (2002). *The arts and the creation of the mind*. New Haven, CT: Yale University Press.

Fesmire, S. (2003). *John Dewey & moral imagination: Pragmatism in ethics*. Bloomington, IN: Indiana University Press.

Foster, W. (1986). *Paradigms and promises: New approaches to educational administration*. Buffalo, NY: Prometheus Books.

Frick, D. M. & Spears, L. C. (Eds.). (1996). *On becoming a servant leader: The private writings of Robert K. Greenleaf*. San Francisco, CA: Jossey-Bass.

Gadamer, H. (1975). *Truth and method* (G. Barden & J. Cumming, Eds. and Trans.). New York: Seabury Press.

Green, J. M. (1999). *Deep democracy: Community, diversity, and transformation*. Lanham, MD: Rowman & Littlefield.

Hargreaves, A. & Shirley, D. (2009). *The fourth way: The inspiring future for educational change.* Thousand Oaks, CA: Corwin.

Henderson, J. G. (2010). *The path less taken: Immanent critique in curriculum and pedagogy.* (J. L. Schneider, Ed.). Troy, NY: Educators International Press.

Henderson, J. G. & Gornik, R. (2007). *Transformative curriculum leadership* (3rd ed.). Upper Saddle River, NJ: Merrill/Prentice Hall.

Henderson, J. G. & Kesson, K. R. (2001). Curriculum work as public intellectual leadership. In K. Sloan & J. T. Sears (Eds.). *Democratic curriculum theory and practice: Retrieving public spaces* (pp. 1–23). Troy, NY: Educator's International Press.

Henderson, J. G. & Kesson, K. R. (2004). *Curriculum wisdom: Educational decisions in democratic societies.* Upper Saddle River, NJ: Merrill/Prentice Hall.

Kesson, K. R. & Henderson, J. G. (2010). Reconceptualizing professional development for curriculum leadership: Inspired by John Dewey and informed by Alain Badiou. In K. den Heyer (Ed.). *Thinking education through Alain Badiou* (pp. 62–77). West Sussex, UK: Wiley-Blackwell.

Klimek, K. J., Ritzehein, E., & Sullivan, K. D. (2008). *Generative leadership: Shaping new futures for today's schools.* Thousand Oaks, CA: Corwin Press.

Langer, E. J. & Moldoveanu, M. (2000). The construct of mindfulness. *Journal of Social Issues, 56*(1), 1–9.

Lugg, C. A. (2011). Leading public schools in an oligarchial age. *Scholar-Practitioner Quarterly, 4*(4), 371–373.

Nancy, J.-L. (2010). *The truth of democracy* (P.-A. Brault & M. Naas, Trans.). New York: Fordham University Press.

The National Commission of Excellence in Education. (1983). *A nation at risk: The imperative for excellence reform.* Washington, DC: National Commission of Excellence in Education. Retrieved from www2.ed.gov/pubs/nationatrisk/risk.html

Noddings, N. (1984). *Caring: A feminine approach to ethics and moral education.* Berkeley, CA: University of California Press.

Noddings, N. (2002). *Educating moral people: A caring alternative to character education.* New York: Teachers College Press.

Noddings, N. (2009). The aims of education. In D. J. Flinders & S. J. Thorton (Eds.). *The curriculum studies reader* (3rd ed.) (pp. 245–438). New York: Routledge.

Ryan, F. X. (in press). *Transaction: An introduction to the philosophy of John Dewey and Arthur F. Bentley.* Great Barrington, MA: The American Institute for Economic Research.

Ryan, J. (2010). The way in which leadership is conceived. *Scholar-Practitioner Quarterly, 4*(4), 346–348.

Schwab, J. J. (1969). The Practical: A Language for Curriculum. *School Review, 78*(1), 1–23.

Starzyk, E. (2011). Former Washington educational leader says Cleveland schools need leader with "fire in the belly". *Cleveland Plain Dealer.* March 18, 2011. Retrieved from http://blog.cleveland.com/metro/2011/03/michelle_rhee_brings_her_educa.html

Tyler, R. W. (1949). *Basic principles of curriculum and instruction.* Chicago, IL: University of Chicago Press.

U.S. Department of Education. (1983). *A Nation at risk: The imperative for educational reform: A report to the nation and the Secretary of Education United States Department of Education by The National Commission on Excellence in Education.* Washington, DC: Department of Education.

Wagner, T. (2008). *The global achievement gap.* New York: Basic Books.

Walker, D. & Soltis, J. (2004). *Curriculum and aims.* New York: Teachers College Press.

Wang, H. (2004). *The call from a stranger on the journey home: Curriculum in a third space*. New York: Peter Lang.

Westbrook, R. B. (1991). *John Dewey and American democracy*. Ithaca, NY: Cornell University Press.

Ylimaki, R. M. (2011). *Critical curriculum leadership: A framework for progressive education*. New York: Routledge.

Ylimaki, R. M. & McClain, L. (2009). Wisdom-centered educational leadership. *International Journal of Leadership in Education*, *12*(1), 13–33.

CHAPTER 8

Maximize Time Spent on Quality Curriculum and Instruction

Rose M. Ylimaki and Lynnette Brunderman

KEY TOPICS

- The Nature of Time in Schools
- High-Quality Curriculum and Instruction
- Rethinking and Extending Time
- A Framework for Time Allocation

According to ISLLC Standard 2, effective instructional leaders maximize time spent on quality curriculum and instruction. In this chapter, aspiring leaders will consider the various relationships among time, curriculum, and quality instruction. It will begin by exploring the nature of time and its relationship to quality curriculum and instruction. Next, the chapter discusses how to rethink time in school and provides a framework for using time effectively during and beyond the school day. In other words, effective principals have effective time management skills; they can prioritize among seemingly disparate activities that occur throughout a day or school year. By providing these understandings and relevant learning activities for application, we develop leaders who take strategic actions to maximize time spent on quality curriculum and instruction. Before you read what research says about relationships among time, curriculum, and instruction, take a few minutes to reflect on your experiences with the use of time for curriculum and instruction in schools.

EXTENDED REFLECTION 8.1

Document how you spend your time in a typical day. Try not to look at the master schedule, but rather keep a journal where you write down how much time you spend on various activities. Refer to the journal as you read this chapter. How does your time journal reflect your priorities? How does your journal reflect the school priorities? Do your priorities mirror the priorities of your principal? Think about how you might be able to rethink how you spent your time. In some cases, this may require conversation with colleagues and your principal.

TIME, CURRICULUM, AND INSTRUCTION

Research overwhelmingly demonstrates a connection between effective use of time and effective instruction in schools (e.g. Farbman & Kaplan, 2005; Hoxby, Muraka, & Kang, 2009; Jacobson et al., 2005). These researchers identified schools that have produced high student performance over several years and then try to unpack the characteristics that make these schools successful. In study after study, both expanded time and the particular ways in which time is deployed and managed are identified as essential elements of creating an effective school. In an international (qualitative) study, for instance, Jacobson and colleagues (2005) found effective use of curriculum and instructional leadership time as part of successful principals' practices. They described how one U.S. principal opened a community center near her school in order to provide before- and after-school tutoring services. In the same study (Jacobson et al., 2005), another U.S. principal gained district support and 21st century grant funds to extend the academic school year by one month. In both of these cases, teachers attended professional learning sessions while students participated in intervention and/or enrichment classes with volunteers. Using interviews with the principals, teachers, and parents, Jacobson et al. (2005) demonstrated that such creative uses of time were essential for professional learning, instructional quality, and gains in student performance.

Other scholars (e.g. Cooper, 2009) have used quantitative methods to explicitly connect learning time to student outcomes. For instance, some scholars have conducted experiments to identify the link between time spent learning in schools and academic outcomes. These studies showed that the amount of time spent on learning is clearly related to how much students learn, both in terms of *content* knowledge and *application* of knowledge. In addition, some researchers have shown that time out of school can have a negative effect on student performance. A meta-analysis of studies on summer learning loss found that all students experience a loss of approximately one month in math, while in reading, such losses were limited to students of lower-socioeconomic status. Understanding these relationships requires an exploration of the nature of time.

The Nature of Time in Schools

There are five interrelated dimensions of school time that aspiring and current principals should consider in order to improve learning and minimize academic losses in schools:

1. allocated time
2. engaged time
3. time-on-task
4. academic learning time
5. transition time.

Allocated time refers to the time that the state, district, school or teacher provides the students. For example, an elementary school may require that reading and language arts be taught in 90-minute blocks every day. In some studies, researchers refer to allocated time as "opportunity to learn". *Engaged time* is usually defined as the time that students appear to be paying attention to materials or presentations that have instructional goals. *Time-on-task* is engaged time on particular learning tasks. The concept is not synonymous with engaged time because it deals with engagement in planned learning experiences. A student may be deeply engaged in math homework or reading a book during a time period allocated to math, but the student is not engaged in the desired learning task. *Academic learning time* is that part of allocated time in a subject-matter area (e.g. physical education, science, math) in which a student is engaged successfully in the activities and materials related to valued educational outcomes. This is a complex concept made up of other concepts, such as allocated time (the amount of time provided for the task), time on task (engagement in tasks that are related to outcome measures or assessments in use) and success rate (the percent of engaged time that a student is experiencing a high success experience in class). *Transition time* is the non-instructional time before and after some instructional activity, such as when the teacher takes attendance or gives back homework at the beginning of an instructional activity. The next sections review dimensions of high quality curriculum and instruction and then consider how to maximize and rethink time to improve teaching and learning.

High Quality Curriculum and Instruction

Chapter 3 discusses the dimensions of a high quality curriculum or the content of education. In this section, we review these curriculum dimensions and then discuss characteristics of high-quality instruction (Danielson, 2007). The final subsection considers the impact of time on quality teaching and learning in schools.

High Quality Curriculum

As a brief review, quality curriculum dimensions include:

- **Intended Curriculum (Expectations)**—the *content* we expect students to learn, using standards (e.g. common core), frameworks, and other guidelines. The intended curriculum is overt, explicit, and written in some documentation as part of formal instruction of the schooling experience (Cuban, 1992; Porter, 2006).
- **Enacted Curriculum (Instruction)**—The enacted curriculum refers to instruction of content or what is actually taught in all classrooms (Porter, 2006). According to Porter (2006), the enacted curriculum is the content delivered and presented by each teacher. The enacted curriculum (instruction) is important because what students are actually taught is a powerful predictor of student learning and achievement.

- **Assessed Curriculum (Formative and Summative)**—refers to student outcomes on various assessments, including formative and summative (Porter, 2006). Formative assessments occur during the learning process, and summative assessments occur after a learning process has been completed.
- **Learned Curriculum (Outcomes)**—The learned curriculum is much more inclusive than the overt, intended curriculum and the assessed curriculum (Eisner, 1970). In other words, the learned curriculum is the effects (unintended and intended) of the educational program experiences. The goal of teaching is to minimize the gap between the enacted (taught) curriculum and the learned curriculum.
- **Hidden Curriculum**—Beyond the written (intended) curriculum, students learn a hidden curriculum that is implied in curricular choices, exclusions and the very ways in which schools are structured in daily educational routines.

Effective principals prioritize time for curriculum dialogue during faculty meetings, professional learning community meetings, and professional development sessions. Further, these prioritized curriculum sessions must examine and share research-based instructional approaches to deliver a quality curriculum in all classrooms.

High Quality Instruction

Robert Marzano (2009) has categorized high quality instruction into three broad areas—namely, routine segments (e.g. learning goals and feedback), content specific segments (e.g. interacting with new content), and segments enacted on the spot (e.g. student engagement, relationships). Danielson (2007) devised a similar framework, including proven instructional strategies to engage students in learning. Danielson's framework is divided into domains, with an instructional domain that incorporates: (a) clear directions and explanations; (b) interactive instructional strategies; (c) engagement; (d) assessments; and (e) flexibility and responsiveness. Commonalities in the Marzano (2009) and Danielson (2007) frameworks are described in the following paragraphs.

Clear goals, directions and feedback. According to Danielson (2007), students must receive clear directions and explanations in order to become engaged in the learning process. Marzano likewise recommends purposeful teaching with clear directions and feedback, and he adds the importance of clear goals. Marzano further emphasizes the use of classroom rules and procedures. Both frameworks emphasize the importance of clear explanations, specific language (written and oral), and clear directions that aid students in learning. Specifically, for many lessons, the teacher should communicate the big ideas that students will learn, what is important, and why it is important (e.g. Danielson, 2007; Marzano, 2009). For discovery type of lessons, students learn the big ideas as they progress through the lesson. However, the lesson's purpose should be clear by the end of the instructional session (Danielson, 2007).

When teachers present new concepts and content, instructional clarity is extremely important because content presentation affects student understanding of new content or concepts. Skilled teachers have great clarity in their explanations, frequently using analogies to convey concepts or stories to illustrate key points. Further, skilled teachers select examples and metaphors that illuminate the new ideas or skills, connecting new content to students' backgrounds (cultural and otherwise), knowledge, and interests.

Moreover, excellent teachers consider students' ages, funds of knowledge or backgrounds (see Chapter 2), and discipline-specific language.

Interactive instructional strategies. Marzano's (2009) work includes a sequential framework for content-focused segments as well as specific research-based instructional approaches. Content specific segments include interacting with new content, practicing and deepening knowledge, and generating and testing hypotheses. Research-based strategies feature identifying similarities and differences, summarizing and note-taking, nonlinguistic representation, cooperative learning, advanced organizers and questioning/dialogue strategies. Students must learn to synthesize or compare similarities and differences in authors, specific books, concepts and so forth. Marzano also recommends teaching students how to write summaries based upon notes. In order to have necessary information for summaries or synthesis activities, students must learn to take notes and use headings effectively. Nonlinguistic strategies, such as Venn diagrams, are very helpful for students to understand similarities and differences in new content. At the same time, in order to maximize learning, students need to be clear about rules and procedures for working in groups. Advanced organizers, such as K-W-L (What I Know, What I Want to Learn, What I Learned), are very effective to help students access prior knowledge. Finally, effective instruction includes questioning and dialogue strategies to assess students' understanding during the instructional process.

Danielson (2007) focuses her instructional domain on questioning and discussion (dialogue) techniques. According to Danielson, good questions tend to be divergent rather than convergent, framed in such a way to invite students to formulate hypotheses, make connections, or challenge previously held views. Excellent questions, then, promote critical thinking by students, encouraging them to make connections among prior knowledge, new content unrelated concepts or events, and to arrive at new understandings of complex material. Even when there is a "right answer" to a question, such as math computation, questions can be posed that promote student thinking and engagement.

When teachers use questions skillfully, they engage their students in an exploration of content. Carefully framed questions enable students to reflect on their understanding and consider new possibilities. In other words, good questions rarely require a simple yes/no response but rather have many possible correct answers. Experienced teachers allow students to think before they must respond to a question, using Socratic methods to facilitate dialogue. Questions and prompts such as the following are very effective:

1. **Clarification**—What did you mean by . . .?/Give me an example of . . .
2. **Probe assumptions**—What are you assuming?/What is underlying what you said?
3. **Probe reasons/Evidence**—How do you know?/What are your reasons for saying that?/What evidence do you have?
4. **Probe implications and consequences**—What are you implying by that?/Because of that, what might happen?
5. **Viewpoints on perspectives**—What might someone say who believed that?/What would an opponent say?

Initial questions for Socratic dialogue should be developed prior to the lesson; however, questions that arise during the discussion should be posed in response to the dialogue.

FIELDWORK 8.1

Spend a class period observing students when they are engaged in some kind of discussion. How did the dialogue compare to the Socratic method described above. How much time did it take for students to get involved in the discussion or dialogue? Then, if students were not engaged in this Socratic kind of dialogue, try to develop a lesson that includes this type of discussion. Did it help students engage more in the lesson? Why or why not?

In a well-facilitated discussion, all students are engaged. In other words, a few students and the teacher do not dominate the dialogue. Rather, all students are drawn into the conversation; the perspectives of *all* students are sought, and *all* voices are heard. The students themselves ensure high levels of participation because they respond to each other and support each other to engage in deep conversations.

Engaging students in learning. Active engagement is essential for students to learn complex content (Cambourne, 1988; Danielson, 2007; Marzano, 2009). Student engagement is not always easy to identify, however. Some students are able to multi-task and actually need to doodle on paper in order to actively listen and participate in a discussion. As Cambourne (1988) notes, student engagement goes beyond activity; the activity should represent new learning (see Chapter 4 for additional information about Cambourne's conditions of learning). And Danielson (2007) agrees, "What is required for student engagement is *intellectual involvement* with the content or active construction of understanding" (p. 83). Further, teachers must often engage students with a range of backgrounds and abilities in the same content. In other words, engagement requires differentiated instruction in several different elements. These elements are: (a) activities and assignments; (b) grouping of students; (c) instructional materials and resources; (d) structure and pacing.

- **Activities and assignments**—When students are actively engaged in learning, their activities and assignments challenge them to think broadly and deeply, to solve problems or to otherwise engage in creative thinking.
- **Groupings of students**—Students may be grouped in many different ways to enhance their level of engagement, including think-pair-share, large groups, led either by the teacher or a student, or small groups working on homogeneous skill areas or heterogeneous groupings.
- **Instructional materials and resources**—Instructional materials can include any items that help students engage with content, including textbooks, readings, lab equipment, maps, internet, videos, math manipulatives and so forth.
- **Structure and pacing**—A well-designed lesson has a defined structure, and students know where they are in that structure. Some lessons have a distinguishable beginning, middle and end with a clear introduction and closure.

Using assessment in instruction. As discussed in Chapter 6, assessment is an integral part of high quality instruction. As the lesson progresses, teachers engage in continuous monitoring of student learning. Teachers monitor everything, including student engagement in the lesson, the appropriateness of materials, and student learning during the lesson and/or unit. As part of the lesson design, teachers will have prepared specific techniques (questions, activities and so forth) to elicit from students evidence of their learning so that intervention or acceleration can be provided. (See Chapter 6 for additional information about formative assessments.) Providing feedback to students is an important aspect of aligning assessment and quality instruction. At the same time, if students do not use the feedback in their learning, it is of little value. Thus, teachers need to help students build their confidence and interest in attaining and using feedback to improve their learning.

Flexibility and responsiveness. Teachers must decide to adjust a lesson plan in midstream if necessary to improve students' learning experiences (Danielson, 2007). An activity, for instance, may require understandings that students have clearly not yet acquired. Teachers then must drop back and teach the required concepts before moving on to the planned lesson. According to Danielson (2007), teachers can demonstrate flexibility and responsiveness in three types of situations. First, teachers must respond when the planned instructional activity is not working. Second, a teachable moment occurs, including momentous events (e.g. September 11 events) or opportunities that capture students' interest (a student brings an interesting object in to class). The third instance relates to teachers' sense of efficacy and commitment to the learning of all students. When some students experience difficulty in learning, a teacher who is responsive and flexible persists in the search for alternative approaches, not blaming the students, the home environment or students' funds of knowledge/home culture. In many ways, flexibility and responsiveness are the mark of experience. At the same time, new teachers can and should learn to respond to students' needs and relevant events. Marzano (2009) adds the importance of student/teacher relationships, reminding us that teachers must cultivate positive and trusting relationships in order to know how to respond to each individual student's needs.

High quality instruction, then, should be culturally appropriate for students being served and prepare all students for a multicultural world. The term "culturally responsive" instruction is often used interchangeably with culturally relevant pedagogy, culturally appropriate teaching, and similar phrases. The purpose of culturally relevant instruction is the maximization of learning for racially and ethnically diverse students. It is important to recognize, however, that all students—regardless of race or ethnicity—bring their culturally influenced cognition, behavior, and dispositions with them to school. Thus, the efficacy of culturally relevant instruction is not limited to students of color even though the term is most often used to describe effective teaching of racially and ethnically diverse students.

Culturally relevant instruction or pedagogy builds upon the premise that "how people are expected to go about learning may differ across cultures. In order to maximize learning opportunities, teachers must gain knowledge of the cultures represented in their classrooms, then translate this knowledge into instructional practice" (Villegas & Lucas, 2002, p. 23). However, student achievement is not the only purpose of a culturally relevant pedagogy. Teachers must also assist students to change the society not simply to exist or survive in it. Ladson-Billings (1995) outlined three criteria for culturally relevant pedagogy:

1. An ability to develop students academically. This means effectively helping students read, write, speak, pose and solve higher order problems, and engage in peer review of problem solutions.
2. A willingness to nurture and support cultural competence in both home and school cultures. The key for teachers is to value and build on skills that students bring from the home cultures.
3. The development of a sociopolitical or critical consciousness. Teachers help students recognize, critique, and change social inequities.

Thus, high quality instruction must be culturally relevant and academically rigorous for all students. Effective principals rethink time within and beyond the school day in order to provide culturally relevant, rigorous instruction in all classrooms. As demographics change and student populations become increasingly diverse, teachers will need opportunities for professional learning and dialogue about how to develop high quality, culturally relevant curriculum, instruction, and assessment strategies in schools. In sum, high quality curriculum and instruction is:

• Engaged and differentiated: All students should receive high-quality responsive universal academic instruction that is supportive, motivating and differentiated for students with varying backgrounds and abilities
• Curriculum (standards) based: Quality instruction should be aligned with the Common Core State Standards (if approved by your state) as well as any additional state and local standards.
• Clear and assessment driven: Teachers should use data from multiple sources that indicate high quality instruction is happening for most students at a universal level. In reviewing student achievement data, for instance, teachers may notice that a group of students is not meeting certain learning targets. Curricular adjustments should be made before considering additional support, such as Response to Intervention. Further, educators must be vigilant in assuring that student achievement data collected can prove that the instruction is of high quality and matches student needs. Additionally, data needs to be gathered to show that a majority of the students are doing well in the instruction. This means looking at data in different ways, such as "disaggregated groups" to ensure the instruction is high quality for all, not just specific groups of students.
• Research and evidence based: The principal and teachers should work as a faculty and in small groups to read and process research about high quality curriculum, instruction, and assessments.
• Flexible, responsive, and relational: Teachers must decide to adjust a lesson plan in midstream if necessary to improve students' learning experiences. Further, students respond better when they have positive, trusting relationships with their teachers.
• Culturally responsive: Curriculum and instruction should be grounded in the culturally responsive practices of relevance, identity, belonging and community in order to best engage all students.

Effective leaders rethink and extend school time in order to prioritize efforts aimed at continuous improvement of curriculum and instruction.

RETHINKING AND EXTENDING TIME

In this section, we consider ways to rethink existing time and extend time beyond the school day or school year. In particular, we emphasize the importance of job-embedded approaches to maximize available professional learning time during the school day. When principals prioritize job-embedded professional learning, teachers engage in continuous instructional improvement that benefits student learning. Further, in order to provide services for the whole child, many districts and schools have extended interventions, enrichments, and social services beyond the school day or academic year. Time for learning regularly built into the routine and school day is needed and the principal should consider two strategies for extending learning time:

- Rearranging existing time
- Creating additional time

Rearranging Existing Time for Job-Embedded Learning

Some scholars have recommended that at least 20 percent of teachers' work time should be devoted to professional study and collaborative work (e.g. Zepeda, 2007). Rather than traditional in-service or district professional development days, professional learning time must be part of every school day. Specifically, school leaders can work toward one-fifth of learning in teachers' work by rethinking teachers' work conditions (e.g. job-embedded professional learning). The notion of job-embedded learning is critical to maximizing the relationship among time, curriculum, and instruction. Sparks and Hirsch (1997) noted,

> Job embedded learning . . . links learning to the immediate and real-life problems faced by teachers and administrators. It is based on the assumption that the most powerful learning is that which occurs in response to challenges currently being faced by the learner and that allows for immediate application, experimentation, and adaptation on the job.
>
> (p. 22)

In other words, job-embedded learning embeds continuous learning into the culture of the school. Zepeda (2007) identified three attributes of successful job-embedded learning: (a) it is relevant to the individual teacher; (b) feedback is built into the process, and (c) it facilitates the transfer of new skills into practice.

Job-embedded learning addresses professional development goals and concerns of the individual teacher. In addition, job-embedded learning occurs at the teacher's job site. Further, through job-embedded learning, feedback is built into the process. Processes that can generate feedback include mentoring, peer coaching, reflection and dialogue, study groups, videotape analysis of teaching and discussion about the events on tape, and journaling. Teachers can also use these tools for reflection on the implementation of new instructional strategies and for planning use of new tools. Finally, job-embedded professional development supports application of new skills into routine teaching practice. When ongoing support through the tools of job-embedded professional development is linked with the instructional supervision and coaching efforts, the transfer of skills into practice becomes part of the job.

Zepeda (2007) identified four principles to ensure successful implementation of job-embedded professional development. The four principles are:

- *Learning needs to be consistent with the principles of adult learning*: Learning goals are realistic; learning is relevant to the teacher, and concrete opportunities for practice of skills being learned are afforded.
- *Trust in the process, in colleagues, and in the learner him-/herself*: For learning to occur on the job, teachers must be able to trust the process (e.g. peer coaching, videotape analysis), their colleagues and themselves. Teachers need to know that feedback will be constructive, not personal.
- *Time within the regular school day needs to be made available for learning*: Traditionally, professional development takes place after hours, usually at some remote site. Job-embedded learning requires time to be available within the context of the normal working day at the teacher's school site.
- *Sufficient resources must be available to support learning*: Providing release time for teachers' professional development requires the creative use of human resources. In addition, outside facilitators are sometimes needed to assist teachers in learning new skills. Funding must be made available to meet these costs.

Using these principles, school leaders can examine the school day to rearrange and maximize opportunities for collaboration about curriculum and instruction. For instance, many principals have taken advantage of substitute teachers or volunteers to cover for teachers as they work in professional learning communities. Many districts have also approved early release dates on a monthly basis in which students leave school early and teachers meet in grade level or cross-grade level teams.

In addition to finding creative ways to carve out time for professional meetings/ development, principals also must explore the most efficient ways to use whatever time is available. Some districts/schools have become extremely creative in the use of technology through strategies, such as video-conferencing, Internet conferences and so forth. Fine (1994) notes, "Technologies can support and broaden professional learning communities and help teachers make better use of their time. Through a range of technologies (e.g. the Internet and video- and audio-conferencing), teachers can access both instructional resources and collegial networks" (pp. 5–6). Some technology platforms (e.g. Adobe Connect) can enable teachers to meet from various locations, allowing teachers to work from home if necessary for childcare.

Most principals coordinate professional learning as part of faculty meetings (weekly, bi-weekly, or monthly); however, faculty meetings can become one-way communication sessions. Announcements can be shared in faculty memos, and the last ten minutes of the meeting may be devoted to question or discussion about these items. When principals free up one-way communication time traditionally used to communicate district policies and so forth, much of the meeting time can be used for professional learning and dialogue about teaching and learning.

Research (Guskey & Sparks, 1991) also indicates that faculty meetings become powerful learning sessions when teachers take a leadership role in planning the faculty meetings/learning sessions in which they share their expertise and engage in professional dialogue about teaching and learning. Zepeda (2007) likewise recommends the following suggestions for framing faculty meetings as learning opportunities:

- Introduce the teacher and the name of the conference or seminar the teacher attended.
- Publicize the topic and presenters in a memo or meeting agenda.
- Allow sufficient time by asking the teacher to project how much time is needed.
- Include time for teachers to ask questions, discuss implications, or to work in small groups.
- Videotape the presentation and upload the video and accompanying power point and professional readings onto the school website. By the end of the year, there should be a sizable collection of learning materials available online and/or in the school library for both current teachers to review and for new teachers to view in subsequent years.
- Assist teachers with developing a PowerPoint, handout, and professional readings before the faculty meeting.
- Follow-up after the faculty meeting with a summary of the discussion. Seek additional learning materials for faculty based upon needs or interests generated during the faculty meeting. Consult with district staff to obtain additional resources.

A subgroup of teachers could help plan the professional learning segments of the faculty meetings. When teachers have a voice in their professional learning and have a good level of trust in their peers, they are more likely to talk about teaching practices, share any struggles, and offer advice for improvements. Many principals develop a year-long calendar featuring topic and teachers/presenters who will facilitate each professional learning session. At the same time, principals should interject topics, instructional techniques, or assessment results as foci for these meetings (e.g. Common Core alignment, inclusion processes). Sometimes, simply sharing a specific instructional techniques or formative assessment results can stimulate dialogue throughout the entire allotted timeframe.

Faculty meetings alone do not adequately support teacher growth. A comprehensive plan is needed that promotes continuous learning, both individually and collectively. Guskey and Sparks (1991) and others (e.g. Marzano, 2009) have offered similar suggestions for rethinking time in ways that support teachers' professional learning. To begin, Guskey and Sparks (1991) suggest planning for large-scale professional development and then rethinking or extending available time in order to meet these professional goals.

1. Identify the objectives and goals of the plan.
2. Identify the target population (e.g. first-year teachers, math teachers, etc.).
3. What are the needs of teachers and staff who will be on the receiving end of the professional development?
4. How were the needs determined?
5. Who will be involved in the planning of the program?
6. How will these people be involved in planning?
7. What resources are needed? What are the costs of these resources?
8. Detail the workings of the plan: What will be involved? What will teachers be doing (ideally more than listening to a presenter)? What activities are planned for teachers? Identify the types of learning activities that will be embedded in the day-to-day work of teachers and how these activities will be embedded in the workday.
9. What types of ongoing support will be provided for teachers?
10. How will the plan be monitored?

By working through these questions, teachers (or a planning subgroup) and the principal will be in a much better position to plan and deliver professional development that is responsive to the needs of teachers at the site. Along with planning strategies for job-embedded learning, principals can be creative with the school day and academic year.

Extended Time Beyond the School Day

Effective principals can extend the school day (adding time before and after school) and the school year (adding time into the summer) in order to minimize academic losses, maximize knowledge application, and provide community and health services.

Strategies for extended academic time are featured below.

Schools will want to work closely with parents to shape these activities around the needs of their community and may choose to provide extra services in response to parental demand. The core services ensure that all children and parents have access to a minimum of services and activities. How these services look and are delivered can vary by school. Children with disabilities or special educational needs must be able to access all the new services. Schools will want to actively seek parental feedback and feedback from the wider community to review and improve their services. Some of these services, such as health and social care, will be provided free of charge. These sorts of services will need to be funded often by local authorities and their children's trust partners such as primary health care. For other services, such as childcare, charges may be made to cover some service costs. Such strategies extend education beyond the academics. When schools provide much-needed services to support the whole child (e.g. health, arts, social care, parent education), they also support student readiness for academic work. At the same time, extended services do not substitute for high quality instruction in schools.

EXTENDED SCHOOL DAY EXAMPLES

- High quality childcare provided on the school site or through other local providers, with supervised transfer arrangements where appropriate, available 8 am–6 pm all year round.
- A varied menu of activities to be offered, such as homework clubs and study support, sports (at least two hours a week beyond the school day for those who want it), music, dance and drama, arts and crafts, special interest clubs such as chess and first aid courses, visits to museums and galleries, learning a foreign language, volunteering, business and enterprise activities.
- Parenting support including information sessions for parents at key transition points, parenting programs run with the support of other children's services and family learning sessions to allow children to learn with their parents.
- Swift and easy referral to a wide range of specialist support services such as speech therapy, child and adolescent mental health services, family support services, intensive behavior support for young people, and sexual health services. (Some may be delivered on school sites.)
- Providing wider community access to health, sports, and arts facilities including adult learning.

FIELDWORK 8.2

Ask a Principal

Interview a good principal about how he/she uses time for professional learning. Questions may include:

1. Describe a typical meeting that is focused on professional learning.
2. How much of your faculty work time is devoted to professional learning?
3. What strategies, if any, do you use to embed professional learning into the workday?
4. How, if at all, do you use time beyond the school day or school year for student and teacher learning?

Be prepared to share your results with the class.

A FRAMEWORK FOR TIME ALLOCATION

In sum, as the following figure suggests, effective principals prioritize time allocation in terms of professional development and student services/tutorials. Principals/ instructional leaders rethink time during and beyond the school day in creative ways. Staff and student learning needs are at the center of time priorities.

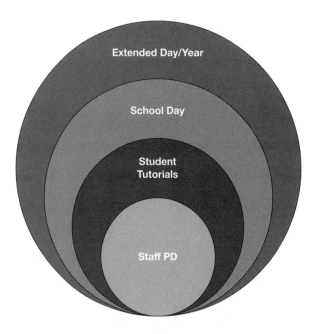

Figure 8.1 Framework for Time Allocation

TIME MANAGEMENT

Some principals work very hard but fail to produce gains in student learning on various assessments. How can that be? The answer lies in time management. In other words, these principals spend too much time on activities that are not connected to instructional leadership (particularly curriculum, instruction, and assessment). Without a clear sense of priorities and research-based work, principals may struggle to attain results from their hard work. The challenge is in figuring out which activities should get the highest priority in the school day and school year, setting directions and then developing people and designing the organization to attain these goals (Leithwood & Riehl, 2005). Consider the following activity for rethinking time.

FIELDWORK 8.3

Making It Fit

This activity is one that Stephen Covey uses to illustrate time management. The rocks represent the major tasks (i.e., instructional supervision, professional learning) that a principal might need to do in a day, and the sand represents all of the other tasks.

Students are divided into teams of three. Each team has a glass container, rocks of varying sizes, and sand. The teams are asked to fill their containers with the materials (rocks and sand) so that it all fits without extending beyond the plane of the opening. (Hint: The only way to make it work is to place the rocks in first, and pour the sand in last to fill in the gaps. This represents the way that an administrator should place the major tasks on the calendar first and fill in around them.)

Discuss with students why this is necessary, and what happens if you fill up the container with sand first and then try to fit in the rocks. This activity also demonstrates the value of strategic planning. Once leaders put a clear strategic plan in place, it's much easier to say no to activities that take you off course, to be present for students and faculty, and to manage distractions more efficiently.

TEN BIG ROCKS FOR PRINCIPALS

According to the National Association for Secondary School Principals, the following ten big rocks (noted throughout this volume) are worthy of the principal's highest priority:

- Mission—clear sense of direction.
- Climate—the school as a safe place.
- Alignment—meshing curriculum, instruction, and assessments.
- Resources—getting teachers the resources they need to be effective.

- Instruction—nurturing the best possible teaching in every classroom.
- Hiring—using every vacancy to bring in excellent teachers.
- Formative Assessments—using data to continuously improve teaching.
- Collaboration—fostering constant sharing of ideas and resources.
- Results—keeping supervision, professional development, and teams focused on outcomes.
- Parents—maximizing and developing family support and funds of knowledge for students' education.

STRATEGIES FOR LEADERS: RETHINKING TIME FOR TEACHING AND LEARNING

This section provides ideas for principals to rethink time during and beyond the school day.

Time

In many states, a minimum number of instructional minutes are mandated per year. In addition, many districts mandate minimum blocks of instructional time for language arts and mathematics.

It is also important to consider how you communicate to the greater community. Are they aware of the professional learning and collaboration that occurs at the school? This communication becomes of greater importance if/when there is consideration of changing school hours to accommodate the needs. For example, many elementary school sites have added additional minutes to four days per school week in order to provide early release time on the fifth day, enabling staff to meet together for a longer period of time. At the secondary level, it is not unusual to see creative scheduling in which

---

FIELDWORK 8.4

A school principal must be knowledgeable about these expectations and build their own building schedule around the parameters. In preparation for your own planning, think about the following:

- What is the purpose of restructuring a schedule? What is our vision at the school?
- Am I more concerned with meeting teacher preferences or professional learning needs through the way we schedule?
- What special area subjects or electives are available for students during the school day in order to free up groups of teachers to work together?
- Are there certain subject areas/classes in which larger groups of children can be taught together?
- In what ways should teachers be grouped for collaboration? (grade level, content area, cross-grade articulation groups, etc.)

students follow a more traditional schedule three days per week, and on the other two days they meet with half of their classes for a slightly longer time period, releasing a bit earlier on those two days. Whatever the strategy, be sure that you are clear about your vision and values, and make decisions that are aligned with your school goals.

During the School Day

Seek to create a master schedule that enables your identified groups of teachers to meet collaboratively during the school day. Some examples follow in Figure 8.2.

Beyond the School Day

As mentioned earlier, many schools seek additional funding for extended day programs designed to support and enhance student learning. With this model often comes the need to provide transportation for students to return home on a different schedule from the one most students may follow. During these times, additional work in Language Arts/Reading and Mathematics may be delivered, as well as other enrichment activities such as native language instruction, different forms of dance, or other skills such as creative writing, sewing, and basic carpentry. Often parents will willingly pay for these services, but in many communities, this is not feasible.

STRATEGIES FOR LEADERS

How do instructional leaders put all of this background on the relationships among time and learning into practice? This section provides guidance for what today's instructional leaders need to know and be able to do as well as example strategies for practice. Instructional leaders need to:

Know:

*   the nature of time in schools
*   high quality curriculum
*   high quality instruction.

Be able to:

*   rethink time for instruction during the school day
*   rethink time for teacher learning during the school day
*   rethink time for student and adult learning beyond the school day
*   prioritize and manage time effectively
*   develop a master schedule that maximizes student and teacher learning.

Use time effectively for:

*   job-embedded professional development
*   collaborative team meetings focused on curriculum and instruction

- common formative assessments
- data analysis teams
- Funds of Knowledge research traditions
- consideration about the hidden curriculum and inclusive practice
- student interventions
- parent involvement and education.

High School Example of Modified Schedule

	Monday	Tuesday	Friday
7:50–8:45	Period 1	Period 1	Period 1
8:50–9:45	Period 2	Period 2	Period 2
9:50–10:45	Period 3	Period 3	Period 3
10:50–11:45	Period 4	Period 4	Period 4
11:50–12:30	Lunch	Lunch	Lunch
12:35–1:30	Period 5	Period 5	Period 5
1:35–2:30	Period 6	Period 6	Period 6
2:35–3:15	Tutorial	Tutorial	Tutorial

	Wednesday	Thursday
7:50-9:20	Period 1	Period 2
9:25-10:55	Period 3	Period 4
11:00-11:40	Lunch	Lunch
11:45-1:15	Period 5	Period 6
1:20-1:55	Tutorial	Tutorial
2:00-3:155	PLCs	PLCs

Elementary Example

	Monday	Tuesday	Wednesday	Thursday	Friday
8:00	Music-6C P.E.-6A CompLab-6B	Music-6A P.E.-6B CompLab-6C	P.E.-6A CompLab-6C Art-6B	Music-6C P.E.-6B Art-6A	Music-6A P.E.-6C Art-6B
8:25	Music-6B P.E.-6C Art-6A	Library-6B CompLab-6A Art-6C	Music-6B P.E.-6C Library-6A	P.E.-6A CompLab-6B Art-6C	P.E.-6B Library-6C CompLab-6A
8:50	Music-5C P.E.-5A CompLab-5B	Music-5A P.E.-5B CompLab-5C	P.E.-5A CompLab-5C Art-5B	Music-6C P.E.-5B Art-6A	Music-5A P.E.-5C Art-5B
9:15	Music-5B P.E.-5C Art-5A	Library-5B CompLab-6A Art-5C	Music-5B P.E.-5C Library-5A	P.E.-5A CompLab-5B Art-5C	P.E.-5B Library-5C CompLab-5A
9:40	Music-3C P.E.-3A CompLab-3B	Music-3A P.E.-3B CompLab-3C	P.E.-3A CompLab-3C Art-3B	Music-3C P.E.-3B Art-3A	Music-3A P.E.-3C Art-3B

Figure 8.2 Schedule Examples

	Monday	Tuesday	Wednesday	Thursday	Friday
10:05	Music-3B P.E.-3C Art-3A	Library-3B CompLab-3A Art-3C	Music-3B P.E.-3C Library-3A	P.E.-3A CompLab-3B Art-3C	P.E.-3B Library-3C CompLab-3A
10:30	Music-4C P.E.-4A CompLab-4B	Music-4A P.E.-4B CompLab-4C	P.E.-4A CompLab-4C Art-4B	Music-4C P.E.-4B Art-4A	Music-4A P.E.-4C Art-4B
10:55	Music-4B P.E.-4C Art-4A	Library-4B CompLab-4A Art-4C	Music-4B P.E.-4C Library-4A	P.E.-4A CompLab-4B Art-4C	P.E.-4B Library-4C CompLab-4A
11:20 11:45	Specialists collaborate and eat lunch at this time				
12:10	Music-1C P.E.-1A CompLab-1B	Music-1A P.E.-1B CompLab-1C	P.E.-1A CompLab-1C Art-1B	Music-1C P.E.-1B Art-1A	Music-1A P.E.-1C Art-1B
12:35	Music-1B P.E.-1C Art-1A	Library-1B CompLab-1A Art-1C	Music-1B P.E.-1C Library-1A	P.E.-1A CompLab-1B Art-1C	P.E.-1B Library-1C CompLab-1A
1:00	Music-KC P.E.-KA CompLab-KB	Music-KA P.E.-KB CompLab-KC	P.E.-KA CompLab-KC Art-KB	Music-KC P.E.-KB Art-KA	Music-KA P.E.-KC Art-KB
1:25	Music-KB P.E.-KC Art-KA	Library-KB CompLab-KA Art-KC	Music-KB P.E.-KC Library-KA	P.E.-KA CompLab-KB Art-KC	P.E.-KB Library-KC CompLab-KA

Please note that specialists without classes can be scheduled to do interventions with small groups of children at the discretion of the principal.

Figure 8.2 Schedule Examples

CASES: RETHINKING TIME

This chapter concludes with two case studies to help candidates consider how to rethink and prioritize their time as school leaders.

CASE 8.1 IS BEING BUSY NECESSARILY PRODUCTIVE?

(Gorton & Alston, 2009, pp. 244–247)

Driving to school, Steve Fuller slowed reluctantly for a traffic light. As he waited for the signal to change, the new principal of Franklin School speculated idly about what the day might bring. It seemed that he was always busy, regardless of how a day started out.

Today, for example, he didn't have any conferences or meetings scheduled until later in the afternoon, to the best of his memory. He was certain, however, that something would come along to dominate the morning. He had hoped to get into some classrooms and do some supervision, but he hadn't mentioned anything to the teachers yet, in case something were to come up to prevent him from accomplishing that task.

Finally, the green light appeared, and Steve accelerated the car to compensate for lost moments. By 7:55 he pulled into the school parking lot at his usual time, parked the car, and entered the school. His secretary had arrived some time earlier, and after five minutes of chit- chat with her, the principal was interrupted by a teacher who wanted to talk about the faculty party that was to occur in about two weeks. The conversation lasted until 8:25, at which time the teacher had to leave for a class that began at 8:30.

At 8:40 Steve Fuller was sitting in his office thinking about what he should do next, when he remembered that he had hoped to do some classroom supervision that morning, As he started to leave, his secretary intercepted him, asking whether they could talk now about revising some of the office procedures. Since there was a lull in her work schedule, it seemed to her like a good time to discuss the matter. The principal momentarily experienced some mixed feelings, but he didn't reveal them to his secretary. Instead, he smiled and said that he would be happy to discuss those matters with her.

At 9:20 the principal and his secretary were still talking (although they had been interrupted by two telephone calls to the principal), when the secretary brought to the attention of the principal his scheduled conference with a parent, Mrs. Channing, at 9:30. The principal was mildly surprised, as he had anticipated that the parent conference was to be held in the afternoon. He thought to himself that the classroom observation would have to wait until after the parent conference.

At 9:45 Mrs. Channing finally appeared for her conference with the principal. Mr. Fuller was a little frustrated because he had expected her to arrive at 9:30, and he hadn't been able to get much done except to talk with a student who had dropped by his office. He concealed his frustration and tried to be as friendly and helpful to Mrs. Channing as possible. The parent wanted to talk with him about her son's discipline difficulties in school, but it quickly became clear that she should have talked to the assistant principal or the counselor instead, each of whom could have been more helpful to her. Unfortunately, when he asked his secretary to contact one of them, neither was free at that time.

As the conference with the parent dragged on and on, the principal became more and more frustrated. Finally, at 10:40, the parent concluded her conference with the principal and thanked him for his help. The principal thought to himself that he really hadn't been very helpful, but he was happy that he was finally rid of the parent.

Since it was now 10:45, the principal decided that he needed a coffee break, and he left his office to go down to the faculty room. After he had poured his coffee, he decided to sit in the back of the faculty room where he hoped to be somewhat alone, and perhaps clear his head from the parent conference. Almost immediately, however, a couple of teachers came over and initiated a discussion about last Sunday's pro football game. The principal had hoped for some privacy, but he was reluctant to turn away the two teachers and besides, he really liked football. So the conversation continued, and before he knew it, it was 11:15.

Excusing himself, the principal left the faculty room and returned to his office. While he was sorting through some papers on his desk, a teacher stopped by and asked if he was busy. The principal thought to himself that he really wasn't busy yet, but there were some things that he knew should be done. On the other hand, at this point, he hadn't started anything specific, and since he had told his faculty that he had an open-door policy and they could see him anytime he wasn't busy, he indicated to the teacher that he would be happy to see her.

The principal's conference with the teacher was about the possibility of the school's or the district's purchase of a television set for her classroom so that she could begin to teach students to become more critical consumers of television. The conference lasted until 11:45, when the principal had to excuse himself to go to lunch with the PTA president.

After returning from lunch, Mr. Fuller answered several telephone messages on his desk, and attempted to open and process his mail. This took about 40 minutes, until nearly 1:45 p.m. At this point, his secretary came in to remind him of the meeting he had to attend at the district office at 2:30. The principal had forgotten about the meeting, although he knew that there was some type of meeting that he was supposed to attend later in the afternoon. He thanked his secretary for reminding him and decided that he'd better prepare to leave, as it would take about 30 minutes to drive downtown to the district office.

At 4:00 the district office meeting concluded. Mr. Fuller decided against returning to the school and instead proceeded home. It had been a boring meeting and, in general, a frustrating day. He felt he had been busy all day but wondered what he had really accomplished. He knew there was something important that he meant to do that he hadn't accomplished, but he couldn't remember anymore what it had been. He thought to himself that he needed to relax, and that perhaps tomorrow would bring a more satisfying and productive day.

Questions

1. If you were the principal, what planning steps might you have taken before arriving at work to improve your productivity?
2. Analyze the different activities in which the principal engaged during the day and suggest how he might have handled things more efficiently.
3. To what extent should an administrator be concerned about how efficiently time is used?
4. What costs are there to not being well organized or efficient?
5. What costs are there to being too organized and efficient?
6. What are some strategies a principal needs to use in order to use time effectively? Have you seen your own principal employ these strategies?

CASE 8.2 HOW TO FIT IT ALL IN?

The administrative team of Duffy High School—Principal Debra Gonzales and one assistant principal—meets in early August to develop a long-term plan for supervising and evaluating the 73 teachers in their building. The district policy mandates that each teacher be formally observed at least twice, with each observation lasting at least the full class period, 50 minutes.

The math is simple:

66 teachers x 2 classroom observations each = 132 observations
132 observations/2 administrators = 66 observations per administrator

At 50 minutes per observation, this amounts to 55 hours each—not including the pre- and post- observation conferences. Gonzales also has set as a priority to conduct informal observations because she wants teachers to feel supported and to be visible in classrooms— both formally and informally.

EXTENDED REFLECTION 8.2

Take another look at the time journal you developed at the beginning of the chapter. How could you rethink your time during the school day to maximize curriculum and instructional work? How would you characterize the quality of your collaboration time with regard to the chapter's recommendations? Remember to consider how you are spending time on the arts, humanities, and community service as well as academic subjects. How could your school extend time beyond the school day to the benefit of students? How can your time journal better reflect your personal and school priorities?

Questions

Every K–12 supervisor faces this dilemma, and there are no clear answers.

1. As a prospective supervisor, brainstorm possible approaches that Gonzales and her assistant principal might consider.
2. Think about how to prioritize the supervisory needs within the school year.
3. What strategies would you employ? Why is it important?

SUMMARY

This chapter examined the relationships among time, quality curriculum, and quality instruction. The chapter began with a consideration of the nature of time during and beyond the school day. There are five interrelated dimensions of school time that aspiring and current principals should consider in order to improve learning and minimize academic losses in schools:

1. allocated time
2. engaged time

3. time-on-task
4. academic learning time
5. transition time.

Next, the chapter reviewed the essential dimensions of high quality curriculum or the content of education:

1. intended
2. enacted
3. assessed
4. learned
5. hidden.

High quality instruction is (a) engaged and differentiated; (b) curriculum-based (standards); (c) clear and assessment driven; (d) research and evidence based; and (e) flexible and responsive. Moreover, high-quality curriculum and instructional practices should be culturally responsive to increasingly diverse students. Research has demonstrated indirect links between effective use of time and effective curriculum and instruction in schools (e.g. Farbman & Kaplan, 2005; Hoxby, Muraka & Kang, 2009; Jacobson et al., 2005). The chapter asked aspiring leaders to rethink time during and beyond the school day, including job-embedded professional learning and extended school opportunities. At the same time, the chapter provided information and activities to help aspiring leaders develop time management skills. This chapter concluded with learning experiences, case studies, and a framework to help instructional leaders maximize time spent on quality curriculum and instruction work.

REFERENCES

Cambourne, B. (1988). *The whole story: Natural learning and the acquisition of literacy in the classroom.* Aukland, New Zealand: Ashton-Scholastic.

Cooper, H. (2009). *Research synthesis and meta-analysis: A step-by-step approach* (4th ed.). Thousand Oaks, CA: SAGE Publications.

Cuban, L. (1992). Managing dilemmas while building professional communities. *Educational Researcher, 21*(1), 4–11.

Danielson, C. (2007). *Enhancing professional practice: A framework for teaching* (2nd ed.). Alexandria, VA: Association for Supervision and Curriculum Development.

Eisner, E. W. (1970). Curriculum development: Sources for a foundation for the field of curriculum. *Curriculum Theory Network,* (5), 3–15.

Farbman, D. & Kaplan, C. (2005). *Time for change: The promise of extended-time schools for promoting student achievement.* Boston, MA: 2020.

Fine, M. (1994). *Chartering urban school reform: Reflections on public high schools in the midst of change.* New York: Teachers College Press.

Gorton, R. & Alston, J. (2009). *School leadership and administration: Important concepts, case studies, and simulations* (8th ed.). New York: McGraw-Hill.

Guskey, T. & Sparks, D. (1991). What to consider when evaluating staff development. *Educational Leadership, 49*(3), 73–77.

Hoxby, C. M., Muraka, S., & Kang, J. (2009). *How New York City's charter schools affect achievement, August 2009 Report. Second report in series*. Cambridge, MA: New York City Charter Schools Evaluation Project.

Jacobson, S., Johnson, L., Ylimaki, R., & Giles, C. (2005). Successful school leadership in changing times: cross national findings in the third year of an international research project. *Journal of Educational Administration*, *43*(6), 607–618.

Ladson-Billings, G. (1995). Toward a theory of culturally relevant pedagogy. *American Educational Research Association*, *32*(3), 465–491.

Leithwood, K. & Riehl, C. (2005). What we know about successful school leadership. In W. Firestone & C. Riehl (Eds.). *A new agenda: Directions for research on educational leadership*. New York: Teachers College Press.

Marzano Research Laboratory. (2009). Meta-analysis database. Retrieved August 24, 2012 from www.marzanoresearch.com/research/meta_analysis_database.aspx

Porter, A. C. (2006). Curriculum assessment. *Handbook of complementary methods in education research*, 141–159.

Sparks, D. & Hirsch, S. (1997). *A new vision for staff development*. Alexandria, VA: Association for Supervision and Curriculum Development.

Villegas, A. & Lucas, T. (2002). Preparing culturally responsive teachers rethinking the curriculum. *Journal of Teacher Education*, *53*(1), 20–32.

Zepeda, S. (2007). *Instructional supervision: Applying tools and concepts, 2nd edition*. Larchmont, NY: Eye on Education.

CHAPTER 9

Promote the Use of the Most Effective and Appropriate Technologies to Support Teaching and Learning

Seann M. Dikkers

KEY TOPICS

- Expectations for Technology
- Technology for Learning
- Technology for Professional Development
- Technology for Leadership

According to ISLLC Standard 2, instructional leaders foster effective and appropriate technologies to support learning and teaching in schools. This chapter is about technology for learning and the role leaders play in shaping technology use for learning, teaching, and leading. More specifically, school leaders who effectively influence technology use understand both *what* to promote and *how* to use technology as part of preparing students for participation in the 21st century workplace. Today leaders face a public demand for student fluency with relevant workplace technologies, but the tools themselves are quickly upgrading and changing like never before. These rapid changes and upgrades affect both personal and professional dimensions of our lives. Take a minute to record your reflections about technology changes you have experienced.

EXTENDED REFLECTION 9.1

Write your ideas about the digital technologies that have essentially changed personal and workplace practices. Are students being introduced to the same tools in school? Are they learning to use these tools? As you read this chapter add to this list, considering all the ways that technology impacts learning in and out of schools.

DIMENSIONS OF TECHNOLOGY IN SCHOOLS

Technology is a broad term that includes any system, device, or process that renders an activity easier, more efficient, or of higher quality. As such, technology is clearly more complex and involved than the specific tools purchased, or the skills hopefully learned while using and teaching with new technology. When asked to discuss technology, teachers and administrators often speak in terms of what is being used *in* classrooms; however, there are other equally important dimensions of technology— those dimensions of technology used outside of school. Instructional leaders' communication around technology can be sharpened with a simple and quick understanding of the five dimensions that influence education. The dimensions of technology in schools include:

- ubiquitous technology
- available technology
- siloed technology
- personal technology
- contextual technology.

Ubiquitous technology—Includes technology so embedded in school practices that we can forget that it too is a technology. Ubiquitous technology (like notebooks, pencils, grades, public schooling, and/or chalkboards) is everywhere, easily available, and often assumed essential. Almost all schools have and all teachers know how to use ubiquitous technologies for learning. These technologies can be enshrined as part of a definition of education, however they too were invented, introduced, and intended to make learning easier.

Available technology—Includes technology in the schools that is readily accessible to every teacher. Unlike ubiquitous technologies, available technologies may be present, but the teachers may not know how to, or want to, use them for learning. These include mounted televisions in classrooms as well as video cameras, mobile devices, and other tools available to teachers through a check out/sign up process.

Siloed technology—Includes technology that a school has access to, but only some teachers/personnel are allowed access. These technology investments can be highly specialized for a specific skill or segregated from use because of security or other concerns. For instance a sewing machine, table saw, or computer-aided design (CAD) program may be in the school and used for learning, but not available to all teachers.

Some technologies, like grading programs or maintenance tools may not be available to students or teachers respectively. These technologies, though siloed, are still part of the school system.

Personal technology—Includes any and all technology that administrators, teachers, and students make use of to perform their duties. Students' access to technology at home is a significant consideration for their learning. In addition, teachers often buy their own supplies and needed tools for their classrooms. Although administrators do not necessarily budget for these things, (but could consider more) they still should be aware of them and balance them into a technology plan for the school.

Contextual technology—Includes all other technologies that are perceived as relevant by the larger culture in which school institutions reside. For instance, contextual technologies like mobile smart phones and video conferencing are changing the work environment nationally and internationally. To have globally competitive graduates, school leaders must be aware of relevant technologies at use at home, at work, and even at play.

FIELDWORK 9.1

Use the dimensions of technology above to create a chart that shows the technologies currently available in your school setting. If you need to stop by the office, media center, or interview some students to further fill in the chart, do so. Consider adding a survey of personal technologies used by students and teachers to get a better sense of what technology is used. What dimension shows the most technology use? Which is the weakest? What suggestions would you make to the leadership team based on this data?

Leaders must have a clear understanding of how the larger culture defines relevant learning (symbiotically tied to technologies used), the types of technologies that are valuable for learning, and a clear eye for the outcomes expected from the use of new technologies (like interactive whiteboards, pads, mobile devices, clickers, digital simulations and games, production tools, laptops, or online professional networks) in regards to both professional development and student learning. For instance, the use of online networks at home (personal) and at school (available) will take on essentially different shapes and meaning—yet because both can serve as learning assets for students and teachers, leaders should plan strategies to leverage both. Mastering effective and appropriate use of technologies is a key standard for school leaders today. The first step is establishing research-based expectations for what technology should do in learning contexts.

SETTING EXPECTATIONS FOR TECHNOLOGY

New digital technologies are arriving much faster than they have over the past twenty-five years, and these rapid technological advances present completely new ways for people to interact with information. Mobile technologies, in particular, are globally showing the fastest and most ubiquitous adoption rate *ever* seen in a new technology (Comer & Wikle, 2008; Horst & Miller, 2006), especially among youth (Rideout, Foehr, & Roberts, 2010; Squire & Dikkers, 2012).

School leaders must stay "on top" of new technologies, implement district policies, shape budgets, and provide professional development for teachers learning with technology. In addition to increasing demands for accountability about *how much* is learned (NCLB), leaders face pressures and public expectations regarding "21st century skills" or "literacies". When new digital technology is applied appropriately and effectively, instructional leaders should see:

- production over consumption
- engaging over passive activity
- "flow" over boredom/frustration
- new affordances over "remapped" uses
- social learning over individual learning
- effective over complex
- professional development over "drop-in" technology.

Production over Consumption

Youth consume digital media at an average of seven and a half hours daily, including an average of three and a half hours per day in which they are multitasking (Rideout, Foehr, & Roberts, 2010). Yet all of this consumption of media does not necessarily mean that students will be able to make media. The ability to present ideas or represent new ways of thinking, via writing, filming, editing, or programming, is still the goal of education despite the medium used. School leaders should seek out technologies that allow learners to produce or make their own products.

Engaging over Passive Learning

Learners mediate not only simple information with tools, but also by the context and terms under which learning can be constructed. Leaders and teachers are essentially creating a "sandbox" for learning that places engaging tools, people, and activities in the path of learners. Interesting technologies can foster mentor-based inquiry and challenges that captivate the learner within the learning space. Leaders need to be aware of a natural progression from "hanging out", to "messing around", to "geeking out", observed in the research of digital media use (Ito et al., 2008). As with reading and writing, early activities are designed to "hook" students in a process that can take years of investment in the child.

Flow over Boredom/Frustration

Have you ever played a game or worked on a project and just lost track of time? When properly engaged, this is a common human experience—coined as "flow" (Csikszentmihalyi, 1990). Natural inquiry and mentorship can be stifled with overt controls, uninteresting/redundant spaces, and tasks that are either too easy or too difficult to create a natural learning or work "flow" where effective learning can happen. For instance, think of how you lost yourself in the last great book you read. Think of how you "forgot" about bedtime at night because you were playing a computer game, like Civilization V, negotiating peace with the Babylonians for hours. In addition to being engaging, flow is revealing itself to be an optimal state for learning too. Reviews of learning studies show that working or playing in "flow" improves mental health, learning, memory, and mastery development (Pink, 2009) for the finest athletes, artists, designers, writers, administrators, and thinkers—the sorts of vocations that are defining the 21st century workplace.

New Affordances over Remapped Uses

New technologies often offer new ways to interact with learning. Effective leaders are open to new teaching practices and new learning models that best complement the tools available. When ignored, technology can simply be an expensive tool for an old practice or remapped to do a task already done effectively with an earlier technology (like using bad math games to replace flash cards). When technology is seen through the lens of what activities it allows, or affordances, it can be leveraged more powerfully for learning.

For instance, Klopfer and Squire (2008) describe learning affordances of mobile tools and provide a useful guide. Notice their focus on activity allowed:

- **Portability**—can move wherever the learner is
- **Social interactivity**—can share data, collaborate, and maximize face-to-face time
- **Context sensitivity**—can gather data unique to the current location
- **Connectivity**—can seamlessly move data, conversations, and people together
- **Individuality**—can provide outlet for teacher and student use and production.

For administrators with potential budget considerations, I would add:

- **Flexibility**—can facilitate varied pedagogies and can be expanded later
- **Durability**—can reasonably endure constant use and wear of students.

Social Learning over Individual Learning

Learning and quality technology use actually leads to increased *social* activity (Klopfer & Squire, 2008). A constructivist view of cognitive development has long brought learning activity and social activity together (Bruner, 1961; Dewey, 1933/1910; Piaget, 1950; Vygotsky, 1978). As multimedia technology and communication applications become more and more robust, these learning theories seem much more relevant than ever before as does the cultural context of our observations of learning (Wertsch, 1991). Effective technologies are more than tools; they enable strong social and cognitive internalizations and can affect the context and culture of learning in positive and negative ways.

Effective over Complex

Care should be taken not to confuse either the *complexity* or the *presence* of a technology with the *effective use* of a technology. Effective technology is easily adopted because it is effective. The ISLLC standards, for instance, are a fairly non-complex tool of guidance for leaders, yet they are rooted in the latest research as well as powerful analytic technologies—making for highly effective use. Likewise, teachers can use non-digital games as motivation strategies to increase grades (Castranova, 2010). Both examples are widely used and effective low-tech tools in a high-tech environment. The number of buttons on the controller does *not* equate to effective technology use, nor does complexity equate to effectiveness.

Professional Development over "Drop-In" Technology

Simply dropping technology into learning spaces will not improve teaching and learning; high-tech tools do *not* necessarily equate to highly effective learning environments. For this reason, technology is all too easy to dismiss because initial efforts are inconclusive in the research. *How* these tools are used, the *context* where they are used, and the *guidance* provided is far more predictive to improved learning than the tool itself. Tools can be exciting, but still must be employed with mastery and appreciated for the 21st century skills they are intentionally designed to amplify.

EXAMPLE: DROP-IN TECHNOLOGIES WITH LIMITED IMPACT

Interactive whiteboards have sold over one million units in the two years from 2011–2012, with both school and government support. There remains limited research showing impact on student learning (Moss et al., 2007). Yet virtually all teachers/users adopt them enthusiastically (Kennewell, 2006) and facilitate more interactive teaching styles (Armstrong et al., 2005).

Laptops increase motivation, increase attendance, and improve academic performance, but some of the gains are short-lived and hard to quantify (Fisher & Stolarchuk, 1998; Gardner, 1994; Lowther, Ross, & Morrison, 2003); laptops appear less predictive when key factors such as teacher training, access, and positive teacher attitudes were accounted for (Penuel, 2006).

At Essa Academy in the United Kingdom, leaders funded iTouches for all students. The significant *learner* changes were not clearly detected in traditional math and reading scores, but were found in creativity, personalization, access to information, and heightened learning conversations (Chohan, 2011).

In addition to having a clear set of expectations for technology use, leaders need to be ready to identify and defend what results they see with a working understanding of 21st century skills in order to make effective decisions, explanations, and evaluations of new technology use. Next, this chapter will give an overview of the term "21st century skills" and provide a guide to better communicating the use of technology through a skills-based framework.

IDENTIFYING 21ST CENTURY SKILLS

What are 21st century skills? How does a school leader know when 21st century skills are in place? How can leaders provide instructional leadership towards 21st century skills? Digital skill lists are growing in number and detail. Essentially, these lists are efforts to clarify what the larger context of education is now asking school leaders to build among their learners. So, while the particular definitions of 21st century skills are still being resolved, school leaders should get a sense of what kinds of skills are being called for across these lists. Briefly summarized you can see the growing scope of these efforts to define 21st century skills.

Early work by the New London Group (1996) summarized research that identified broad "new skills" like situated practice, overt instruction, critical framing, and transformed practice. The language describing emergent skills clarified *and* shifted to the act of learning in the next four years to include specific dispositions like ownership, personalization, play, "generativity", and competence (diSessa, 2000). Practices that surrounded technology and media were to be defined as "literacies" to emphasize that these skills were becoming relevant to working in participatory digital systems.

Experts from media, communication, education, and literacy studies pooled their findings for both the New Media Consortium (2005) and The International Society for Technology in Education (ISTE, 2009) to create standards of 21st century learning. These added to the dialogue: the ability to work in multi-modal settings, learn new grammars, participate in interactive communication (digital citizenship), transform media to build new meanings, operations, and concepts, and digital versions of traditional competencies like creativity, collaboration, critical thinking, problem solving, and decision making.

According to literacy experts Colin Lankshear and Michele Knobel (2008), these 21st century skills began to translate to both digital and non-digital formats. Students should be able to independently both "push" and "pull" information through multiple modes; including traditional ones. Their work informed the MacArthur Foundation report (Jenkins et al., 2009) that summarized education for the 21st century to include the abilities of play, simulation, performance, appropriation, distributed cognition, collective intelligence, and networking. The Partnership for 21st Century Skills sponsors one of the more recent listings. Writers for the partnership identify 13 skills for learning, tech literacy, and work-ready skills (Trilling & Fadel, 2009). Other interesting studies also highlight digital skills for learning that include "hanging out", "messing around" and "geeking out" (Ito et al., 2008), losing/failing (Juul, 2009), and even redefined aspects of "cheating" in game studies (Consalvo, 2007) as a path to learning. As an administrator, I made a simple summary checklist (Table 9.3), useful for clarifying and sharing the attributes of new technologies and learning. For school leaders, this checklist carries the collective knowledge of the last decade of digital technology studies in a portable, sharable tool.

Table 9.1 21st Century Literacies and Skill Iterations

New London Group 1996	diSessa 2000	New Media Consortium 2005	ISTE 2007	Lankshear & Knobel 2008	MacArthur/ Jenkins 2009	P21/Trilling & Fadel (reduced categories) 2009	Other
Situated practice	Ownership of learning	Multimodal	Creativity & innovation	Reading and understanding digital and non-digital formats	Play	Critical thinking & problem solving	Hanging out
Overt instruction	Personalization of work	Creative fluency & interpretive facility	Communication & collaboration	Creating and communicating digital information	Simulation	Complex communication	Messing around
Critical framing	Play in work	Learning a new grammar	Research & information fluency	Evaluation of information	Performance	Applied imagination & invention	Geeking out
Transformed practice	Generativity	Interactive communication	Critical thinking, problem solving, & decision making	Information literacy – "pull"	Appropriation	Information literacy	Losing
	Regime of competence	Use media to evoke emotional responses	Digital citizenship	Media literacy – "push"	Multi-tasking	Media literacy	Cheating
		Transform the way we learn	Technology operations and concepts	Independent learning	Distributed cognition	ICT literacy	Piracy
				Moral and social literacy	Collective intelligence	Flexibility & adaptability	Intertextual creation
					Judgment	Initiative & self-direction	
					Transmedia navigation	Social & cross-cultural	
					Networking	Productivity & accountability	
					Negotiation	Leadership & responsibility	

Table 9.2 21st Century Literacies/Skills Listings

21st Century Skills	New London Group 2000	diSessa 2000	Prensky 2006	Gee 2007	Lankshear & Knobel 2008	Hughes 2009	Trilling & Fadel 2009	Jenkins et al. 2009	Ito et al. 2008
Appropriation/ Media Use	✓		✓	✓	✓		✓	✓	✓
Generativity/ Design	✓	✓		✓			✓	✓	✓
Transmedia Navigation/ Multimodal expression/ Redesigning	✓		✓	✓	✓	✓		✓	✓
Judgment/Critical Framing/ Critical Thinking	✓		✓	✓	✓		✓	✓	✓
Negotiation/Shifting Views/ Cross-Cultural Communication	✓		✓	✓	✓	✓	✓	✓	✓
Simulation/ Situated Practice	✓		✓	✓				✓	✓
Play in Work/ Motivation		✓	✓	✓	✓		✓	✓	✓
Ownership of Learning/ Identity Construction		✓	✓	✓		✓			✓
Personalization/Customized/ Performance (multiple-IDs)		✓	✓	✓		✓		✓	✓
Regime of Competence/ Collective Intelligence/ Collaborative ethos		✓	✓	✓		✓	✓	✓	✓
Distributed Cognition/ Multilinear Authoring			✓	✓	✓	✓		✓	✓
Networking/Audience Focus/ Affinity/Moral-Social Connectedness			✓	✓	✓	✓		✓	✓
Multitasking/ Productivity				✓			✓	✓	✓
Emergent Leadership/Peer-Based Learning							✓		✓
Personalized Technology						✓			✓
Global Information Awareness					✓				
Informal "Hanging"/"Messing"									✓

Table 9.3 21st Century Skills Observation Guide

Attributes Students will...	Learn at different paces	▣
	Show initiative and self-direction	▣
	Play in work	▣
	Immerse or 'geek out' in work	▣
	Show ownership of learning	▣
	Show creativity & innovation	▣
	Multi-task	▣
Abilities Students can...	Read and understand digital and non-digital formats	▣
	Manipulate and mix media	▣
	Critically process simulated spaces	▣
	Distribute cognition using digital tools	▣
	Critically frame/evaluate incoming and created content	▣
	Personalize work environments	▣
	Learn a new grammar through experiences	▣
	Use judgment to critically think & solve problems	▣
	Create online identities	▣
	Communicate multimodally	▣
	Express digital citizenship	▣
Social Graces Student display the ability to...	Interact and effectively communicate	▣
	Interact in social and cultural diversity	▣
	Network	▣
	Learn from and/or mentor other students	▣
	Collaborate with others effectively	▣
	Negotiate ideas and resolve differences	▣
	Interact flexibly & adapt	▣
	Participate in a local or online collective intelligence	▣
Unique items Students also...	Use media to evoke emotional responses	
	Express moral and social negotiation	
	Hanging out	
	Messing around with new media	
	Show leadership & make decisions	
	Negotiate new media 'Cheating', 'losing', and/or 'pirating'	

FIELDWORK 9.2

Choose any new technology being used in a colleague's classroom. Use the above observation guide to evaluate that technology. What insights does this tool allow? What is the intended use of the technology? How is the technology actually being used? How might this technology be used in the workplace?

School leaders are challenged to assess classroom learning using technologies unfamiliar to them. Regardless of the technology or topic, school leaders can know if 21st century work is being done if they are aware of what tools are available and the degree to which they facilitate 21st century work. In the final three sections, this chapter provides an overview of specific types of and resources for learning, professional development, and leading.

TECHNOLOGY FOR LEARNING

There are hundreds of recently minted new technologies for learning. By the time of this printing, there will be more. Administrators cannot be expected to keep up with every tool that is created; yet too many educators are unfamiliar with many of today's technology tools. One solution is to seek out filtered lists of effective technologies. Without any technical expertise, school leaders can simply share resources and encourage teachers to try new things. For example, look at the website noted in the Fieldwork 9.3, below. Consider technology for learning in terms of new classroom tools, concept delivery, assessment tools, and digital environments for learning.

Classroom learning opportunities can be amplified by the introduction of new tools. When students are given the chance to learn with these new tools (Squire & Barab, 2004) they can become more engaged and enthusiastic. In this case, the problem is not encouraging the use of digital technology, but in recognizing the effectiveness of each instance. These tools essentially transform what learning looks like—*simply by using them*. Leaders should encourage teachers to simply allow new technologies for current work.

FIELDWORK 9.3

Set down this book for a moment and look at this "toolbox" of resources for teaching: tinyurl.com/ISLLCToolbox. Over 300 teachers created this list, across the country, that have helped build tool links over the last three years. For most of the applications on this list, teachers claim they will *never teach without them again*. Now, pick out one from each category that you haven't seen before and take 15–20 minutes to try them out, view their tutorials, or get a sense of what they can offer in terms of production and learning for students.

In addition, new online tools are making it ever easier to bring new concepts into classrooms. For instance, emergent digital conversations (like CommonCraft, TED Talks, iTunes University, or P2PU) give instant access to new people and ideas; requiring the bare minimum of technological skill. Start by letting teachers experience for themselves how powerful it can potentially be by using or sharing samples from these resources or passing along one or more of the many new tools available. Find out what challenges exist and advocate for new hardware and policy to free up classroom use.

Familiar formative assessment tools are providing new ways to assess student learning in traditional categories like reading and math skills. In addition, new tools like KidGrid, allow teachers to use an iPhone/iPod Touch, as they work with students to enter assessments, notes, photos, and even grades. In its final iteration, KidGrid will link students, teachers and parents to learning in the classroom in real-time, allowing assessment and parental involvement to overlap.

Finally, new technology is also enabling *environments* that facilitate learning. Sasha Barab and his team in Indiana developed Quest Atlantis—a full three-dimensional simulation of a fantasy community dealing with water pollution and in need of scientists to identify and address the problem (Barab et al., 2009). The groundbreaking Quest2Learn school (New York) has reshaped an entire middle school on the idea that all learning comes through design and play spaces (Salen, 2008). Recent work suggests that even the allowed presence of some hardware tools (like smart phones) can influence learning in a positive way and encourages learning behaviors (Dikkers, Martin, & Coulter, 2012; Squire & Dikkers, 2012).

TECHNOLOGY FOR PROFESSIONAL DEVELOPMENT

Effective instructional leadership can and should mean allocating a budget for learning technologies; however, this should be seen as an end point, not a starting point. In other words, leaders should seek to build the demand for tools because teachers are already experimenting, using, and sharing great 21st century tools with each other—moving contextual and personal technology use to siloed, available, and even ubiquitous technology use where appropriate.

Adult learning follows a developmental process when it comes to adoption of new tools—just like students do. Mimi Ito's team at the University of California, for instance, tracked technology tool acquisition in a large study of over 8,000 hours of online behavior (Ito et al., 2008). They found that before users attained mastery of online settings ("geeking out"), they tended to ease into it gently with what would appear to be "hanging out" and then "messing around". In addition, our nation's most awarded technology-savvy teachers consistently note the importance of trial and error, playing around at home, online communities to talk about learning, and supportive administrators in the professional development process (Dikkers, 2012). Adult learners also need to be eased into new technology use and be internally motivated to try new things because they see or imagine the benefits. Specifically, I advise today's instructional leaders to focus on six professional development activities for technology use:

- Find exemplars of effective use.
- Encourage lifetime learning in all respects.

- Integrate new technology into current professional development.
- Encourage involvement in professional networks (on and offline).
- Introduce virtual tools for collaboration and student work.
- Provide leadership with attitude, aptitude, and planning for technology use.

Instructional leaders look for teachers who are already doing innovative work and share technology exemplars widely. Experts inspire novices to experiment and master new technologies *because* they make teaching more effective and efficient. Professional development led by practicing experts serves to define a workplace that is good for teaching and learning (Leithwood, 2006). Peer-to-peer professional development dovetails with current standards for how teachers learn and develop professional skills best (Hammerness, Darling-Hammond, & Bransford, 2005).

Promoting effective technology means promoting effective professional development that engages teachers with tools that amplify *their own* learning. Many online tools are already available for on-demand professional development including services such as TeacherTrainingVideos.com and other online resources that provide ways for teachers to learn in privacy—reducing the stigma of fumbling with technology in front of your peers. Streaming and online tools allow for teachers to learn as they go and some paid services allow principals to track usage for professional development. These are simple solutions. Complex solutions are seen in the growing effort to build professional learning communities and networks.

Professional networks around teaching are some of the most robust learning environments already in place. Teachers who are new to technology can find access to key mentors (Hobson et al., 2008) in digital settings too. These digital settings have already served as a connection point for teachers that learn in community with other practitioners as both experts and mentors. Often the activity in these digital spaces surrounds lesson ideas (Thinkfinity, Connexions, or 4Teachers), resources for class (California Free Textbooks, OpenCourseware, Eztakes, or The Jason Project), or communication between distant students or teachers (ePals, Listenup!, or Edmodo). Teachers organize units for class and simply bookmark digital resources for each— and then share them with each other (Delicious, Google Reader, or NetNewsWire). These access points are exactly how innovative teachers are already connecting to new ideas.

Virtual classrooms are not limited to virtual schools. Tools used in virtual learning spaces are often available to teachers for free. Communication tools like Google Groups or WikiSpaces are available for anyone seeking to coordinate the activities of groups of people. Paid services provide more specificity and some security with technical support (In2Books, EDU20, and Edmodo) for teachers that are ready to go one step further.

Finally, the role of the leader is essential for school achievement (Heck, Larson, & Marcoulides, 1990), teaching quality (Blasé & Blasé, 1998; Quint et al., 2007), and any transformation in practice (Hallinger, 2005; Sheppard, 1996). Without the expectation of digital competency and practice of 21st century skills, teachers have every motivation to teach as they always have, and new teachers follow suit. Leadership matters. Developmental learning towards the use of technology requires leaders to respect and value all the stages of technology learning, allow time for individual teacher development, and provide appropriate resources at each stage to facilitate growth. Formal supervision of 21st century teaching and learning in the teacher evaluation processes is one way to show its importance. Perhaps more importantly, the principal should show informal support for 21st century teaching and learning in conversations, faculty meetings, and professional learning community meetings.

CASE 9.1 JON TANNER'S LEADERSHIP

Technology Director Jon Tanner has one of the most invigorated staffs I had ever encountered doing technology workshops. Their use of new tools, collaboration, sharing, and transformed practice was palatable to the point I had to pull Jon aside and ask, "How are you getting so many teachers to try new technologies with such energy?"

Jon's answer was that he never assigns new technology to teachers. He asks them to take a seminar within the district (taught by himself or another teacher) and use the seminar work time to develop new unit plans that integrate the tools being requested. The seminar is largely a survey of the concepts in this chapter so far—What is technology? What defines appropriate and effective use of technology? What are 21st century skills and why are they important? What resources are available for learning and professional development?

Teachers plan new curriculum then consider what technologies would be useful in the delivery of content and in helping students produce their representations of knowledge. Because the technology budget saves by not "dropping-in" technology where it will not be used, teachers that request new technology with a curricular plan, get it.

These "early adopting" teachers then have effective technology rich classrooms that encourage their neighbors to think about their own practice and what activities would be compelling enough to take the course themselves. The result has been a gradual, growing enthusiasm for seeking, developing, and trying new practices in the classroom. Jon's instructional leadership practices, including his technology budgeting program, have had a positive, cost-saving impact on his school and the entire district.

Questions

1. In what ways did Jon Tanner successfully practice the six professional development activities listed above?
2. How does a program like this play off of natural human practices and networks?
3. What would you change in your district in order to create a program like this?

STRATEGIES FOR LEADERS

New digital technology also influences leadership preparation and development. Digital skills need to be learned by students, teachers, *and* leaders. Leaders who are equipped with knowledge of new technologies, can filter good ones from bad ones, and have experience with technologies are well prepared to provide 21st century leadership in schools. More specifically, new instructional leaders:

Know:

- dimensions of technology (ubiquitous, available, siloed, personal, contextual)
- 21st century learning skills
- how to cultivate a grounded vision and values
- technology skills and strategies (through ongoing learning).

Grounded Vision and Values

Technology does not learn, people do; technology does not teach, teachers do; and technology does not lead, leaders do. Again and again, research bears witness that it is not revolutionary technologies that reform school environments, but a community of passionate, connected, and effective educators grounded in shared values and a vision for continuous school improvement (e.g. Elmore, 2004; Goldring & Rallis, 1993; Hallinger, 2005; Halverson, Kelley, & Kimball, 2004; Leithwood et al., 2004). Technology, at best, serves to make the user more effective and efficient—it serves an existing need and fills it. At worst, technology becomes a distracting focal point and wastes precious time and money. Good technology does not need selling; it sells itself by filling existing needs and enabling innovative practices.

Effective school leaders need to understand and have context for their work in terms of technology in and out of schools—both informing the other and how their decisions are only part of the larger context of students' lives. In other words, the new instructional leader is committed to technology as means for democratizing access to high quality education.

CASE 9.2 C. CRYSS BRUNNER'S EXPERIENTIAL SIMULATIONS© (ES) MODEL

Using standard online development tools—website, chat room, threaded discussion, video, and audio clips—I have developed virtual instructional/preparation/task-oriented experiences and processes in which participants, first with real identities masked and later altered completely, meet online to collaborate on an assigned problem-based learning and/or decision-making task (the simulation). Experiential Simulations (ES) involve the immersion of participants (who are unaware of the shifts in their identities) in an environment in which they are perceived by the others as having an identity unlike their "true" identity (Brunner, Hammel, & Miller, 2003). For example, the altered identity reflects a gender/racial/class/positional identity other than that to which they are accustomed (women may be men; whites may be people of color). While interacting with others in this virtual environment, participants "walk in the shoes" of someone constructed differently from themselves. The interactions occur in carefully designed leadership/policy forming situations, intended to illustrate how perceptions and understandings of others' identity shapes the way leaders enhance or restrict others' participation in decision-making and task completion. At the same time, through private communication with me [the instructor], participants reflect on questions posed related to identity constructs (gender, race, class, age, etc.), power conceptions, and the decision-making dynamics at play within the group (Brunner, Opsal, & Oliva, 2006). Essentially, there are two main aspects of this innovation. One entails using computer technology to modify a person's appearance and voice. Simply modifying a person's appearance and voice to get a different response from an audience is not new. What is new is the modification of a person's appearance in order to get a different response from an audience, *and* having the person with the modified persona learn lessons, pertinent to social justice, from their experience of immersion in that response (Miller & Brunner, 2008).

Ongoing Acquisition of Skills and Strategies

Technology for leadership also includes tools that keep leaders current. Useful tools like the annual Horizon Report (Johnson et al., 2011) summarize what experts in new media technologies see coming for education. This report provides overviews of emerging technologies, sample projects, as well as additional resources for ongoing learning. For instance, this year's review includes summaries of electronic books, mobile use, augmented reality, game-based learning, gesture based computing, and learning analytics; all topics that school leaders should be prepared to make learning decisions around and assessments for when they find their way into classrooms.

Professional technology networks are available for leaders, too. "Staying connected" in isolation is antithetical. Effective leader network and digital technologies can amplify this. Online communities (e.g. ConnectedPrincipals) are an invaluable source for leaders to gather input on technology practices with regards to learning. Although these online communities have some similarities to teacher networks and toolboxes, but they are personalized and specialized for leadership. It is. For more on school leadership networks, visit the American Association of School Administrators (AASA) listing of leadership networks (www.aasa.org/LeadershipNetworks).

FIELDWORK 9.4

Set up and maintain your own accessible list of resources for professional development. This can be kept on a hyperlinked spreadsheet, a set of RSS feeds and a "reader", or use bookmarking tools in your browser. Find tools, networks, and news services that will keep you current in your own practice.

Be able to:

- effectively use technologies for managing data
- effectively use technology for formative assessment
- capitalize on technology to support engagement or flow
- use technology to support social and professional learning
- provide ongoing professional development in technology.

Effective use of technologies for managing data

Effective instructional leaders also stay current in using technology to access data that guides school decision-making processes (e.g. Abrutyn, 2006; Earl & Katz, 2002; Halverson & Thomas, 2007; Knapp, Copland, & Swinnerton, 2007). The use of data-driven decision-making has to be led by local school leaders who understand how to measure, what to measure, and have a focus on student learning (Halverson & Thomas, 2007; Knapp et al., 2007; Robinson, Lloyd, & Rowe, 2008). All technology adoption should be measured in terms of student learning (Wayman, Midgley, & Springfield, 2006). For instance, leaders must use data to monitor student and program effectiveness. Effective instructional leaders must have familiarity with current technology, skills to identify redundancy (i.e., digital surveys instead of paper ones—*in the classroom*), and strategies to increase outcomes (i.e., digital surveys instead of paper ones—*for parent feedback)* for each situation.

Effective use of technology for formative feedback

In Chapter 6, formative assessment of student learning is addressed as a key tool for teachers to guide student learning during the instructional process. Formative assessment systems also examine leadership development, using technology-driven data to inform practice. Formative school data, such as that provided by ValEd, CALL, or SCS, allow leaders descriptive and (soon) prescriptive lenses for leading their schools (Halverson, 2010; Halverson et al., 2004) with reflective, data-driven distributed leadership (Knapp, Copland, & Talbert, 2003). Built upon a decade of leadership research work (Leithwood, Mascall, & Strauss, 2009) these tools also exemplify high-tech manifestations of technology-informed research. 21st century administrative programs should prepare leaders with experience in using formative assessment tools, instruction in how to interpret data, and in how to identify research-based processes aimed at improved student learning.

CASE 9.3 BRANCHING NARRATIVES FOR LEADERSHIP DEVELOPMENT

Dr. Richard Halverson and colleagues experimented with an educational leadership class that asked prospective administrators to build an online interactive narrative for their final project (Halverson, Blakesley, & Figueiredo-Brown, 2010). Students in Dr. Halverson's class build each "conversation path" into a sort of game (much like the "Choose your own adventure" books of the 1980s) only for school leaders. Future classes can play these student-created games, modify them, and build their own based on future class topics.

Similarly, in Dr. Halverson's Introduction to Leadership course, adult learners needed to learn how to make complex decisions by weighing a range of options available to leaders. Chris Blakesley, a specialist in interactive narrative design, and two former principals were brought in to help Richard Halverson design a course that placed this problem solving skill at the center of the classes' activity. The challenge was to get students to think like experienced administrators through a design challenge.

The focus was on post-observation conferences with teachers. Instead of a lecture on the topic, students were asked to build a game where the player would have conversational options that would lead to different outcomes. Students had to learn "realistic" conversation threads and then test them on each other and field studies to make a design that represented their understanding of leadership options. Not only did the future leaders learn more about the complex choices leaders make (because they had to build them), but they discovered that the design challenges drew more of their natural interest; they reported spending far more time on the class, but enjoyed the collective problem solving, challenge, and found pride in the final product and its contribution to other future learners.

EXTENDED REFLECTION 9.3

At the beginning of this chapter, you developed a list of all the ways technology impacts learning in and out of schools. What did you add to this list as you read the chapter?

SUMMARY

This chapter explored the dimensions of technology that are important for today's instructional leaders: production, engagement, flow, new affordances, social learning, and effective use informed by professional development. In addition, this chapter also reviewed 21st century skills expected of learners. This chapter reviewed specific examples of technology for professional development, leadership tasks, and formative assessment of school practices. Technology for learning is not only a central topic for changing learning practices; in many cases, it *is* the change. Effective instructional leaders are *always* learning more about technology for learners, technology for teachers, and technology for their own practices.

REFERENCES

Abrutyn, L. (2006). The most important data. *Education Leadership, 63*(6), 54–57.

Armstrong, V., Barnes, S., Sutherland, R., Curran, S., Mills, S., & Thompson, I. (2005). Collaborative research methodology for investigating teaching and learning: The use of interactive whiteboard technology. *Educational Review, 57*(4), 457–469.

Barab, S. A., Scott, B., Siyahhan, S., Goldstone, R., Ingram-Goble, A., Zuiker, S. J., & Warren, S. (2009). Transformational play as a curricular scaffold: Using videogames to support science education. *Journal of Science Education and Technology, 18*(4), 305–320.

Blasé, R. & Blasé, J. (1998). *Handbook of instructional leadership: How really good principals promote teaching and learning.* Thousand Oaks, CA: Corwin Press.

Bruner, G. (1961). The act of discovery. *Harvard Educational Review, 31*(1), 21–32.

Brunner, C. C., Hammel, K., & Miller, M. D. (2003). Transforming leadership preparation for social justice: Dissatisfaction, inspiration, and rebirth—An exemplar. In F. Lunenburg & C. Carr (Eds.). *Professors and practitioners: Building bridges through leadership: NCPEA yearbook—2003* (pp. 70–84). Toronto, Ontario: Scarecrow Education.

Brunner, C. C., Opsal, C., & Olivia, M. (2006). Disrupting identity: Fertile soil for raising social consciousness in educational leaders. In C. Marshall & M. Oliva (Eds.). *Leading for social justice: Making revolutions in education* (pp. 214–232). Thousand Oaks, CA: Sage.

Castranova, E. (2010). Build your own Sheldon syllabus. Retrieved from http://terranova.blogs.com/terra_nova/2010/03/build-your-own-sheldon-syllabus.html

Chohan, A. (2011). Learning without frontiers talk: Essa Academy. Paper presented at the Learning Without Frontiers conference, London.

Comer, J. C. & Wikle, T. A. (2008). Worldwide diffusion of the cellular telephone, 1995–2005. *The Professional Geographer, 60*(2), 252–269.

Consalvo, M. (2007). *Cheating: Gaining advantage in videogames*. Cambridge, MA: The MIT Press.

Csikszentmihalyi, M. (1990). *Flow: The psychology of optimal experience*. New York: Harper and Row.

Dewey, J. (1933/1910). *How we think: A restatement of the relation of reflective thinking to the educative process*. Boston, MA: D. C. Heath and Company.

Dikkers, S. (2012). The professional development trajectories of teachers successfully integrating and practicing with new information and communication technologies. (Ph.D. dissertation). University of Wisconsin, Madison.

Dikkers, S., Martin, J., & Coulter, R. (Eds.). (2012). *Mobile media learning: Amazing uses of mobile devices for learning*. Pittsburgh, PA: ETC Press.

diSessa, A. (2000). *Changing minds: Computers, learning, and literacy*. Cambridge, MA: The MIT Press.

Earl, L. & Katz, S. (2002). Leading schools in a data-rich world. In K. Leithwood & P. Hallinger (Eds.). *Second international handbook of educational leadership and administration*. Dordrecht, The Netherlands: Kluwer.

Elmore, R. F. (2004). *School reform from the inside out: Policy, practice, and performance*. Cambridge, MA: Harvard Universtiy Press.

Fisher, D. & Stolarchuk, E. (1998). The effect of using laptop computers on achievement, attitude to science and classroom environment in science. Paper presented at the Western Australia institute for Educational Research Forum 1998 [Online].

Gardner, J. (1994). *Personal portable computers and the curriculum*. Edinburgh, UK: Scottish Council for Research in Education.

Gee, J. P. (2007). *What video games have to teach us about learning and literacy*. New York: Palgrave Macmillan.

Goldring, E. B. & Rallis, S. F. (1993). *Principals of dynamic schools: Taking charge of change*. Newbury Park, CA: Corwin Press.

Hallinger, P. (2005). Instructional leadership and the school principal: A passing fancy that refuses to fade away. College of Management, Mahidol University, Thailand.

Halverson, R. (2010). School formative feedback systems. *Peabody Journal of Education, 85*(2), 130–146.

Halverson, R., Blakesley, C., & Figueiredo-Brown, R. (2010). Video game design as a model for professional learning. In C. Lankshear, M. Knobel & M. Peters (Eds.). *Learning to play: Exploring the future of education with video games* (pp. 9–28). New York: Peter Lang.

Halverson, R., Kelley, C., & Kimball, S. (2004). Implementing teacher evaluation systems: How principals make sense of complex artifacts to shape local instructional practice. In W. K. Hoy

& C. G. Miskel (Eds.). *Educational administration, policy and reform: Research and measurement research and theory in educational administration* (Vol. 3). Greenwich, CT: Information Age Press.

Halverson, R. & Thomas, C. (2007). *The roles and practices of student services staff as data-driven instructional leaders*. Madison, WI: Wisconsin Center for Educational Research.

Hammerness, K., Darling-Hammond, L., & Bransford, J. (2005). How teachers learn and develop. In L. Darling-Hammond & J. Bransford (Eds.). *Preparing teachers for a changing world* (pp. 358–389). San Francisco, CA: Jossey-Bass.

Heck, R., Larson, T., & Marcoulides, G. (1990). Principal instructional leadership and school achievement: Validation of a causal model. *Educational Administration Quarterly, 26*, 94–125.

Hobson, A. J., Ashby, P., Malderez, A., & Tomlinson, P. D. (2008). Mentoring beginning teachers: What we know and what we don't. *Teaching and Teacher Education, 25*(1), 207–216.

Horst, H. A. & Miller, D. (2006). *The cell phone: An anthropology of communications*. New York: Berg.

Hughes, J. (2009). New media, new literacies and the adolescent learner. *E-Learning, 6*(3), 265–288.

The International Society for Technology in Education (ISTE) (Producer). (2009). International Society for Technolgoy in Education Website: ISTE Standards. Retrieved from www.iste.org/AM/Template.cfm?Section=NETS

Ito, M., Horst, H., Bittanti, M., Boyd, d., Herr-Stephenson, B., & Lange, P. G. (2008). *Living and learning with new media: Summary of findings from the digital youth project*. Chicago, IL: The MacArthur Foundation.

Jenkins, H., Purushotma, R., Weigel, M., Clinton, K., & Robinson, A. J. (2009). *Confronting the challenges of participatory culture: Media education for the 21st century*. The John D. and Catherine T. MacArthur Foundation Reports on Digital Media and Learning. Cambridge, MA: The MacArthur Foundation.

Johnson, L., Smith, R., Willis, H., Levine, A., & Haywood, K. (2011). *The 2011 Horizon Report*. Austin, TX: The New Media Consortium.

Juul, J. (2009). Fear of Failing? The many meanings of difficulty in video games. In M. J. P. Wolf & B. Perron (Eds.). *The video game theory reader 2* (pp. 237–252). New York: Routledge.

Kennewell, S. (Producer). (2006). Reflections on the interactive whiteboard phenomenon: a synthesis of research from the UK Swansea School of Education. Retrieved from www.aare.edu.au/06pap/ken06138.pdf

Klopfer, E. & Squire, K. (2008). Environmental detectives—the development of augmented platforms for environmental simulations. *Education Tech Research Development, 56*, 203–228.

Knapp, M. S., Copland, M. A., & Swinnerton, J. A. (2007). Understanding the promise and dynamics of data-informed leadership. In P. A. Moss (Ed.). *Evidence and decision making* (pp. 74–104). Malden, MA: Blackwell.

Knapp, M. S., Copland, M. A., & Talbert, J. F. (2003). *Leading for learning: Reflective tools for school and district leaders*. Seattle, WA: Center for the Study of Teaching and Policy, University of Washington.

Lankshear, C. & Knobel, M. (Eds.). (2008). *Digital literacies: concepts, policies, and practices* (Vol. 30). New York: Peter Lang.

Leithwood, K. (2006). *Teacher working conditions that matter: Evidence for change*. Toronto, Ontario: Elementary Teachers' Federation of Ontario.

Leithwood, K., Mascall, B., & Strauss, T. E. (2009). *Distributed leadership according to the evidence*. New York: Routledge.

Leithwood, K., Seashore Louis, K., Anderson, S., & Wahlstrom, K. (2004). *Executive summary: How leadership influences student learning*. New York: The Wallace Foundation.

Lowther, D. L., Ross, S. M., & Morrison, G. M. (2003). When each one has one: The influences on teaching strategies and student achievement of using laptops in the classroom. *Educational Technology Research and Development, 51*(3), 23–44.

Miller, M. D. & Brunner, C. C. (2008). Social impact in technologically-mediated communication: An examination of online influence. *Computers in Human Behavior, 24*(6), 2972–2991.

Moss, G., Jewitt, C., Levaaic, R., Armstrong, V., Cardini, A., & Castle, F. (2007). *The interactive whiteboard, pedagogy and pupil performance evaluation: An evaluation of the schools whiteboard expansion (SWE) project*. London: London Challenge.

New London Group. (1996). A pedagogy of multiliteracies: Designing social futures. In B. Cope & M. Kalantzis (Eds.). *Multiliteracies: Literacy learning and the design of social futures*. New York: Routledge.

New Media Consortium. (2005). *A Global Imperative: The Report on the 21st Century Literacy Summit*. Stanford, CA: The New Media Consortium.

Penuel, W. (2006). Implementation and effects of one-to-one computing initiatives: A research synthesis. *Journal of Research on Technology in Education, 38*(3), 329–348.

Piaget, J. (1950). *The psychology of intelligence*. New York: Routledge.

Pink, D. (2009). *Drive: The surprising truth about what motivates us*. New York: Riverhead Books.

Prensky, M. (2006). *Don't bother me Mom—I'm learning*. St. Paul, MN: Paragon House.

Quint, J. C., Akey, T. M., Rappaport, S., & Willner, C. J. (2007). *Instructional leadership, teaching quality, and student acheivement: Suggestive evidence from three urban school districts*. New York: MDRC.

Rideout, V., Foehr, U. G., & Roberts, D. F. (2010). *Generation M2: Media in the lives of 8- to 18-year-olds*. Kaiser Family Foundation Studies. Menlo Park, CA: Henry J. Kaiser Family Foundation.

Robinson, V. M., Lloyd, C. A., & Rowe, K. J. (2008). The impact of leadership on student outcomes: An analysis of the differential effects of leadership types. *Educational Administration Quarterly, 44*(5), 635–674.

Salen, K. (2008). *The ecology of games: connecting youth, games, and learning*. Cambridge, MA: MIT Press.

Sheppard, B. (1996). Exploring the transformational nature of instructional leadership. *The Alberta Journal of Educational Research, XLII*(4), 325–344.

Squire, K. & Barab, S. (2004). Replaying history: Engaging urban undeserved students in learning world history. Paper presented at the 6th international conference on Learning sciences, Los Angeles, CA.

Squire, K. & Dikkers, S. (2012). Amplifications of learning: Use of mobile media devices among youth. *Convergence: The International Journal of Research into New Media Technologies*. Retrieved from http://con.sagepub.com/content/early/2012/02/15/1354856511429646.full.pdf+html

Trilling, B. & Fadel, C. (2009). *21st century skills: Learning for life in our times*. San Francisco, CA: Jossey-Bass.

Vygotsky, L. S. (1978). *Mind in Society: The development of higher mental processes*. Cambridge, MA: Harvard University Press.

Wayman, J. C., Midgley, S. & Springfield, S. (2006). Leadership for data-based decision making: Collaborative educator teams. Paper presented at the Annual meeting of the American Educational Research Association.

Wertsch, J. (1991). *Voices of the mind: A sociocultural approach to mediated action*. Cambridge, MA: Harvard University Press.

CHAPTER 10

Monitor and Evaluate the Impact of the Instructional Program

Lynnette Brunderman and Thad Dugan

KEY TOPICS

- Organizational Learning and the Instructional Program
- Systemic Program Evaluation
- The Importance of Teams
- The Importance of Capacity

According to ISLLC Standard 2, effective leaders monitor and evaluate the impact of the instructional program. The No Child Left Behind Act and related policies have clearly increased the demand for instructional leaders who can do this. In order to monitor and fully evaluate specific instructional programs, leaders need to have a strong self-awareness, relationships with others, and a recognition of the interdependent nature of schools as complex social systems. In other words, today's instructional leaders must be able to build capacity for deep democratic learning (Hackney & Henderson, this volume) and continuous improvement at all levels of the system. Planned school changes must address root causes of problems as these problems affect all aspects of the system (e.g. curriculum, instruction, decision-making processes, parent involvement). Evaluation occurring daily as part of everyday work can provide the basis for self-awareness, organizational learning, and continuous improvement of the system. Reflections, fieldwork, and cases help develop leaders who are able to monitor and evaluate the impact of their instructional programs as part of organizational learning and continuous improvement.

ORGANIZATIONAL LEARNING

Organizational learning (or organizational change theories) share a common belief that organizations are complex but flexible entities. Mitchell and Sackney (2000), for instance, define organizational learning as the capacity to use past experience to make better decisions in the future. Individual learning, the flow of knowledge, and subsequent changes in individual and institutional behavior are necessary functions for organizational change (Huber, 1991). Moreover, we contend that capacity involves a simultaneous development of individual and organizational learning and growth. Such development requires leaders to cultivate self- and collective-awareness as well as organizational change. In other words, the individual develops the organization and the organization develops the individual. Individual and organizational growth depend on leaders who cultivate a deep consciousness and action-orientation toward equity and justice.

DiBella and Nevis (1998) proposed an integrated strategy to build the capacity of an organization to learn. They contend that an organization's capacity to learn is related to learning orientations or mental models. If an organization has the ability to learn, it can change to build a desired future (Senge, 1990). Organizations capable of adapting and learning have been characterized by Senge (1990) according to five core "disciplines" or aptitudes:

1. personal mastery
2. mental models
3. shared vision
4. team learning
5. systems thinking.

Each of these disciplines is described below.

PERSONAL MASTERY

Organizations only learn through individuals, so successful organizations must be populated with employees who are always learning (Senge, 1990). If institutions depend on individual learning, professional development is key. In spite of the growing emphasis on accountability, many educators are not "data literate". Personal mastery of assessment literacy is critical for school improvement processes in today's schools. Assessment literacy includes proficiency with using formative and summative data, research designs, and methods. Schools should develop systematic procedures to improve the personal capacity of staff to use data and understand evaluation reports. At the same time, leaders must cultivate self- and collective-awareness that there is anonymity in numbers. In other words, assessment literacy is about people engaged in democratic under-standings of individual and collective growth as well as learning and achievement. Take a few minutes to develop your personal mastery in how to observe and use student assessment data.

FIELDWORK 10.1

Discover Your Data

David Baker, Flowing Wells School District, Tucson, Arizona

Data-driven decision making is almost a universal statement for school improve-ment. Unfortunately, our school systems are often inundated with data and the challenge is to make operational interventions. In a two-step process, it is possible to observe facts from a data set and swiftly establish a path for improvement.

Step 1: Form a team of stakeholders, usually the department or grade level teachers, and identify *facts* about the data set. In order to provide clarity and focus in the observation process, the team should compare its data against a benchmark. Three easily accessible benchmarks may be frequency, internal variance, and external variance.

- **Frequency:** Identify number of items in a tested strand or concept relative to the entire assessment.
- **Internal variance:** Identify the variance between standards, concepts, teachers, programs or other data found in the site-level data.
- **External variance:** Identify the variance between overall performance of the site against external data like the state performance, national performance, similar demographic schools/districts or expected level of performance.

Step 2: Stakeholders review the data based on the established benchmark and then ask a question or make an inference about the observational facts. Stakeholders should commit in writing to a question and/or inference in order to focus the discussion and serve as a reference document. This process creates a focused discussion that can lead to an immediate and actionable step.

Once stakeholders identify an area of focus, it is important to review the standard or assessment to check for understanding. In other words, does everyone under-stand how the data is measured in the assessment. It is a necessary and often overlooked step to actually review the publicly released standards, assessment items, or assessment instructional reports to develop an understanding of how a student or group of students is measured. Once a clear understanding of the assessment is developed, the stakeholders can decide on a course of action that may include re-teaching, pulling out support, reorganization of instructional units, creating a formative assessment, or rethinking the utility of a district assessment.

Discussion

With materials prepared, a principal-led discovery can be completed in about 30 minutes. By condensing the process into a succinct meeting, the potential for creating and implementing an intervention(s) increases significantly. Time management, actionable plans, and administrative feedback are important variables in school improvement. The meeting may end with the *identifying resources* and *calendaring* dates to monitor progress. Approach this meeting as an opportunity to establish your expectations about using student achievement data, building a relationship with stakeholders, and focusing on improvement. These meetings can be productive by eliminating any discussion discounting the data and focusing on a team approach to increasing student achievement. We all want the best for our students and no one can do it alone.

When working with staff on this kind of data analysis activity, you will quickly observe various mental models or perceptions in action.

MENTAL MODELS

Deeply ingrained assumptions about the world influence perception, personal behavior, and organizational behavior (Senge et al., 2000). These beliefs provide a basis for decisions and operations and promote organizational improvement. Mental models in education would change school improvement expectations beyond "quick fixes" to long-term outcomes, unexpected results, and more sophisticated analyses of programs connected to democratic aims. Because organizational change takes time, mental models should include an expectation that three to five years will be required, but continuous progressive improvements should be expected. Outside evaluations help determine continuation or abandonment of newly implemented programs, establish a tradition in which learning builds over years, and provide the basis for improvements to slowly integrate into the organization. Evaluations, which are used to improve programs, can help to revise mental models when accountability, programs, and evaluations are designed congruently involving the staff, sufficient support, and democratic leadership.

FIELDWORK 10.2

Confronting Mental Models

You are an elementary school principal, and your faculty is all female, except for the physical education teacher. As you work with your teachers on the development of curriculum and lesson plans, you begin to notice a subconscious prejudice about expectations for students depending on gender. When you observe classes, you notice that boys are called upon more in science lessons, and that they typically take the lead in the labs and experiments. You also notice that girls are called upon more frequently to answer questions in reading lessons. As the teachers lead discussions about the reading selections, the teachers express an obvious opinion about gender roles in the family. If you hadn't looked at the calendar, you'd think you were in the 1950s, as indicated by some of the comments made by the teachers about the roles of moms and dads in discussions and stories about families. You also notice that boys and girls are disciplined differently at recess. Some of the aggressive behavior that the boys exhibit is not tolerated in the girls when they exhibit the same behaviors. The teachers seem to dismiss the boys' behavior as "boys will be boys". But they are quick to criticize the girls by saying, "Young ladies don't act that way."

Although you have a very dedicated and collaborative faculty, you realize that they most likely are influencing student success based on gender. As you look at the state test scores, you notice that the boys score significantly higher in math and the girls score significantly higher in reading. You could dismiss this as typical of the interests of boys and girls at this age, but you strongly suspect that your faculty members might unknowingly be contributing to this achievement gap.

As principal of this school, what would you do? Explain, in bulleted format, a process for handling this challenge.

(Excerpted from Midlock, 2011, p. 135)

SHARED VISION

Without a common vision—and the humility to learn from each other and develop a common vision—members of an organization may be guided by individual values and interpretations that result in personal agendas and limit productivity. Senge (1990, p. 9) defines shared vision as "the capacity to hold a shared picture of the future we seek to create". Effective leaders facilitate a shared vision of the ideal future by providing quantifiable benchmarks that bring it closer to the ideal (DuFour, 1999). Organizations help or hinder this process, depending on the degree to which members discuss, identify, and agree on goals and share the vision for the common good (Goodstein, Nolan, & Pfeiffer, 1992). In schools with a shared vision, it is easier to promote improvements and develop effective programs supported by teachers, administrators, and staff. Top-down accountability cannot force shared vision and often faces resistance. Nor does vision alone stand in an environment of unyielding accountability. If vision and leadership support school accountability, schools can link student outcomes, curriculum goals, instruction, students' funds of knowledge, and decision-making to an overarching plan.

As indicated in Chapter 6, schools should also seek to provide timely and more specialized formative feedback. School leadership can use formative evaluations to develop a shared vision and a shared vision can promote a culture that values formative evaluations. For example, a vision in which "all students will learn" can be supported if the school develops and implements a comprehensive data-based system documenting individual student progress. By recording student growth, schools develop feedback systems supporting and sharing the reality of "all students will learn". See specific formative assessment strategies in Chapter 6.

TEAM LEARNING

Organizations must have collective wisdom that transforms individual thoughts into organization problem-solving in order to resolve complex issues. Coaches, mentors, and leaders facilitate groups within organizations that have a capacity to learn; leaders help teams suspend ineffectual patterns and collectively arrive at desired results (Senge, 1990; Senge et al., 2000). Effective feedback encourages team learning by presenting information useful to the group once data is made available, understood, and used for decision-making. If used effectively, the results of program evaluations can promote team learning. At the same time, team learning will promote improved program evaluations and better applications of results. Consider the team learning strategies required in the case study below.

CASE 10.1 BUILDING CAPACITY FOR TEAM LEARNING

After profiling the faculty at Taylor High School, the principal, Ed Jackson, realizes that there are seven veteran teachers with over twenty years of experience. Although Ed knows that these seven teachers will be retiring in four years, he is concerned about providing vital learning opportunities for them. He does the math: a teacher who teaches thirty students per class period, five periods a day, will teach some 600 students in four years. Those last four years of these veterans' careers could and should be as invigorating as the beginning years.

The faculty profile also shows that for the past few years, Taylor High School has hired approximately eleven new teachers each year to replace retiring teachers. Jackson and his administrative team develop a mentoring strategy that pairs new teachers with veteran teachers nearing retirement. A defining feature of the strategy is that these teachers will go through professional development as pairs, learning with and from one another.

- If you wanted to implement a program such as this, what would you need to do to ensure that both the veteran and the beginning teacher could learn from each other?
- What types of support would teachers need to participate in such a plan?
- How could such a plan be implemented in the school where you work?

(Excerpted from Zepeda, 2012, p. 222)

SYSTEMS THINKING

Organizations are composed of interdependent components that function together, hopefully toward shared goals that are driven by policies, strategies, and so forth. Systems thinking requires that organizational components constantly review, re-evaluate, and stabilize in the short term so that entire system plans can be strategically aligned with resources and processes (Senge, 1990). "Systems thinking" drives continuous improvement and discourages organizations and individuals from repeatedly making the same mistakes.

Schools that design and implement effective feedback are able to illuminate factors associated with effective instruction, diverse learning, complex interactions, and intentional and unintended outcomes. Such formative feedback is a component of program evaluation and helps promote systems thinking by measuring impacts of various interactions across the school. Knowledge and analysis of interactivity and effectiveness within a school expands institutional skill and capacity when members are involved in team learning. Staff members can develop the ability to distinguish among short-term improvements, symptoms, and root causes of problems, and they can learn to discriminate between low-level or first-order changes and more meaningful second-order changes (Marzano, Waters, & McNulty, 2005). In other words, these schools have high levels of capacity to develop and sustain substantive changes. See the Systematic Program Evaluation activity in the Appendix, which provides a needs assessment for capacity building at all levels of the system.

Organizations with these five disciplines in place have evidence of high capacity for organization learning and growth (Mitchell & Sackney, 2000). Specific characteristics of high capacity schools are described below. As you read these characteristics, think about your own school. Would you characterize your school as a "high capacity school"? Why or why not?

HIGH CAPACITY SCHOOLS

High capacity schools are learning communities capable of resiliency, democratic learning, and development. Mitchell and Sackney (2000) use an ecological metaphor to explain systems thinking in learning communities, meaning that the system is self-regulating and self-sustaining. He warns, however, that ecosystems are fragile and that certain conditions can damage the system's ability to thrive or to survive. Here organizational learning occurs in ebbs and flows, depending on the focus for improvement at particular times. Similar to Senge's (1990) five disciplines, learning communities consider three aspects: (1) personal; (2) interpersonal; and (3) organizational (Mitchell & Sackney, 2000). That is, the development of a learning community comes about through the interplay among personal abilities, interpersonal relationships, and organizational structures. Growth occurs as personal, interpersonal, and organizational capacities increase; it is limited as they decrease.

Building personal capacity

From the perspective of schools, personal capacity is an amalgamation of all the embedded values, assumptions, beliefs, and practical knowledge that teachers carry with them and of the professional networks and knowledge bases with which they connect. Building personal capacity involves self-awareness and purposeful work on mental models or the assumptions, values, and beliefs in such a way that teachers come to grips with the personal narratives that shape and constrain their professional practice and learning. This work is necessary because new learning always confronts prior knowledge, values, belief systems, and even unconscious biases regarding class, gender, race, and so forth. If these embedded structures operate out of conscious awareness, then their influence on professional renewal is not open to scrutiny, and their tacit operation could undermine professional learning opportunities. Peeling back the embedded layers of prior knowledge, beliefs, and values frees teachers to reconstruct their professional narrative in the face of complex challenges or difficult problems.

When teachers confront their deep-seated beliefs about education and society, they must be willing to engage in an internal assessment of their professional knowledge, beliefs, practices, assumptions, and values. Further, these teachers must be willing to identify gaps in their knowledge and tensions in their beliefs about education. This search for personal awareness/capacity, then, helps the individual understand the degree to which he/she has access to new or different professional ideas. As a result of this internal and external examination, teachers develop a professional narrative. The following questions are very helpful in this process:

- Who am I as a teacher now?
- How am I most skillful?
- Where do I want to grow?
- What inspires me to develop my capacities?

Answers to these questions are the foundation for building personal capacity. Argyris and Schon (1978) write about the importance of congruence between the espoused theory (what we say we believe or do) and the theory-in-use (what we actually do). In other words, do we walk our talk in our classroom and in our schools? When teachers answer these questions honestly, they engage in critical reflection on the relationships among embedded beliefs, actual practices, and the effects of practice (Mitchell & Sackney, 2000). In general, according to Mitchell and Sackney, when unintended effects prevail, there is cause to wonder if the espoused theory is out of alignment with the theory-in-use. Furthermore, if the unintended effects are causing problems for an individual teacher's students, colleagues, or personal learning, there is an indication that the learning community is at risk.

Building interpersonal capacity

Building interpersonal capacity shifts the focus from the individual to the group. At the core of this component lies collegial relations and collective practice. "Relationships, more than information, determine how problems get solved or opportunities exploited" (Mitchell & Sackney, 2000, p. 37). In other words, the construction of professional knowledge is no longer the solitary pursuit of one individual. Instead, it is a heavily contested process of negotiation among different people with different knowledge bases, different histories, different styles, and different values. Under these conditions, the climate within which people work becomes a concern of deep importance because, over time, educators (and others) internalize the expectations and norms that have developed within the school. The process of internalization leads to routine behaviors as educators come to accept open dialogue about practice as "the way we do things around here". In a learning community, where individual and collective learning are deeply embedded in one another, contradictions and paradoxes are welcome (Swieringa & Wierdsma, 1992). What is important is not so much the *solution* to any given problem but *authentic consensus* about how the problem should be solved. The learning arises from solving the problem, and different solutions to the same problem can be found in different contexts and with different group members.

The process of learning also includes an element of unlearning. This too is a difficult process because so much emotional energy is tied up with what is known and valued. The contested and emotional nature of learning, then, implies that attention needs to be paid to the affective and cognitive conditions operating within the school culture. Further, we argue that leaders need to consider the broader sociocultural context as it influences the ways in which students, teachers, and leaders approach curriculum and instructional practice. According to Isaacs (1999), dialogue includes the skills of listening, respecting, suspending, and voicing. Teachers listen with respect to others' ideas and perspectives about practice. They suspend judgment about the value of a particular practice as they listen. At the same time, learning community members have the trust and respect to question each other's ideas and offer constructive feedback. These skills provide the necessary safety net for deep dialogue and critical inquiry that characterize a learning community. In other words, building interpersonal capacity involves a high functioning team of people who work and learn together. Instructional leaders need to model and support the distinctions between advocacy (the advancement of one's opinion or belief) and communication that is characterized by questions as often as by statements (the exploration of a colleague's opinion about practice). Communication patterns characterized by questions and dialogue allow individuals to contribute freely without the fear of recrimination or reprisal and opens spaces for consideration of sensitive issues, problems of purpose, and unarticulated dreams or dreads (Mitchell & Sackney, 2000).

Schools in which teachers engage in an honest assessment of their skills and make their practice public have a strong foundation for the development of a learning organization. Such organizations have the opportunity for authentic dialogue about practice and more difficult conversations, such as racial/ethnic achievement gaps, the hidden curriculum, and other social inequities (see Chapter 3). Principals must learn how to facilitate authentic dialogue and difficult conversations as part of collaboration processes. In many schools, principals stop debates or conflict in favor of polite interaction. While politeness is an appropriate goal for school cultures, teachers must feel comfortable to engage in honest dialogue about practice. Schools that learn through authentic dialogue have interpersonal capacity for learning and continuous improvement.

Shared understandings and new practices do not emerge immediately or easily. Indeed, shared understandings develop through a series of phases that typify team development in many settings. The first phase, which Mitchell and Sackney (2000) have labeled "naming and framing", affords teachers the time and space to define the context and the working parameters of a particular issue. In the first phase, teachers ask, "What is the meaning of this?". They listen not only to others but also to themselves because it is as important for them to confront their own thoughts as to discover the thoughts of others. Once the team members develop personal and shared understandings, they enter what Isaacs (1999) calls a "crisis of collective pain" (p. 363). Here teachers/learning community members analyze and integrate old information and new information; they confront old habits, engage in a genuine dialogue and deconstruct their individual and group narratives. In the final phase, individuals see themselves as part of a collective whole and begin to reconstruct professional practice. Mitchell and Sackney (2000) call this phase "experimenting and applying" because it is here that members find new and creative solutions to the problems they face. Interpersonal capacity generates a shared inspiration and learning power that can lead to increased empowerment and expanded capacity to improve teaching and learning among all members. In so doing, school members build organizational capacity.

Building Organizational Capacity

Organizational capacity begins with the awareness that structural arrangements can open doors for teachers, break down walls between them, or keep people away from one another. That is, personal and interpersonal capacities are deeply affected by the kinds of organizations within which individuals work. A learning community requires a different kind of organizational structure than the traditional structures in place in most schools. Traditional school structures have typically been characterized by separation of individual administrators, teachers and students and power imbalances whereby administrators or groups control the decision-making processes. These conditions have served to isolate teachers and students, to minimize contact among educators, to reduce flexibility and professional discretion, and to engender defensiveness and resistance among the professional staff (and among students). Such conditions are not conducive to the creation of a learning community, nor are they likely to generate profound improvements in teaching and learning.

Mitchell and Sackney (2000) argue that the first walls to be breached are the walls that exist in people's minds. The norms of privacy and individualism, although deeply entrenched in many schools, do not advance professional learning nor do they promote continuous improvement. For these norms to be overcome, structural arrangements need to bring individual educators (teachers and leaders) into close professional contact with one another and to bring the socio-cultural conditions into view. One way to confront socio-cultural norms is to get them out in the open.

Collaborative structural arrangements also have to provide opportunities for educators to engage in professional conversations and to build a culture of inquiry.

FIELDWORK 10.3

Confronting Norms

Staff members can individually identify what they believe to be the socio-cultural norms of the school, placing one idea per post-it note, and then placing them on the wall. By categorizing "like" ideas, staff can see the commonalities and differences among the group members. These commonalities and differences can form the basis for a substantive conversation about norms and values. If sufficient trust and critical reflection have developed and if the school members are in close contact with students, parents, and community members, the dialogue can open people's eyes to implicit values, norms, and unintended consequences of these.

This is not to say that shared decision-making mechanisms can be imposed or rigid. Collaboration has often failed because participants have not had sufficient understandings of shared power, professional development, preparation or flexibility for the necessary changes in deeply entrenched practices and values. As noted in Chapter 8, time needs to be built into the school day for teachers to meet and to talk. Beyond time, the actual meeting structure will need to shift and change depending on the circumstances and the needs of the particular group. Rather than reporting out various agenda topics, leaders need to develop more enabling structures (Mitchell & Sackney, 2000). Enabling structures include (but are not limited to) collective reflection meetings, problem-solving think tanks, formal opportunities for collaboration, connections to educational research, and networking sessions.

Recall from Chapter 6 the importance of maintaining a data-based approach to professional dialogue. Specifically, leaders keep records of formative and summative assessments of student learning. Leaders must also monitor the other components of the system and their overall integrated effectiveness. For example, in this approach, teams collect data on a multitude of indicators, including student retention, formal assessments, student satisfaction surveys, equity audits (see Chapter 6 for more information), and meeting minutes where educators talk about some of the issues that arise in their practice. Data can also be collected from colleagues, parents, community members, and other educators regarding educational, social, financial, and cultural political conditions. The data provide a solid foundation for critical reflection and deep analysis of the relationship between practice and the effects of practice.

According to Mitchell and Sackney, the most important structural arrangement centers on power relationships in the educational hierarchy. Typically, administrators have operated from control functions and teachers from service functions (Mitchell & Sackney, 2000). In that arrangement, administrators have made decisions, and teachers have implemented them. Administrators are responsible for evaluating teacher performance. These conditions have served to disconnect teachers from many of the decisions that have major implications for classroom practice and to disconnect administrators from the daily world of classroom practice. This is more likely to lead to defensiveness and self-protection than experimentation with new practices. Rather, in a learning community, a horizontal stratification is put into place. In other words, hierarchical levels are reduced and power is distributed throughout the school (Spillane, 2003). In that kind of arrangement, administrators serve facilitative functions rather than control functions, and performance appraisals are developmental rather than evaluative. This keeps administrators in touch with daily classroom circumstances and practices, and it keeps teachers in touch with the decisions that affect the ways in which they work with their students. Leadership is also distributed with different individuals taking on leadership roles in different situations. As Mitchell and Sackney (2000) put it, an explicit consideration of power and shared leadership implies the development of a community of leaders.

In sum, a learning community is supported when organizational structures, power dynamics, and procedural frameworks support professional learning for individuals and for groups. According to Mitchell and Sackney (2009), these learning communities have high capacity.

FIELDWORK 10.4

Power and Decision-Making Practices

Cryss Brunner designed the following power protocol, which helps educators recognize the relationships among their views of power and their decision-making practices. Have each staff member complete the protocol. During a meeting, ask small groups to categorize the results in terms of "views of power". Then have staff members read Brunner and Schumacher (1998), which explains the ways in which power has been thought about and practiced in schools. Further, Brunner and Schumacher's (1998) article illustrates the explicit links between conceptions of power and decision-making processes. This activity helps educators recognize that their views of power are deeply ingrained and need to be considered as they affect the ways in which they interact with others.

Power protocol:

1. Define power.
2. How do you get things done?
3. How do you make decisions?

HIGH CAPACITY SCHOOLS AND ORGANIZATIONAL LEARNING

Mitchell and Sackney (2009) conducted interviews and observations in Canadian schools over a ten-year period and identified seven themes that must drive practices for sustainable improvement in an era of accountability:

1. shared vision
2. collaborative work culture
3. collective inquiry (i.e., reflective practice, presence of knowledge systems and data-based decision making, collective learning)
4. authentic community involvement
5. an action orientation (i.e., innovation, experimentation, risk-taking in pedagogy and curriculum)
6. commitment to continuous improvement
7. a results orientation.

Schools with evidence of all seven themes developed into high capacity professional learning communities and improved student learning and achievement. Specifically, three embedded but interactive layers of capacity-building leadership were necessary to develop the school organization into high capacity learning communities: building people, building commitments, and building schools.

Building people

Building people was defined as a commitment to growth, expressed in a desire to help others grow as they have grown (Mitchell & Sackney, 2009). Staff works hard to build a culture of trust and encouragement that fosters risk-taking. People are honored and thrive as they grow as members of a connected community. Teachers develop habits of inquiry and reflection, and are continually searching for new knowledge to expand their curriculum understandings and instructional practices. Through this growth, teachers build a practice that does not abandon the standards curriculum, but balances the written curriculum with student needs and interests.

Building commitments

Building commitments requires the development of deep trust, collective responsibility, and appreciation of diversity. Administrators trust teachers to "complete the tasks that they take on and teachers trust students to complete their tasks to the best of their abilities" (Mitchell & Sackney, 2009, p. 79). Collaboration is developed through working together in teams with tasks aimed at helping teachers learn the value of professional teamwork. Administrative support for collaboration is guided by facilitating open communication, opening spaces for teachers to talk with one another, and by providing unmanaged team times for joint planning as well as organizing meeting times (Mitchell & Sackney, 2009).

Building schools

Building schools is based in several areas: (a) building networks, (b) building knowledge systems, (c) building leadership infrastructure, and (d) organizing to build capacity. Building networks refers to the interdependency of the staff within the school. Teachers develop connected planned units that support student learning throughout the whole school. Knowledge is built through professional development activities that "link professional knowledge with professional practice" (Mitchell & Sackney, 2009, p. 117). These professional development activities influence teacher practice that emphasizes using student data that is linked with instructional practices and educational decisions. Moreover, instructional leaders must consider the role of context in building capacity and developing organizational learning. In particular, Day (2007) and others have noted the contextual nature of capacity building in persistently underperforming schools.

THE ROLE OF SCHOOL CONTEXT: BUILDING CAPACITY IN PERSISTENTLY UNDERPERFORMING SCHOOLS

In high capacity schools, leaders incorporate both formal leadership and informal leadership capacities aimed at academic and democratic/social change. Leadership is emergent and is not a role or set of tasks, but it is an inherent element of life for all staff. Capacity-building leadership, however, cannot emerge without an explicit consideration of context. For instance, Day (2007) noted that leaders of high-need or high-poverty schools build capacity in layers. Specifically, Day (2007) found that principals in high-poverty, diverse schools build capacity in four phases of development:

- **Phase 1: Coming out of Special Measure**—Practices in this phase include (a) enriching the teaching and learning environment; (b) providing security; (c) establishing a student behavior policy and improving attendance; (d) gaining community acceptance; (e) modeling teaching and learning in classrooms.
- **Phase 2: Taking Ownership of an Inclusive Agenda**—Practices include (a) examining vision and values to deepen the school mission; (b) distributing leadership; (c) inclusivity or integration of students from different social and cultural environments; (d) providing continuous professional development to improve teaching performance; (e) becoming a school that prioritizes pubic thinking about teaching.
- **Phase 3: Going Deeper and Wider: Sustaining the Momentum**—Practices include (a) restructuring leadership; (b) involving the community; (c) student-centered learning; (d) placing staff development and well-being at the center of school improvement; (e) broadening horizons to help students gain a global perspective on the environment, etc.
- **Phase 4: Continuing Excellence and Creativity**—Schools in high-poverty areas can never "coast"; they must always strive to find new ways to attain excellence. There are no final phases or steps in the school improvement process here. Practices started and developed in earlier phases will continue. "The improvement journey is one that will not end" (Day, 2007, p. 48).

In Arizona Tier III (high-poverty, culturally diverse) schools, Ylimaki et al. (2012) found similar evidence of layered leadership. Further, in response to the Arizona border context, they noted that Arizona turnaround leaders build capacity through community relationships, professional learning communities, and assessment literacy. Ylimaki et al. (2012) drew on Leithwood, Harris, and Strauss' (2010) turnaround stages to develop the Tier III leadership program. Specifically, Leithwood, Harris, and Strauss (2010) identified three overlapping turnaround stages: (1) stopping the decline and creating conditions for early improvement; (2) ensuring survival and realizing early performance improvements; and (3) achieving satisfactory performance and aspiring to much more. Leithwood et al. (2010) also found that schools in turnaround settings must gradually distribute leadership and develop capacity for school improvement beyond the principal's leadership. These phases and stages must be addressed in order to support organizational learning in persistently underperforming schools.

SYSTEMIC PROGRAM EVALUATION AND ORGANIZATIONAL LEARNING DESCRIPTION

Program evaluation provides organizational leaders with data on implementation levels, goal attainment, and program effectiveness. Although the data may not be sufficient for sweeping improvements, carefully planned formative assessments often provide structured feedback to improve systems. Basic program evaluations provide insight into the merits and values of a single program and data on immediate outcomes. Program evaluations should provide more global measures of broad implications and a systemic view of the interrelationships of the program to the organization as a whole in a particular community context.

Learning organizations successfully convert information into action, whether the source of knowledge is internal (the result of doing) or external (the result of observing others). Learning organizations will measure effectiveness, and if a gap in performance is found, such organizations initiate and facilitate change. In particular, gaps in student performance must be addressed at all areas of the system. Thus, systemic program evaluation is an important component of organizations with the capacity to use knowledge for learning and development (DiBella & Nevis, 1998).

STRATEGIES FOR LEADERS

How do instructional leaders put all of this background on curriculum rigor, relevance, coherence, and cultural politics into the curriculum dimensions discussed in this chapter? This section provides guidance for what today's instructional leaders need to know and be able to do as well as example strategies for practice. Instructional leaders need to:

Know:

- themselves and their inherent values, inspirations, and biases
- principles of systems thinking
- organizational learning
- relationships among power and decision-making.

Be able to:

- build capacity among staff (see Chapter 7)
- confront mental models and norms
- develop a shared vision
- develop teams
- conduct needs assessments and systemic program evaluations.

The following case and needs assessment activity provides students with an opportunity to put all of these strategies into practice. The first activity requires students to take on two different roles: principal and superintendent. In both roles, students must consider what makes a school program successful. The second related activity asks students to incorporate evaluation into a professional development model.

CASE 10.2 THE BOARD IS LOOKING CAREFULLY

New Day School District has selected a new superintendent, Roberto White. A recent Ph.D. graduate from a major research university in a different state, he is a nationally recognized educational leader. The school board has informed him that significant budget cuts loom on the horizon, yet his most important assignment is to bring about significant educational reform by creating effective schools for all students, not only for the academically oriented ones.

Dr. White believes that if he is to be successful in meeting the school board's expectations, he first needs to determine the leadership capabilities of the school principals. To help him make that determination, he asks each principal in the district to prepare a three- to five-page report outlining the programs currently at the school and the success of each, showing data to support the conclusions. He would like each principal to rank in order of importance the programs that they deem necessary, and those that might be eliminated, including the impact of each program on the students and the community.

Assume that you are the principal of the school in which you are currently employed, and that your school is part of New Day School District. Prepare the report requested by the superintendent, identifying the name of the school and your name at the beginning of the report.

When responding to the submissions of your classmates, assume you have been appointed by the superintendent to a committee that has the responsibility for reviewing the reports and recommending which programs should be cut and which maintained at each site. Working with your fellow committee members, reach consensus on these recommendations. Submit the decisions of the committee with the rationale for your final decisions.

Students should learn to build in evaluation in all phases of their decision-making. The field experience asks that students apply program evaluation to a professional development design.

SUMMARY

Systemic program evaluations can promote learning through dissemination of information because organizational learning relates to acquisition, development, and utilization of information. Such program evaluations should shift from a focus on the merit of a single program to assessments of impact of programs within the whole organization or organizational improvement overall. To understand the impact of a single instructional program (e.g. a new reading series) or how a program fits within the entire system, a more holistic, organic approach is needed. "Systems thinking" offers a broad view by exploring program interactions and relationships. With a comprehensive approach to organizational learning, effective change will become an influential aspect of the organizational culture or "how we do things around here".

FIELDWORK 10.5

Staff Development Workshop and Needs Assessment

The student will work with their principal to plan and conduct a needs assessment, analyze the data, and subsequently plan a staff development workshop. The student will deliver the actual workshop to the staff at the school site. The student

continued . . .

is also expected to design multiple ways to monitor and evaluate progress, addressing the timeline for evaluation. The student should include a proposal for revising the plan if necessary.

Table 10.1 Field Experience—Staff Development Workshop and Needs Assessment (50 points possible)

	Exceptional	*Admirable*	*Acceptable*	*Amateur*
Needs assessment *10 points* (ISLLC Standards 1, 2, 4, 5)	Extremely well organized; logical format that was easy to follow; data collected and used to identify goals that are tightly aligned; collaboration with school staff integral *(9–10)*	Presented in a thoughtful manner; there were signs of organization; data collected and used to identify goals; collaboration with school staff discussed *(8)*	Somewhat organized; ideas were not presented coherently; data collected, but goals are only loosely tied to data; collaboration with school staff implied *(7)*	Choppy and confusing; format was difficult to follow; data was not collected and goals not tied to data; no indication of collaboration with school staff *(6 and below)*
Workshop plan *10 points* (ISLLC Standards 1, 2, 4, 5)	Plan designed to achieve organizational goals tightly aligned with needs assessment; plan develops the instructional capacity of staff; plan drives improvement of instructional program; plan developed in collaboration with staff; job-embedded; includes significant ongoing development *(9–10)*	Plan designed to achieve organizational goals aligned with needs assessment; plan develops the instructional capacity of staff; plan drives improvement of instructional program; job-embedded; includes ongoing development *(8)*	Plan designed to achieve organizational goals aligned with needs assessment; plan develops the instructional capacity of staff; plan drives improvement of instructional program; job-embedded *(7)*	Plan is not designed to achieve organizational goals; not aligned with needs assessment; plan does not develop the instructional capacity of staff; not job-embedded; designed as one-time workshop; no collaboration with staff *(6 and below)*

continued . . .

Table 10.1 Continued

	Exceptional	*Admirable*	*Acceptable*	*Amateur*
Continuous and sustainable improvement *10 points* (ISLLC Standards 1, 2, 4, 5)	Plan promotes continuous and sustainable improvement over time; addresses resources needed; proposes multiple ways to enhance and extend learning *(9–10)*	Plan promotes continuous and sustainable improvement; addresses resources needed; proposes one way to enhance and extend learning *(8)*	Plan promotes continuous and sustainable improvement; addresses resources needed *(7)*	Plan does not promote continuous and sustainable improvement; does not address resources needed; does not propose ways to enhance and extend learning *(6 and below)*
Evaluation of plan *10 points* (ISLLC Standards 1, 2, 4, 5)	Plan includes multiple ways to monitor and evaluate progress; addresses timeline for evaluation; includes proposal for revising plan if necessary *(9–10)*	Plan includes at least one way to monitor and evaluate progress; addresses timeline for evaluation; includes proposal for revising plan if necessary *(8)*	Plan includes at least one way to monitor and evaluate progress; addresses timeline for evaluation; omits proposal for revising plan *(7)*	Plan does not address any way to monitor and evaluate progress; does not address timeline for evaluation; omits proposal for revising plan *(6 and below)*
Conducts workshop *10 points* (ISLLC Standards 1, 2, 4, 5)	Implements plan to achieve goals; collects 4 or more artifacts as evidence (videotape, workshop materials, lesson plan; participant feedback, etc.) *(9–10)*	Implements plan to achieve goals; collects 2-3 artifacts as evidence (videotape, workshop materials, lesson plan; participant feedback, etc.) *(8)*	Implements plan to achieve goals; collects one artifact as evidence (videotape, workshop materials, lesson plan; participant feedback, etc.) *(7)*	Does not implement plan to achieve goals; does not collect artifacts as evidence *(6 and below)*

Name: _____   ____/50

REFERENCES

Argyris, C. & Schon, D. (1978). *Organizational learning: A theory of action perspective*. Reading, MA: Addison-Wesley.

Brunner, C. C. & Schumaker, P. (1998). Power and gender in "New View" public schools. *Policy Studies Journal, 26*(1), 30–45.

DiBella, A. J. & Nevis, E. C. (1998). *How organizations learn*. San Francisco, CA: Jossey-Bass.

Day, C. (2007). Sustaining the turnaround: What capacity building means in practice. *International Studies in Educational Administration (ISEA), 35*(3), 39–48.

DuFour, R. (1999). Help wanted: Principals who can lead professional learning communities. *NASSP Bulletin, 83*(604), 12–17.

Goodstein, L. D., Nolan, T. M., & Pfeiffer, J. W. (1992). *Applied strategic planning: An introduction*. San Francisco, CA: Jossey-Bass/Pfeiffer.

Huber, G. (1991). Organizational learning: Contributing processes and the literatures. *Organization Science, 2*(1), 88–115.

Isaacs, W. (1999). *Dialogue and the art of thinking together*. New York: Doubleday.

Leithwood, K., Harris, A., & Strauss, T. (2010). *Leading school turnaround: How successful leaders transform low-performing schools*. San Francisco, CA: Jossey-Bass.

Marzano, R., Waters, T., & McNulty, B. (2005). *School leadership that works: From research to results*. Alexandria, VA: Association for Supervision and Curriculum Development.

Midlock, S. F. (2011). *Case studies for educational leadership: Solving administrative dilemmas*. New York: Pearson Education, Inc.

Mitchell, C. & Sackney, L. (2000). *Profound improvement: Building capacity for a learning community*. Lisse, The Netherlands: Swets and Zeitlinger.

Mitchell, C. & Sackney, L. (2009). *Sustainable improvement: Building learning communities that endure*. Rotterdam, The Netherlands: Sense Publishers.

Senge, P. (1990). *The fifth discipline: The art and practice of the learning organization*. New York: Doubleday.

Senge, P., Cambron-McCabe, N., Lucas, T., Smith, B., Dutton, J., & Kleiner, A. (2000). *Schools that learn: A fifth discipline fieldbook for educators, parents, and everyone who cares about education*. New York: Doubleday.

Spillane, J. (2003). Educational leadership. *Educational Evaluation and Policy Analysis, 25*(4), 343–346.

Swieringa, J. & Wierdsma, A. (1992). *Becoming a learning organization*. Amsterdam, The Netherlands: Addison Wesley.

Ylimaki, R., Brunderman L, Dugan, T., & Bennett, J. (2012). Promising results from a turnaround leadership development project in persistently low-performing, culturally diverse schools. A paper presented at the European Conference on Educational Research, Cadiz, Spain, September, 2012.

Zepeda, S. J. (2012). *Instructional supervision: Applying tools and concepts, third edition*. Larchmont, NY: Eye On Education Inc.

Systemic Program Evaluation

SCORING SUMMARY SHEET

SCHOOL AND DISTRICT LEADERSHIP CAPACITY

The district and school leadership focuses on improved student achievement.

		Exceeds the Standard → 3	Meets the Standard → 2	Approaches the Standard → 1	Falls Far Below the Standard → 0
Indicators		3	2	1	0
1.1	The district/charter holder commits administrative support and professional development to create a student-centered, teacher-led learning community.	③	②	①	⓪
1.2	District/charter holder leadership blends both expectations and support to ensure that systems (i.e., fiscal, curricular, instruction, effective practices, assessments) are aligned to goals that focus on student achievement.	③	②	①	⓪
1.3	Leadership (i.e., governing board, district administration, and principals) has led an inclusive process of developing a sustained and shared philosophy, vision and mission that promotes a culture of excellence.	③	②	①	⓪
1.4	Leadership is developed and involved at all stakeholder levels, with a strong emphasis on teacher leadership.	③	②	①	⓪
1.5	Leadership actively promotes ongoing, two-way communication among multiple stakeholder groups.	③	②	①	⓪
1.6	All administrators have growth plans focused on the development of effective leadership skills that include the elements of the *Standards and Rubrics for School Improvement*.	③	②	①	⓪

continued . . .

Continued

Indicators		*Exceeds the Standard*	*Meets the Standard*	*Approaches the Standard*	*Falls Far Below the Standard*
		3	2	1	0
1.7	Leadership works to build coherency and alignment by "reculturing" around state and federal accountability systems.	③	②	①	⓪
1.8	District/school leadership systematically uses disaggregated data in planning for diverse student needs, and then communicates data analysis information to school staff.	③	②	①	⓪
1.9	Leadership ensures that all instructional staff receives appropriate curriculum and instructional materials and are provided with professional development/training necessary to effectively use curricular, instructional, and data resources relating to the Arizona Academic Standards.	③	②	①	⓪
1.10	Leadership ensures that time is allocated and protected to focus on curricular and instructional issues.	③	②	①	⓪
1.11	Leadership promotes and sustains continuous school improvement by allocating resources (e.g., fiscal, human, physical, time), monitoring progress and resource use, and providing organizational structure.	③	②	①	⓪
1.12	The school is organized to maximize equitable use of all available fiscal resources to support high student and staff performance.	③	②	①	⓪
1.13	The principal demonstrates the skills necessary to lead a continuous school improvement process focused on increasing student achievement.	③	②	①	⓪

ANALYSIS OF RATINGS FOR CAPACITY

Top 2–3 Strengths

Top 2–3 Limitations/Areas Needing Improvement

SCORING SUMMARY SHEET

CURRICULUM, INSTRUCTION, AND PROFESSIONAL DEVELOPMENT

Rigorous curriculum and instruction provide all students the opportunity to meet or exceed ***Curriculum Standards****.*

	Indicators	Exceeds the Standard — 3	Meets the Standard — 2	Approaches the Standard — 1	Falls Far Below the Standard — 0
2.1	The school or district has developed an explicit, written curriculum that is aligned with Academic Standards.	③	②	①	⓪
2.2	A systematic process for monitoring, evaluating, and reviewing the curriculum (including the hidden curriculum) is in place.	③	②	①	⓪
2.3	The curriculum expectations are communicated to all stakeholders.	③	②	①	⓪
2.4	A comprehensive curriculum and access to academic core standards are offered to all students.	③	②	①	⓪
2.5	The staff monitors and evaluates curriculum and instructional programs based on student results, and makes modifications as needed to ensure continuous school improvement.	③	②	①	⓪
2.6	Instructional planning links Academic Standards and aligns curriculum, instruction, practice, formative assessment, summative assessment, review/re-teaching and appropriate interventions to promote student achievement.	③	②	①	⓪
2.7	Instructional materials and resources are aligned to Academic Standards and performance objectives, and there is research-based evidence of their effectiveness.	③	②	①	⓪
2.8	Technology is integrated effectively into classroom instruction and is used as a teacher resource tool for instructional planning, instructional delivery, assessment, monitoring student progress, and communicating information.	③	②	①	⓪
2.9	Differentiated instruction (i.e., adjustment of concept, level of difficulty, strategy for instruction, amount of work, time allowed, product or performance that demonstrates learning) is used to meet the learning needs of all students.	③	②	①	⓪
2.10	A variety of scientifically research-based strategies and best or proven practices focused on increasing student achievement are used effectively in classroom.	③	②	①	⓪

continued . . .

Continued

		Falls Far Below the Standard			
		Approaches the Standard			
		Meets the Standard			
		Exceeds the Standard			

Indicators		3	2	1	0
2.11	The long-term professional growth of individual staff members is required and focuses directly on increasing student achievement.	③	②	①	⓪
2.12	Teachers and staff promote high expectations of students and recognize and accept their professional role in student success and failure.	③	②	①	⓪
2.13	Professional development is continuous and job-embedded.	③	②	①	⓪
2.14	The district/school provides a clearly defined evaluation process and focuses directly on increasing student achievement.	③	②	①	⓪
2.15	Teachers exhibit sufficient content knowledge to foster student learning.	③	②	①	⓪

ANALYSIS OF RATINGS FOR CURRICULUM, INSTRUCTION, AND PROFESSIONAL DEVELOPMENT

Top 2–3 Strengths

Top 2–3 Limitations/Areas Needing Improvement

SCORING SUMMARY SHEET

FORMATIVE ASSESSMENTS

*The school uses multiple **standards**-based assessments, strategies and **data** to measure and monitor student performance and to revise curriculum and instruction as needed.*

		Exceeds the Standard	Meets the Standard	Approaches the Standard	Falls Far Below the Standard
Indicators		*3*	*2*	*1*	*0*
3.1	School leadership designs and implements an assessment system that supports the needs of all stakeholders (i.e., students, teachers, administrators, parents, governing board members, community members) when appropriate.	③	②	①	⓪
3.2	Multiple and varied assessments and evaluation strategies are used appropriately and effectively, including equity audits.	③	②	①	⓪
3.3	Teachers assess learning, formulate classroom benchmarks based on standards, and communicate the results to students and families with respect to students' abilities to meet Arizona Academic Standards.	③	②	①	⓪
3.4	School and classroom assessments are aligned to the Arizona Academic Standards and/or performance objectives.	③	②	①	⓪
3.5	Assessments are used to re-focus student learning on targets to enable them to meet/exceed standards.	③	②	①	⓪
3.6	Test scores are used to identify gaps in curriculum or between groups of students for instructional implications.	③	②	①	⓪
3.7	The district/school implements specific steps for monitoring and reporting student progress in learning the Arizona Academic Standards.	③	②	①	⓪
3.8	District/school leadership coordinates implementation of state-required assessment and accountability program.	③	②	①	⓪

ANALYSIS OF RATINGS FOR ASSESSMENTS

Top 2–3 Strengths

Top 2–3 Limitations/Areas Needing Improvement

SCORING SUMMARY SHEET

SCHOOL CULTURE, CLIMATE, AND COMMUNICATION

*The school functions as an effective **learning community**, supports a climate conducive to student achievement, and possesses an effective two-way **communication** system.*

Indicators		Falls Far Below the Standard — Approaches the Standard — Meets the Standard — Exceeds the Standard —			
		3	2	1	0
4.1	There is a shared philosophy of commitment, ownership, vision, mission and goals that promote a culture of excellence.	③	②	①	⓪
4.2	Facilities support a safe and orderly environment conducive to student learning.	③	②	①	⓪
4.3	There is policy, leadership, and staff support for an equitable code of discipline that supports students' understanding of rules, laws and expectations for responsible behavior that enables teaching and learning.	③	②	①	⓪
4.4	There is leadership, staff, student and community involvement in the development and implementation of safety plans that meet state requirements.	③	②	①	⓪

continued . . .

Continued

Indicators		3	2	1	0
	Exceeds the Standard — *Meets the Standard* — *Approaches the Standard* — *Falls Far Below the Standard* —				
4.5	Teachers and staff build positive, nurturing relationships with students and work to improve student attendance, dropout rates, and graduation rates.	③	②	①	⓪
4.6	Student achievement is highly valued and publicly celebrated.	③	②	①	⓪
4.7	A healthy school culture promotes social skills, the humanities, and students FofK so that students are prepared and supported to learn.	③	②	①	⓪
4.8	A culture of respect exists where relationships, trust, communication and collaboration are valued within the entire school community.	③	②	①	⓪
4.9	Change is accepted as a normal and positive process that leads to continuous district/school improvement.	③	②	①	⓪
4.10	All members of the school community are active partners in governance, and support and participate in school-wide improvement efforts.	③	②	①	⓪
4.11	Students are provided with a variety of learning opportunities within the normal school day; and may receive additional assistance beyond regular classroom instruction to support their academic learning.	③	②	①	⓪

ANALYSIS OF RATINGS FOR SCHOOL CULTURE

Top 2–3 Strengths

Top 2–3 Limitations/Areas Needing Improvement

Excerpted from Needs Assessment Scoring Sheets, Arizona Department of Education, www.azed.gov/improvement-intervention/school-improvement

Contributors

Vanessa Anthony-Stevens is an experienced teacher, having worked with education and educators from the elementary school level through higher education, predominately in multilingual and Native American teaching contexts. She received her doctorate in Language, Reading, and Culture from the University of Arizona. Her research interests are Indigenous education, intercultural education, ethnographic methods, and critical policy studies.

Lynnette Brunderman spent more than thirty years working in public education in the state of Arizona, both in the classroom and in various administrative roles. Currently she is an Associate Professor of Practice at the University of Arizona in the Department of Educational Policy Studies and Practice. Dr. Brunderman is also a project director and researcher for the Arizona Turnaround Leadership Development Project.

Peter Burke is Director of The Education Doctorate (Ed.D.) graduate program in educational leadership and a faculty member in the School of Education at Edgewood College, Madison, Wisconsin. Before assuming the position at Edgewood, he was the bureau director for licensing at the Wisconsin Department of Public Instruction and an administrator for various programs at the University of Wisconsin-Madison School of Education. His research interests focus on leadership, school improvement, and the supervision of instruction.

Seann M. Dikkers is an Assistant Professor in the Educational Technology division of the Patton College of Education at Ohio University. Formerly Dr. Dikkers served as a middle school teacher, high school principal, education consultant, and director of Gaming Matter Labs. Dikkers' work focuses on the integration of new media technologies into formal and informal educational settings. His publications feature mobile media learning and leading with and through technology.

Thad Dugan is an Assistant Principal and Ph.D. student in Educational Leadership and Policy at the University of Arizona. He has also been a teacher, primarily in urban settings in California and Arizona. His research interests include critical perspectives on leadership, turnaround leadership, and linking critical theory to practice. Thad Dugan is the author of several chapters and articles dealing with critical perspectives on leadership preparation and practice.

Norma González is a Professor in the Department of Language, Reading, and Culture at the University of Arizona, and is affiliated faculty with the Second Language Acquisition and Teaching program. She is an anthropologist of education, and her Ph.D. is in sociocultural anthropology. She is the President of the Council of Anthropology and Education. Her research focuses on language processes in the U.S.–Mexico borderlands, immigration and education, language ideologies, and household ethnographies.

Catherine Hackney is an Associate Professor of educational leadership at Kent State University. Her research interests focus on democratic curriculum development, feminist leadership practice, and transformative curriculum practice. She has published numerous works dealing with the role of leadership in democratic curriculum development.

James Henderson is a Professor at Kent State University, where he has taught graduate courses in curriculum studies for nineteen years. He is coordinator of the Curriculum and Instruction Master's and Ph.D. programs and serves as co-editor of the *Journal of Curriculum and Pedagogy*. His research focuses on the arts of democratic curriculum leadership, and he has individually or collaboratively published numerous publications dealing with democratic curriculum education and curriculum-based pedagogy.

Brendan H. O'Connor is Assistant Professor of Language, Literacy, and Intercultural Studies at the University of Texas at Brownsville. He is a linguistic anthropologist of education whose interests include knowledge and identity in classroom interaction, youth language and culture, and the cultural context of schooling in the U.S.–Mexico borderlands.

Henry St. Maurice has taught English, special education, and computer science in a variety of settings including elementary, secondary, and rehabilitation programs. He has been a Professor at the University of Wisconsin-Stevens Point and a faculty member at Edgewood College. Dr. St. Maurice has been involved in the Supervision and Instructional Leadership special interest group (SIG) for many years and has published numerous articles on effective supervision.

Rose M. Ylimaki is an Associate Professor in the Department of Educational Policy Studies and Practice at the University of Arizona. She previously served as a curriculum leader and teacher in the Midwest. She has published numerous works on curriculum leadership and school leadership in underserved schools. She also studies leadership development in schools with underserved populations.

Index